The Historian and the Believer

THE HISTORIAN

AND

THE BELIEVER

The Morality of Historical Knowledge
and Christian Belief

Van A. Harvey

THE WESTMINSTER PRESS
Philadelphia

Published by The Westminster Press ®
Philadelphia, Pennsylvania

PRINTED IN THE UNITED STATES OF AMERICA
9 8 7 6 5 4 3 2 1

Library of Congress Cataloging in Publication Data

Harvey, Van Austin.
   The historian and the believer.

   Reprint of the ed. published by Macmillan, New
York.
   Includes bibliographical references and index.
   1. History (Theology)   2. Bible — Criticism,
interpretation, etc. — History — 19th century.
3. Bible — Criticism, interpretation, etc. — History —
20th century.   I. Title.

[BR115.H5H44 1981]   230'.044'0904   80-27941
ISBN 0-664-24367-3

ACKNOWLEDGMENTS

The author wishes to thank the following for permission to reproduce copyrighted material: S.C.M. Press, London, for *A New Quest of the Historical Jesus* by James M. Robinson, distributed in the U.S.A. by Allenson's, Naperville, Illinois, *Demythologizing and History* by Friedrich Gogarten; *The New York Times* for an interview with Martin Agronsky, © 1963 by The New York Times Company; Harcourt, Brace & World for *Murder in the Cathedral* by T. S. Eliot; J. C. B. Mohr (Paul Siebeck) for *Gesammelte Schriften* and *Die Absolutheit des Christentums* by Ernst Troeltsch, *Glauben u. Verstehen I* and *Glauben u. Verstehen II* by Rudolf Bultmann, *Zur Frage nach dem historischen Jesus* by Ernst Fuchs; Oxford University Press for *Epistle to the Romans* by Karl Barth, *Collected Essays*, Vol. 1 by F. H. Bradley, *The Idea of History* by R. G. Collingwood, *Laws and Explanation in History* by William Dray, *The Nature of Historical Explanation* by Patrick Gardiner, and *The Oxford Dictionary of the Christian Church;* Charles Scribner's Sons for *God Was in Christ* by D. M. Baillie, *Theology of the New Testament*, Vol. I & II and *Jesus Christ and Mythology* by Rudolf Bultmann, *History and the Gospel* by C. H. Dodd, *Resurrection and Historical Reason* by Richard R. Niebuhr; T & T Clark for *Church Dogmatics* by Karl Barth; Doubleday & Company for *This Hallowed Ground* by Bruce Catton, Copyright © 1955 by Bruce Catton, *The Renewal of Man* by Alexander Miller, Copyright © 1955 by Alexander Miller, *The Philosophy of History in Our Time*, edited by Hans Meyerhoff, Copyright © 1959 by Hans Meyerhoff; Westminster Press for *The Reality of Faith* by Friedrich Gogarten, Copyright 1959 W. L. Jenkins, *History Sacred and Profane* by Alan Richardson, © S.C.M. Press Ltd., 1964, published in the U.S.A. 1964 by Westminster Press; Fortress Press for *The Nature of Faith* and *Word and Faith* by Gerhard Ebeling; World Publishing Company for *Existence and Faith,* shorter writings of Rudolf Bultmann, selected, translated, and introduced by Schubert M. Ogden, Copyright © 1960 by Meridian Books, Inc.; Yale University Press for *The Problem of Knowledge* by Ernst Cassirer, *The Courage to Be* by Paul Tillich; Random House, Inc. for *The Historian's Craft* by Marc Bloch; University of Chicago Press for *The Protestant Era* and *Systematic Theology* by Paul Tillich; Cambridge

Contents

[vii]

Contents

. . . however humble the sphere of her rule, yet at least, while within that sphere, criticism is subject to no intrusion and oppressed by no authority. She moves on her path unheedful of the warning, unheedful of the clamour, of that which beyond her realm may be or may call itself religion and philosophy; her philosophy and her religion are the realization and the fruition of herself, and her faith is this, that while true to herself she can never find an enemy in the truth.

—F. H. BRADLEY, *Collected Essays, I.*

. . . faith opens the way to knowledge. It removes the taboos which surround our intellectual life, making some subjects too holy to be inquired into and some too dangerous for us to venture into. Yet it grants reverence to the mind for which now no being is too low to be worthy of a loving curiosity. All knowledge becomes reverent and all being is open to inquiry. So long as we try to maintain faith in the gods, we fear to examine them too closely lest their relativity in goodness and in power become evident, as when Bible worshipers fear Biblical criticism, or democracy worshipers fear objective examination of democracy. But when man's faith is attached to the One, all relative beings may be received at his hands for nurture and for understanding. Understanding is not automatically given with faith; faith makes possible and demands the labor of the intellect that it may understand.

—H. RICHARD NIEBUHR, *Radical Monotheism and Western Culture*

Preface

MY hope is that this book might contribute in a modest way to the clarification of what theologians like to refer to as "the problem of faith and history." As is so often the case with such sweeping references, this problem is really not one but many.

Of these many problems, none has caused more consternation and anxiety in the breasts and minds of Christian believers than the application of critical historical methods to the New Testament and, especially, to the life of Jesus. It is fashionable among contemporary Protestant theologians to consider this aspect of the problem something of a dead issue except, that is, among fundamentalists and other conservative Christians. My conviction is that this attitude is unwarranted, that even the most sophisticated theological programs of the last two or three decades have failed to grapple in any rigorous and clear fashion with the thorny issues created by a revolution in the consciousness of Western man of which critical historiography is but the expression.

This conviction has necessarily led me onto that swampy ground which borders both theology and the philosophy of history, where the philosophy of history refers not to a speculative theory about "the meaning of history" but to the systematic reflection on the nature of historical judgment itself. My concern is with the stance of the historian, with what he seems committed to as an ideal of judgment. This stance is not properly understood until one sees it as the expression of a certain morality of knowledge, and this morality of knowledge, I believe, has the profoundest of implications for religious belief in general and Christian belief in particular. The first part of the book delineates the elements of this morality, especially as they are reflected in the justification of historical explanations and claims. The second part of the book is an assessment of much recent Protestant theology in the light of the ideal of historical judgment delineated in the first part. The final chapter represents my attempts to achieve some solid ground.

Because of my concern for both the philosophy of history and theology, I should like to think that philosophers as well as theologians might find something of interest in these pages, although my own basic concern is theological, as is evident in the first and final chapters. Although philosophers may be put off by the theology, the fact remains that Christian belief, anchored as it is in history, raises a number of interesting philosophical questions about the presuppositions of the historian, presuppositions that stand out in bolder relief when he is confronted by the type of claim frequently staked out by Christian apologists, for example, the claim that the events on which Christianity is based are utterly unique.

My indebtedness in this enterprise is so great and extends in so many directions, I scarcely know where to begin acknowledging it. I would like to thank, first of all, the Bollingen Foundation, the American Association of Theological Schools, and Dean Joseph D. Quillian of Perkins School of Theology for the aid that made it possible to spend an unforgettable year in Marburg, Germany, where so many of these ideas were first conceived. So, too, special thanks is due to the Graduate Council of the Humanities at Southern Methodist University and to the Danforth Foundation, which made that Council possible, for enabling me to devote a part of my time to the writing of this book. I am also grateful to Mrs. Nadell Lightfoot, who spent so many extra hours with the mechanics of its production. My gratitude is especially extended to those students and colleagues who read and criticized the manuscript at various stages: Professors Frederick S. Carney, David Coldwell, Albert C. Outler, Decherd Turner, William C. Robinson, Jr., and, above all, Schubert M. Ogden who was always selflessly available for conversation and help, without which this book scarcely would have taken its present shape.

Finally, may I express my gratefulness and affection for that kindly and fatherly man, now about to celebrate his eighty-first birthday in Marburg, who was as generous with his time as he was incisive in his criticisms and suggestions, Professor Rudolf Bultmann, to whom this book is respectfully dedicated.

Dallas, Texas   V.A.H.
August 4, 1965

Preface
to the Paperback Edition

I am especially grateful to those readers and reviewers of this book who took the pains to comment on or to criticize arguments or conclusions contained in it. I have learned much from these critics and, had it been possible, would have revised or altered those passages that seemed unconvincing or unclear or in error. This paperback edition, unfortunately, does not allow for such a revision, and I have had to be content with a few minor corrections and the resolution to continue to work on the theological model only sketched in the final chapter.

Both friendly and unfriendly critics alike tended to concentrate on this final sketch. Although gratified by this attention, I did not altogether welcome it because I felt that the contribution of the book to contemporary theology, if any, consisted primarily in my analysis of the problem historical inquiry raises for Christian belief. I feared lest this analysis be ignored on the grounds that my synthesis seemed, for various reasons, to be inadequate. Recent developments in theology have not altered my feelings in this regard. Indeed, most of the recent theological fads—the "new hermeneutic," the "God-is-dead" school, and especially the "theology of hope"—continue to rely on philosophically crude or superficial analyses of the basic issues posed by Biblical criticism.

With respect to the final chapter, some critics argued that I did not measure my own point of view by the same standards of rigor

I applied to other theologians. Other critics suggested that even though they found my viewpoint to be "cogent and viable," as one wrote, they doubted that it could "do justice to the Christian faith." Still others, however, said that only some such theological perspective as I proposed enabled them to see any significance in traditional christological confessions, and they urged me to develop the sketch more fully.

It is difficult to know how to reply to such diverse and conflicting evaluations. There is, to be sure, some justice in the first criticism. I hedge with the qualification "some" because it was quite explicitly noted at the close of the first section of the last chapter that what followed was only "the sketch of the outlines of a model" and lacked "any degree of rigor." My purpose was to provide the reader with the glimpse of a theological position which, if it did not rigorously follow from the preceding analysis, was, at least, compatible with it. I felt that the reader, especially the lay reader, was entitled to such a glimpse since, lacking it, he might easily regard (and dismiss?) the earlier argument as but one more destructive attack on the heart of the Christian religion. I wished to make it clear that the basic intention behind the entire book was theological.

To those who said that the intention so expressed did not do justice to the Christian faith, I can only say that they appeared to have missed the thrust of the argument. One of my points was that this objection no longer is a legitimate one because critical historical inquiry of the New Testament and of the entire Christian tradition has uncovered the incredible diversity of Christian symbolism, doctrine, belief, and moral practice. Thus, one can no longer appeal to "the Christian faith" as though this were a self-evident norm by which to measure various theological perspectives. The compelling question today is whether such a norm exists. One might even say that it is precisely the diversity of Christian belief and practice that should be the starting point of theological reflection. My own viewpoint, at least, has the virtue of building on the fact of this pluralism.

Perhaps what the critic meant was that my theological standpoint does not do justice to just this richness and diversity of

Christian belief. But this objection then requires more careful formulation. My argument was that any version of the Christian faith will include many different logical types of assertions: historical, theological, christological, and anthropological. Historical inquiry has rendered some of the historical assertions untenable that appear in most of the many contemporary versions of the Christian faith. One may, of course, dispute this by showing where my analysis is wrong, but it will hardly suffice to ignore the analysis yet measure the conclusion by a standard which the analysis itself has attempted to show is too imprecise to be of any use.

Were I to revise the book, I would develop more fully the point that one cannot legitimately demand the same tight rational justification for a total theological perspective of the logical type I proposed as one can demand for specific historical claims or even for a broader interpretation of history like, say, Marxism. Or, to use the jargon of analytic philosophy, the logic of "seeing as" is quite different from the logic of claiming some event to have happened in a specific way or of assuming some interpretative standpoint regarding history. Correspondingly, the ethics of belief is different in each case. The criteria for deciding whether believing in the trustworthiness of God is a morally responsible act or not are quite different from the criteria appropriate for judging whether a belief that a given event happened in such and such a way or not is justifiable, just as both sets of criteria will differ from that brought forward to assess some historical standpoint.

These are extraordinarily difficult philosophical problems, and the major part of my time is now being spent trying to achieve some clarity about them. But I am convinced that it is precisely because the logic of the matter has not been clearly delineated that the so-called problem of faith and history is as muddled as it is in the contemporary literature. Here I can only express my gratitude to all those who have forced me to think longer and harder about these issues.

VAN A. HARVEY

University of Pennsylvania
September 1968

The Historian and the Believer

I

Faith and History in Contemporary Theology

1 · *The Shadow of Ernst Troeltsch*

OUT of the mists of the nineteenth century, there arise again and again spectral figures that refuse to be exorcised. This is particularly true of Protestant theology. Schleiermacher, Strauss, Feuerbach, Kierkegaard, Ritschl—all continue to stalk the present because they identified and analyzed so profoundly issues that still bedevil us. Yet their presence is embarrassing because the various solutions they proposed now seem so patently dated and, in some cases, comic, that we feel justified in dismissing their work or ignoring them entirely. But just at the most important junctures of our own intellectual enterprises, we are disturbed to discover that we are wrestling with the same old issues, that the same questions have returned again in only a slightly different guise. With that realization, the possibility suggests itself in the back of our minds that the answers once proposed may not be so fantastic as we had so smugly assumed. We find ourselves rethinking the thoughts of those whose conclusions we look upon with disdain. This is always painful.

The writings of Ernst Troeltsch, particularly, evoke this discomfiture. The issue with which he wrestled throughout the greater part of his life was the significance of the historical-critical method for traditional Christian belief and theology. He discerned that the development of this method constituted one of the great advances

[3]

in human thought; indeed, that it presupposed a revolution in the consciousness of Western man. To be sure, Western culture, in contrast to many others, has always been characterized by a sense of history. But only in the nineteenth century did this manifest itself in a sustained and critical attempt to recover the past by means of the patient analysis of evidence and the insistence on the impartiality and truthfulness of the historian. The distinctions between history and nature, fact and myth; expressions like the growth of language and the development of the state; the tendency to evaluate events in terms of their origins; the awareness of the relativity of one's own norms of thought and valuation; all these, Troeltsch saw, are but the by-products of a change in thought so profound that our period deserves to be put alongside those of previous cultural epochs as a unique type.[1]

This revolution in consciousness found its formal expression in the creation of a new science, history. Underlying this new science was an almost Promethean will-to-truth. The aim of the historian, it was declared, was to "tell what really happened." The magic noun was "fact," and the honorific adjective was "scientific." Description, impartiality, and objectivity were the ideals, and the rhetorical phrase and the value judgment were looked upon with disdain. This drive to recover "the facts as they really happened" has, with some justice, been criticized of late, but it should not be forgotten how revolutionary this will-to-truth was or how reactionary the forces were that needed to be overcome. Only when the question "What really happened?" was consistently and radically posed, did it become clear how much of what was previously accepted as fact was, in truth, fiction; how so many long-trusted witnesses were actually credulous spinners of tales and legends. Indeed, it can be argued, all reliable historiography rests on some such distinction as "whether or not something actually happened; whether it happened in the way it is told or in some other way . . . ," as August Wilhelm Schlegel wrote in his review of the Grimm brothers' *Old German Songs*,[2] and it is difficult to quarrel with him and still account for the concepts of myth, legend, and fairy tale that constitute so much of the mental furniture of our age.

This will-to-truth became attached to a method, and the presuppositions of that method, Troeltsch concluded, were basically incompatible with traditional Christian faith, based as it ultimately is on a supernaturalistic metaphysics.[3] This incompatibility was most clearly seen, he thought, in the realm of Biblical criticism. The problem was not, as so many theologians then believed, that the Biblical critics emerged from their libraries with results disturbing to believers, but that the method itself, which led to those results, was based on assumptions quite irreconcilable with traditional belief. If the theologian regards the Scriptures as supernaturally inspired, the historian must assume that the Bible is intelligible only in terms of its historical context and is subject to the same principles of interpretation and criticism that are applied to other ancient literature. If the theologian believes that the events of the Bible are the results of the supernatural intervention of God, the historian regards such an explanation as a hindrance to true historical understanding. If the theologian believes that the events upon which Christendom rests are unique, the historian assumes that those events, like all events, are analogous to those in the present and that it is only on this assumption that statements about them can be assessed at all. If the theologian believes on faith that certain events occurred, the historian regards all historical claims as having only a greater or lesser degree of probability, and he regards the attachment of faith to these claims as a corruption of historical judgment.

Troeltsch poured scorn on those of his contemporaries who attacked the historical method as a manifestation of unbelief while employing something like it to vindicate the truth of their own views. The method, he claimed, did not grow from an abstract theory, nor could one ignore the cumulative significance of its extraordinary results. "Whoever lends it a finger must give it a hand."[4] Nor could the critical method be regarded as a neutral thing. It could not be appropriated by the church with only a bit of patchwork here and there on the seamless garment of belief. "Once the historical method is applied to Biblical science and church history," he wrote, "it is a leaven that alters everything and, finally, bursts apart the entire structure of theological methods employed until the present."[5] Christianity must, therefore, build its religious thought upon it or else be consigned to the limbo of those countless other antiquated forms of religious belief that were unable to make their own accommodation to the *Zeitgeist.*

Actually, Troeltsch believed the church had no real option, because it is impossible even to think without the new assumptions. They have already penetrated to the deepest levels of Western man's consciousness. They are a part of the furniture of his mind. Therefore, one must be willing to see the matter through to its final consequences, to let burn what must burn, hoping that a new synthesis might emerge on the other side, a synthesis all the stronger for having been purged by the fire. Troeltsch himself tried to do this, and if his efforts now appear dated and relative to his own time, that only seems, ironically enough, to vindicate his thesis; namely, that the expressions of the human spirit—its language, art, philosophy, and religion—are intelligible only in terms of their time, that man is immersed in history like a fish in water, that man's failure to transcend history only reveals that he is a creature whose thought is something less than absolute.

The application of the principles of historical criticism to the Bible in the nineteenth century was a traumatic event in the history of Protestantism.[6] It is true, as Emanuel Hirsch has pointed out, that Biblical criticism had been practiced in a modest way since the beginnings of the Reformation.[7] Luther himself was a shrewd critic. But it was only in the third decade of the nineteenth century that it was possible to subject the Scriptures to rigorous analysis without dogmatic presuppositions and limitations. The attempt to do so naturally aroused the hostility of theologians and the ecclesiastical authorities. Did not the entire enterprise rest on unbelieving presuppositions?

The conflict between the critic and authority soon reduced itself, as all such conflicts do in the modern world, to the issue of freedom of inquiry. This, in turn, necessarily assumed the form of the question of intellectual honesty and integrity. It was no easier to make out the friends of truth then than now. The issue was frequently clouded by the fact that the earliest Biblical critics sallied forth into speculative theology in the name of a factual science. D. F. Strauss, for example, after a thousand or so pages of reasoned historical argument in his *Life of Jesus,* took pen in hand and charted a theological program for the future in which the doctrine of the Incarnation was to be supplanted by the idea of the deification of humanity.[8] These fantasies could only cast doubt on the critics' motives and judgments. Furthermore, this new revolution in scholarship, it seemed to some, was merely the ideological expression of the political tide of liberalism that was inundating the Continent, and of which the French Revolution was the living and horrifying consequence. It is no wonder that a defender of the old order like John Henry Newman should have equally abhorred Strauss' *Life of Jesus,* the French flag, and Tom Paine's *Age of Reason,* which he kept locked in his safe lest it stain the imagination of his students.[9]

Happily, there were those less sweeping in their condemnation, men who patiently tried to sift out what was valid in the new enterprise while casting aside what was extreme, programmatic, and revolutionary. They saw in the new science, history, the chance to re-establish the Christian faith on a sound basis, historical fact. It was the great contribution of liberal theology to save Protestantism from obscurantism. Orthodox scholars, for the most part, either rejected criticism outright or practiced it in such a piecemeal fashion that their work now seems like a hopeless mixture of naive credulity and rationalism. Liberalism was not without its own brand of dogmatism, as subsequent research was to disclose, but at least it did not flinch from applying the canons of historical science even when the results did not seem altogether happy for its own position. The bridgehead was won, the practice established, and there was no longer any possibility of retreat. And when the dialectical theology arose after the First World War, it was one of the members of this new movement, Rudolf Bultmann, who wrote that the great contribution of liberalism was not its clarification of history

but above all the education of the critic, which is to say, an education to freedom and truthfulness. We who have come out of liberal theology could not have been or remained theologians had we not been encountered by the seriousness of the radical integrity of liberal theology. We perceived the work of all shades of orthodox theology in the universities as an effort at compromise, on which we could have been inwardly broken. G. Krüger is always to be thanked because he saw, in that oft-named essay on "unchurchly theology," the danger to the soul in the vocation of the theologian, the entrance into doubt, the shattering of naive credulity. Here—so we perceived—was the atmosphere of truthfulness, in which alone we were able to breathe.[10]

It is not my purpose here to relate the very interesting drama of historical criticism but simply to emphasize that, since the early part of the nineteenth century, it has become, to use Hirsch's expression, a "fateful question" for the Christian community.[11] Even when the methods of historical inquiry have been accepted by Protestant theologians, the marriage of theology and criticism has not been a tranquil one. No sooner has a measure of domestic bliss seemed assured than a new disturbing characteristic of one of the mates has emerged and a reappraisal of the relationship has taken place. Liberal theology, for example, welcomed the methods of historical criticism and used them in order to establish its own theological position, only to be unsettled by the further development of that criticism. The picture of the Jesus of history, which it believed had been secured by sound historical methods, came under severe attack by historians using the same critical method; first, by Albert Schweitzer, and then by the form critics. The new dialectical theology, as another example, sought to achieve its *modus vivendi* with criticism by neutralizing it, by insisting that Christian faith, in the nature of the case, did not depend on the changing and relative results of historical inquiry. Yet in the last decade, the problem of the relation of faith to history has moved back into the forefront of theological discussion in just those circles that have taken, as their point of departure, the basic insights of this theology.

Troeltsch would surely smile ironically were he able to scan the journals of contemporary theology, and in this chapter I should like to suggest why. To do this, I shall focus on two related issues which stand out in the contemporary discussion: the problem of the relationship of faith to historical judgments about Jesus of Nazareth and the problem of Biblical interpretation. I do not pretend to give an exhaustive account of the current state of the discussion; rather, I will attempt to unravel a few of the philosophical and theological issues and so reveal why, as Troeltsch saw, nothing less than a systematic treatment of the matter is required. Such a treatment will concern us in the remainder of this book.

2 · The Problem of the Historical Jesus

The so-called problem of the historical Jesus—"so-called" because, as we shall see, it is not one problem but many—has plagued Protestant theologians since the publication in 1834 of David Friedrich Strauss' *Life of Jesus.* Strauss had many purposes in writing this ponderous yet sensational book, but one of them was to apply what he regarded as the canons of scientific historical research to the New Testament in order to separate fact from fiction, legend, and myth. Some of Strauss' predecessors had suggested, albeit with great caution, that the infancy narratives and the temptation and ascension stories in the Gospels were mixed with legendary elements, but Strauss not only questioned these traditions but most of the others as well: the baptism of Jesus by John the Baptist, the mission of the seventy, most of the healing narratives, the "nature" miracles, the transfiguration, and the resurrection.[12] Strauss argued that none of these stories, when carefully examined, could be regarded as historical. They arose, he suggested, as messianic legends and myths that had become attached to Jesus because he was believed to be the Promised One of Israel. The logic of the matter was simple: such and such a deed was associated with the coming of the Messiah; Jesus was the Messiah; therefore, he must have done such and such a deed.[13]

Strauss' analysis is unintelligible without the historical revolution in consciousness of which I have already written. Previous to Strauss, the interpreter of difficult New Testament texts usually employed one of three types of interpretations. He could suggest, as the rationalists did, that the miracle stories were misinterpretations of fact; or he could argue, as the supernaturalists did, that the stories were eyewitness accounts; or he could dismiss them all, as the freethinkers did, as frauds perpetrated by the earliest Christian community. The supernaturalists defended their position against the freethinkers by pointing to the unimpeachable moral character of the witnesses and by asking an apparently unanswerable question: "Why, if the stories were false, weren't they repudiated by other eyewitnesses?" The rationalists, on the other hand, pointed out how easily the miracles could be explained as misinterpreted facts. The miracle of Jesus' calming of the storm, for example, probably arose from a remark Jesus made about the violence of the weather and some prognostication, founded upon a shrewd observation of signs, that the storm would soon subside.

Strauss undermined all of these alternatives by arguing that the writers of the New Testament—in fact, the people of the entire age—were naive and mythologically-minded folk without any conception of natural law or order.[14] They lived in a mythological time in which unusual events of nature and history were attributed to supernatural beings of all kinds. Their standard of reality was different than ours; their writings expressed a picture of the world which, though natural to them, is entirely alien to our own. Strauss, in short, began to think historically.[15]

"Scarcely ever has a book let loose such a storm of controversy; and scarcely ever has a controversy been so barren of immediate result," wrote Albert Schweitzer concerning the reception of Strauss' book. "The fertilising rain brought up a crop of toadstools."[16] The toadstools to which Schweitzer refers were the acrimonious and sterile debates concerning miracles and Strauss' interpretation of the relationship of Jesus to the Christ of faith which expended a considerable amount of the theological energies in the subsequent decades. But there was a more significant and less barren result: a century-long effort to establish the exact nature of the New Testament sources—a problem Strauss had left unresolved—so that on the basis of those sources something positive and supportive of faith could be said about the life of the historical Jesus. This effort was particularly important to the theologians of the Ritschlian school, who dominated Protestant theology in the last quarter of the century. It was essential to the Ritschlians that the Gospel tradition about Jesus be trustworthy, because the object of faith, they thought, is not the dogma of classical orthodoxy but the God-consciousness of Jesus, the force of his religious personality by which he had won a victory over the world. This, in part, accounts for the expenditure of so much energy on the Synoptic problem. Although it was not a victory easily achieved, the widespread consensus at the turn of the century was that Mark was the First Gospel, that it was, in either oral or written form, used by Matthew and Luke, and that the Fourth Gospel could not—or only with extreme caution—be used as a source for historical claims about Jesus. On the basis of this literary solution, it was believed, as Wilhelm Bousset wrote at the time, that there only remained to draw a "life-like portrait which, with a few bold strokes, should bring out clearly the originality, the force, the personality of Jesus."[17]

Grave doubts about the possibility of such a picture were raised by the works of William Wrede, Julius Wellhausen, and, later, the form critics. They all argued, in effect, that the earliest traditions about Jesus actually consisted of sayings, parables, and other vignettes without any apparent chronological order and that Mark collected these and superimposed upon them his own temporal and interpretive scheme. The upshot of this critical development was that even Mark, by common agreement the earliest Gospel, could not be considered a fully trustworthy source for a chronological picture of Jesus' ministry or for an insight into his personality. The Gospels, in short, were regarded less as sources for a life of Jesus than as a picture of the beliefs of the early church.

This conclusion, if true, was devastating to both liberal and orthodox Protestantism, but it troubled not at all the theologically brash young men who became the phalanx of that movement misleadingly called neo-orthodoxy. What was said over the grave of their own teacher, Wilhelm Herrmann, applied equally to them: it sometimes appeared that the results of New Testament criticism could not be radical enough for him. Karl Barth, Emil Brunner, Rudolf Bultmann, and Paul Tillich saw in the collapse of the old quest of the historical Jesus a chance to be once again both Biblical in spirit and historically honest: Biblical in spirit, because the *kerygma* as proclaimed by Paul and the author of the Fourth Gospel was not at all concerned with the religious personality of

Jesus; historically honest, because statements about the "personality" and "life" of Jesus could find no justification in the historical sources. The *kerygma* in the New Testament, they argued, was about God's identification with mankind in the full ambiguity of human history. Jesus was the bearer, the incarnation, of God's Word. But from a historical point of view, his life and personality were as ambiguous as those of any other human.[18] Only faith perceives the divine "incognito" in the man Jesus. Miracle stories are not objects of belief; they are the historically conditioned expressions of the Christian community's faith in God's revelation.

This position seemed paradoxical and unstable to many, as if the new theology had made a virtue out of an unhappy necessity. Consequently, it came increasingly under attack. Among systematic theologians, it was D. M. Baillie who argued that the neo-orthodox theologians had reacted too violently against the excesses of liberalism's emphasis on Jesus and that "there is no stablilty in a position which accepts to the full the humanity of Christ but has no interest in its actual concrete manifestation and doubts whether it can be recaptured at all; which insists on the 'once-for-allness' of this divine incursion into history, but renounces all desire or claim to know what it was really like."[19] Baillie called for a return to the Jesus of history. "If it is true that 'no man can say, Jesus is Lord, except in the Holy Spirit,' " he wrote,

it is equally true that no man can say it, in the truly Christian sense, except through a knowledge of what Jesus actually was, as a human personality, in the days of His flesh. In the ages of authority Christians may indeed have largely dispensed with this, and Christian faith, however impoverished, managed to live without it. But in the modern age of criticism and questioning, the rediscovery of the human historical personality came as a new realization of the historical content of the dogmas: men found in the Gospel story a real human personality which constrained them to say . . . "Jesus is Lord". . . .[20]

Baillie's position seemed so balanced, so eminently sensible, that scarcely anyone pointed out that while he had argued that knowledge about Jesus was a necessity, it still remained to be established whether or not such knowledge was a possibility. Since there is no logical connection between theological necessity and historical possibility, the problem of the fragmentary nature of the sources remained.

It seemed especially significant, then, when a group of Bultmann's own students, who by this time (c. 1950) were occupying the most prestigious university chairs in Germany and Switzerland, also began to express similar doubts about their teacher's alleged skepticism[21] concerning the historical Jesus and the significance of it for faith. This was a happy development for the critics of Bultmann. If the prodigal son, who had wasted his substance in the far and barren country of radical Biblical criticism, would not return, surely there was some cause for rejoicing in the return of the grandsons. James M. Robinson, who more than any other has traced the movement and focused the discussion,[22] regards a paper by Ernst Käsemann in 1954 as initiating the new quest for the historical Jesus, a quest which hopes to ground the Christian faith firmly in fact. How can such a new quest succeed, however, if the old quest was impossible because of the nature of the sources? The answer lies, claims Robinson, in a new conception of the historical method, on the one hand, and of the *kerygma,* on the other. The *kerygma* is about the existential selfhood of Jesus, and the New Testament sources preserve just those sayings and scenes in which his self and intention are made clear. But the aim of history in general is to re-create the existential self-understandings of past human beings and not merely to give a chronological description of their lives. Hence, the formal parallel between the *kerygma* and the new historiography opens up a new possibility for theology.

3 · *The Deeper Issues Involved in the Discussion of the Historical Jesus*

From this very oversimplified sketch, one can gain some idea of the extraordinary complexity of the problems raised by New Testament research. It is clear, for example, how inextricably intertwined the historical and theological issues seem to be. This is why arguments about the New Testament pass so easily from judg-

ments about fact to judgments about the presuppositions of the
investigator, from claims about results to counterclaims that these
so-called results simply reflect the assumptions of the critic. If, say,
the members of the Bultmann circle argue that the sources do not
permit the historian to reconstruct the development of the career
of Jesus, a more conservative critic will argue that this is a skeptical conclusion based upon a prior assumption that the Gospels do
not contain substantial eyewitness material but are primarily made
up of a community tradition transmitted by anonymous and non-
professional persons. This argument soon drifts imperceptibly into
a methodological debate concerning what an eyewitness might
have been expected to have said about Jesus,[23] which then brings
one to the problem of miracles and the problematic nature of the
appeal to supernatural causation. It is not surprising that the lay-
man, confronted with such diversity of argument on so many
different levels, should himself be driven to historical skepticism.
But this skepticism only raises deeper theological questions: Is
Christian faith compatible with a historical skepticism about
Jesus? Can one rest his faith on historical assertions which themselves do not seem capable of a high degree of probability? What is
the relation between faith and the history?

This brings us to the first of the fundamental issues with which
Troeltsch wrestled and which hovers over the subsequent pages of
this book: the degree to which the presuppositions of the historian
determine the conclusions he reaches. This issue, of course, is a
philosophical one, and it transcends the concerns of Christian
theology, although it does arise in a particularly acute form
there.

Troeltsch addressed himself to this philosophical issue, and he
argued that critical historical inquiry rests on three interrelated
principles: (1) the principle of criticism, by which he meant that
our judgments about the past cannot simply be classified as true or
false but must be seen as claiming only a greater or a lesser degree
of probability and as always open to revision; (2) the principle of
analogy, by which he meant that we are able to make such judgments of probability only if we presuppose that our own present
experience is not radically dissimilar to the experience of past

persons; and (3) the principle of correlation, by which he meant that the phenomena of man's historical life are so related and interdependent that no radical change can take place at any one point in the historical nexus without effecting a change in all that immediately surrounds it. Historical explanation, therefore, necessarily takes the form of understanding an event in terms of its antecedents and consequences, and no event can be isolated from its historically conditioned time and space.[24]

Troeltsch himself believed that these principles were incompatible with traditional Christian belief and, therefore, that anyone who based his historical inquiries upon them should necessarily arrive at results which an orthodox Christian would consider negative and skeptical. Consider, for example, the principle of analogy. The historian, Troeltsch argued, must assume that the events of the past are similar to the events of the present, whereas orthodox belief, by postulating the divine nature of Jesus and the supernatural events of miracle and resurrection, shatters this principle. Consequently, it is impossible to assess the degree of probability of orthodox assertions because in the realm of the supernatural any discussion of possibility and probability flounders.

Many theologians agree with Troeltsch that the principle of analogy is incompatible with Christian belief if one interprets it as he does. But they conclude from this not that Christian belief is untenable but that Troeltsch simply reflected the antisupernaturalistic and positivistic bias of the nineteenth century.[25] Troeltsch's criticisms, they claim, are but a version of a naturalistic metaphysics in which the occurrence of genuinely unique events is precluded from the outset. Moreover, these critics continue, these same naturalistic assumptions have dominated most of the New Testament criticism from D. F. Strauss to Rudolf Bultmann, and this accounts for the widespread skepticism concerning the Gospels. It is clear, for example, that Strauss' concept of myth is predicated on the view that "all things are linked together by a chain of causes and effects, which suffers no interruption,"[26] just as Bultmann admits that "the historical method includes the presupposition that history is a unity in the sense of a closed continuum of effects in which individual events are connected by the succession of cause and effect,"[27] a continuum that "cannot be rent by the interference of supernatural, transcendent powers. . . ."[28]

This criticism, it should be said, does not emanate only from obscurantist theological circles anxious to preserve a belief in miracles at all costs, although it has been welcomed and exploited in these circles. The criticism arises from what claims to be a more sophisticated understanding of the nature of historical thinking itself.

Actually, there are at least three versions of this criticism, all of which differ in important respects although they converge at the same point. (1) One may argue, as Richard R. Niebuhr has done in his *Resurrection and Historical Reason,* that the metaphysical presuppositions of Strauss and of Bultmann (and, by implication, of Troeltsch) really destroy genuine historical thinking.[29] Historical thinking, Niebuhr argues, requires an openness to the uniqueness and novelty of past events, and no historian can dogmatically and in advance rule out the possibility of such events. If the resurrection, for example, is what it claims to be, then it challenges the principle of analogy; it cannot be conformed to it. But in this sense, the resurrection represents the problem of all historical understanding, namely, how to understand the genuinely unique and singular. (2) Another related but similar criticism issues from a slightly different philosophy of history. In this view, the mistake of Bultmann and Strauss is that they do not understand that there is no such thing as a disinterested or objective historian. Every historian's judgments reflect his interests, values, and metaphysical beliefs. There are no "bare facts" in history, it is said; there are only interpretations. It follows, writes Alan Richardson, that "it is positivistic philosophy, not historical method, which decrees that the resurrection of Christ cannot be regarded as an historical event."[30] The Christian will have his own unique perspective and write a correspondingly different history. (3) A similar criticism in a slightly different form has been advanced by the proponents of the new quest. They, as we have seen, are also convinced that philosophical presuppositions determine the kind of history the historian writes. But unlike the two views noted above, they do not desire to rehabilitate a belief in the resurrection or in miracles.

They argue that the issue is not between supernaturalism and naturalism but between those historians who think they should be primarily interested in reconstructing a chronicle of external fact and those who think their task is to relive and re-create sympathetically the basic intention and purposes of past historical agents. The "new questers" are critical of Strauss, for example, not because he employed the negative criteria concerning miracles that he did, but because he was so busy looking for facts that he failed to see that the real question was what understanding of existence came to expression in the words and deeds of Jesus. Consequently, these proponents of the new quest accept Troeltsch's formal criteria for historical inquiry without being liable, they think, to the criticism of being positivistic historians.

I do not propose to debate these matters in this chapter. My intention is merely to point out what the deeper issues are and to note that Troeltsch's problems still haunt us. In what sense does the historian necessarily assume the principle of analogy, the similarity of the past to the present? If he does, what does this do to traditional belief? If he does not, in what sense can we talk about probability and improbability at all?

This brings us to a consideration of Troeltsch's first principle of historical judgment, the idea that every historical claim attains only a lesser or a greater degree of probability. This also raises the profoundest of questions for faith and it was on the basis of an answer to this question that the so-called neo-orthodox, or dialectical, theology was established. Barth, Brunner, Bultmann, and Tillich argued, as Martin Kähler and Sören Kierkegaard had done before them, that faith is a passion which becomes comic and distorted if it tries to rest on the "approximation process" of historical inquiry. Faith has, they claimed, its own certitude, and it is a falsification of both faith and historical inquiry if the former is based on the latter: a falsification of faith because faith cannot change with every new consensus of New Testament criticism or hold its breath lest some discovery in the Dead Sea area casts a shadow of doubt over this or that particular belief; falsification of history because it is intolerable to honest inquiry if the New Testament critic or believer decides in favor of one historical judgment rather than another because it is more compatible with his religious beliefs. Consequently, the dialectical theologians argued that the object of faith is not the Jesus reconstructed by the historian but the Christ proclaimed in the *kerygma,* the one who was crucified and revealed to be the Word of God.

This attempt to separate faith from criticism is, as we shall see in Chapter Five, liable to severe and perhaps devastating criticisms. It has been pointed out that while historical inquiry can never prove the belief that Jesus was the Son of God, it can, nevertheless, cast doubts on it, at least in principle. For what if it were confirmed beyond a reasonable doubt that Jesus never lived or that he was not crucified or that his actual words were quite different in content and spirit from those preserved by the church? It is impossible to claim at one and the same time, the critics of dialectical theology insist, both that Christianity is founded on an interpretation of a concrete historical event and that no historical judgments are relevant to its truth or falsity. One cannot have historicity without risk. Consequently, insists Gerhard Ebeling, faith is necessarily "exposed to all the vulnerability and ambiguity of the historical." It has no guarantees in this respect, and this uncertainty is, for the Protestant, the "reverse side of the certainty of salvation *sola fide.*"[31]

These criticisms have some merit, but the problem Troeltsch identified is by no means solved simply by embracing risk in the name of faith. For what is the believer to do when faced by widespread disagreements among New Testament historians concerning what can be known about Jesus? Shall he limit his belief to only those judgments about Jesus which can be said to represent a firm consensus? And what shall he do if any such consensus is lacking? Can he pick and choose his favorite historian because this or that one buttresses his faith? And what shall we say of the Christian historian? What should he do when what he believes as a historian seems to conflict with his faith, or, as is more usual, when the probabilities of history do not seem to justify the certitude of faith? Can one and the same man hold the same judgment tentatively as a historian but believe it passionately as a Christian?

Theologians do not often realize to what extent this problem deeply troubles theological students and informed laymen. Faced with a plurality of views defended by learned men, they find themselves unable to give any convincing grounds why they should choose one rather than another. Nor do more conservative theologians sense the ironic dilemma they face in their attempts to allay the anxiety of those who want to know whether the traditional historical claims can stand the acids of reasoned argument. If the Christian apologist simply assumes the doctrine of inspiration and accepts the principle of supernatural intervention, he begs the issue and arrives at "conclusions" which were in the premises from which he started. This practice inevitably breeds suspicion in the minds of those he is most trying to convince. If, however, the doctrine of inspiration and the principle of supernatural intervention are set aside, the apologist necessarily employs the canons of those with whom he is in debate. When conservative theologians have attempted this approach, their results have been so divergent that they enhance the very skepticism they seek to dissolve. As Rudolf Bultmann has noted:

. . . one can scarcely obtain a stronger impression concerning the uncertainty of our knowledge about the person of Jesus than if he puts together what various scholars have thought about the messianic self-consciousness of Jesus. And it is noteworthy that one has had only a few less thoughts concerning the external course of his life and the reasons for his execution.[32]

4 · *Biblical Criticism and the Problem of the Unity of the New Testament*

As Gerhard Ebeling has pointed out, the entire history of Christian theology may be regarded as the history of Biblical interpretation. This is especially true of Protestant theology, because it has been characterized from the outset by appeal to the Bible as the sole norm of faith and practice (*sola scriptura*).[33] It is just for this reason that Biblical criticism poses such a fateful problem for the Protestant community. It not only raises questions concerning the truth of the historical narratives, but it materially affects the reading of Scripture itself by posing the question of interpretation and meaning. Two related issues come immediately to the fore in this connection: the problem of the unity of the New Testament, and the problem of making intelligible to the present a message which was originally proclaimed in the thought-forms of a pre-scientific and mythologically-minded past.

It is now clear that the traditional Protestant doctrine of the inspiration of the Holy Scripture, which developed in the seventeenth century, obscured these matters.[34] It assumed that the Bible is a book of unified beliefs and that it is possible, therefore, to interpret an unclear utterance of, say, Paul with the aid of a verse from the Fourth Gospel or from the Letter to the Hebrews. If every writer was inspired by the Holy Spirit, how could there be diverse and contradictory doctrinal viewpoints in the Bible? This assumption was directly linked to another: The patterns of thought of the Biblical writers were essentially like our own so that their language and concepts could be taken at face value. It was naively assumed that the only real problem of interpretation was to establish the literal meaning of the text. Few theologians dreamed that it required an act of historical understanding just to reconstruct the intention of the author. Would the Holy Spirit inspire a document that could only be understood by a trained historian?

These traditional assumptions were rendered problematical when they were not shattered by the development of Biblical criticism. As a priori assumptions they had to be suspended, of course, by the historian, since the infallibility of a document is not an affirmation of faith but a conclusion arrived at only after an analysis of the text. But such an analysis did not support the assumption. On the contrary, the Biblical critic was able to give a more intelligible account of the New Testament by showing that there were important differences in point of view among the Biblical authors and that these, in turn, reflected the various cultural and religious environments.

This last point is worth dwelling on, because it both illustrates Troeltsch's insight that no historical phenomenon can be understood apart from its historical context and casts some light on the problem of the interpretation of the New Testament. The various doctrinal viewpoints in the New Testament, the historian claimed, can best be understood in terms of the rapidly changing historical situation of what was called "primitive Christianity."

That situation probably looked something like this: The earliest Christian community was predominantly Palestinian and Jewish in ethos.[35] Consequently, it interpreted the significance of Jesus largely in terms of the hopes and expectations of late Judaism. Jesus was believed to be the Messiah, the fulfillment of the promises made by God to Israel. It is by no means clear, however, what the first-century writers meant by the term "Messiah" or the titles "Son of God" and "Son of Man;" if, indeed, there was any one single meaning at all. It seems likely that there were many diverse and conflicting messianic sects reflecting the various apocalyptic hopes and visions of the time. When one group confessed that Jesus was the Messiah, they may not have meant, for example, that his life actually embodied a messianic pattern; they may have meant that he would come again in the future as the heavenly judge and king. Another group may have believed that Jesus' resurrection was the inauguration of the new messianic age. Still another group may have tried to see some messianic pattern in his life and career. All one can say is that the crucial patterns of interpretation and the symbols in which they were couched were intelligible only to a Jewish audience.

The fact of Jesus' crucifixion obviously constituted a stumbling block to all the prevalent messianic patterns, since the Jews regarded execution as a punishment for sin. That Jesus was executed by the Romans only confused the matter. How could the Messiah be crucified? The Christian community evidently tried to overcome this scandal in at least two ways: by reinterpreting the concept of the Messiah and by interpreting Jesus' death as the will of God. Jesus had to die, it was argued, because his death was a sacrifice, an atonement for sin. Both ideas, at any rate, made use of prevailing cultic patterns of thought.[36]

The delay of the expected end of the world and the second coming of Christ were increasingly embarrassing for the earliest Christian community, as the New Testament literature itself suggests.[37] With the fall of Jerusalem in 70 A.D. and the spread of

Christianity into the Hellenistic world with its different religious ethos, however, it became clear that the Jewish belief in the coming of the Messiah was not only unintelligible but irrelevant to the Gentile. Moreover, the cultic concepts of sacrifice and atonement, which had been used to overcome the scandal of Jesus' death, were also strange. Consequently, the early Christian missionaries had to find a new religious vocabulary.

There is considerable evidence that the missionaries of the Hellenistic Christian church adopted the vocabulary and symbols of the Hellenistic mystery religions and Gnosticism. Herbert Braun of Mainz has made one of the more recent attempts to show how this might have happened.[38] He points out that while the term "Son of God" was a messianic symbol for the Jew, it was associated in the Hellenistic mind with the gods and heroes of the Graeco-Roman world. Common motifs in this religious context were divine procreation, virgin birth, the descent from heaven of a divine-like creature, the misery of the deity during his unrecognized stay on earth, and his victorious vindication and return to heaven. So prevalent are these motifs, that many scholars believe that there was a common archetypal salvation myth widely current in the Near Eastern world, and they profess to see traces of it in the letters of Paul and in the Fourth Gospel. This would not be surprising, were it proved to be true, since it would have been a natural way in which the church tried to make a point of contact with its cultural situation. Just as Isis and Osiris were made gods because of their virtue, and Heracles was made a son of God because of his obedience, Jesus also was raised to heaven and given a name above every name. As Pythagoras, Empedocles, and Asclepius healed men of their diseases and drove away the plague, Jesus healed the sick, brought the dead to life, and banished the evil spirits. On the surface, the difference between these Hellenistic mysteries and the Christian religion was that the Christian assigned mythological features and functions to a concrete historical person while the Hellenist assigned them, for the most part, to mythological, semi-divine beings.

The use of Hellenistic categories did, however, involve a shift in orientation from the Hebraic and apocalyptic modes of thought characteristic of the earliest Palestinian community. Whereas the Jewish messianic titles were functional and placed Jesus on the side of the creatures, so to speak, the Hellenistic titles were metaphysical and tended to place him on the side of divinity.[39] Jesus was regarded as having a part in creation, and the miracles were evidence of his divine nature. Secondly, the rapprochement with Hellenism required a new interpretation of the history of Judaism, the law and cult. Both of these shifts required a new synthesis which would, nevertheless, preserve the distinctive understanding of faith and God's grace. It was the great contribution of Paul and John to formulate this synthesis.

Related to this general understanding of the continuity of the early Christian forms of thought with those of the environment has been the realization of the important differences among the New Testament authors themselves. The Protestant doctrine of inspiration concealed this. It has become clear, however, that those authors closely associated with Judaism and its forms of thought and symbolism differed appreciably from those more identified with Hellenism. Moreover, even among those who stood within the same cultural milieu, there were often divergent emphases. Although Paul and the writer of Luke-Acts, for example, both attempted to mediate the Gospel of Christ to the Hellenistic and pagan world, they differed quite markedly from one another in their conception of faith.[40] So, too, the author of the Letter of James had a significantly different understanding of the faith than, say, the writer of the Fourth Gospel, though both of them, in turn, may be contrasted with the author of the Book of Revelation or of the Letter to the Hebrews.

Now, if this oversimplified picture of the development of primitive Christianity is at all valid, it can be seen why it was historically necessary to assume a great deal of diversity in the New Testament. Nor can this diversity, as F. C. Grant has pointed out, be

limited to choice of language, as if the New Testament writers all meant the same thing but selected different words for saying it. The diversity involves some of the basic ideas of New Testament theology; the religious attitude, ethos, and approach of quite different groups;

and also a variety in practice, in organization, and in types of religious activity, which the studies of the past generation have made so clearly evident that no fair-minded student can ignore them.[41]

It is obvious, then, why orthodox Protestants resisted Biblical criticism so desperately. It seemed to cast doubt on the supernatural origins of Christianity and, more importantly, it shattered the naive conception of unity which was the presupposition of the appeal to the Bible as the norm for belief and practice.

5 · *Biblical Criticism and the Problem of New Testament Interpretation*

This discovery of the diversity of New Testament belief raises the deeper question of historical interpretation. If the emergence of primitive Christianity is described simply in terms of the borrowing of this or that belief, as many historians were inclined to do, then the development of the early church is seen primarily as the assimilation of ideas and symbols from its environment. From this point of view, Christianity is regarded as one syncretistic religion among others, significant largely because of its survival, the fortuitous linkage of its destiny with Rome and Western culture. It is possible, however, to penetrate beneath the external facts and symbols and to ask at a deeper level what understanding of life was being expressed through these primitive and mythological forms and how this differed from the understandings expressed by Christianity's rivals and, furthermore, whether this understanding has any relevance for the present. From this point of view, it is still an open question whether there is a deeper unity concealed by the diversity.

This question was not asked either by the liberal Biblical critics or by the orthodox defenders of the Bible, and, ironically, for a single reason. Both took the myths and symbols at face value as expressing objective and literal beliefs. The difference between the liberal and orthodox parties was that the former rejected these as prescientific and naive beliefs while the latter regarded them as divinely inspired and authoritative.

It is the liberal position that is of interest to us here because it profoundly affected theological interpretation of the Scriptures for several generations. The liberal, so understandably weary of the unedifying spectacle of his orthodox colleagues debating with geologists and evolutionists, desired nothing more than to bring his beliefs into conformity with science. He tended, therefore, to regard the mythical imagery of a miraculously born savior-god as the relic of an outmoded belief-system having no conceivable contemporary relevance. Consequently, the liberal critic rarely, if ever, asked any significant questions about the structure of this mythology, its pattern, form, or "logic." The liberal, rather, looked for relevance and significance in those elements of Scripture that were most free from mythology and the miraculous; that is, in the parables and teachings of Jesus and in his religious consciousness. The upshot was that the religion *of* Jesus was played off against the religion *about* Jesus, the latter having to do with a pre-existent savior-god who was supernaturally conceived, waged an unending war with demons, was crucified as a vicarious sacrifice for sin, raised from the dead, and taken back into heaven.

It is against this background that one must understand the sensation created by the publication in 1919 of Karl Barth's commentary on Paul's letter to the Romans. It was a sensation not only because of its theological content but because of the mode of interpretation Barth practiced and defended. This mode differed radically from that of liberalism, on the one hand, and orthodoxy, on the other. Although accused of being an enemy of historical criticism by his liberal colleagues, Barth obviously was not so much opposed to historical criticism as it had been practiced—the reconstruction of the text, the rendering of the Greek into its precise equivalents, the addition of archaeological and philological notes, the arranging of the whole so that it could be explained in terms of its historical context—as he was convinced that these procedures were "merely the first step towards a commentary."[42] Orthodox interpreters, on the other hand, were only slightly more adequate, because all they achieved was the "first draft of a paraphrase."[43] A commentary, Barth argued, requires understanding, and this demands, in turn, an earnest wrestling with the questions and the subject matter of a text. This wrestling, however, presupposes that regardless of how strange and alien the mode of expression of a document is, one can, in principle, understand its questions and the subject matter with which it deals. Is this true? And if it is true, how can this be explained?

It is true, Barth insisted, because Paul is dealing with the "infinite qualitative difference between time and eternity," with the relationship of man to God. This relationship is the theme of the Bible as well as the essence of all philosophy. "When I am faced by such a document as the Epistle of Paul to the Romans, I embark on its interpretation on the assumption that he is confronted with the same unmistakable and unmeasurable significance of that relation as I myself am confronted with, and that it is this situation which moulds his thought and its expression."[44] If, then, one wants to understand how Paul thought of this relationship, the interpreter must try to follow him. He must be utterly loyal to him and cannot be satisfied until "the document seems hardly to exist as a document; till I have almost forgotten that I am not its author; till I know the author so well that I allow him to speak in my name and am even able to speak in his name myself."[45]

Barth's commentary ushered in a new theological era. In the first place, it enabled him and those who followed him to accept fully the methods of historical inquiry and yet to use that inquiry in such a way that the Scriptures could be interpreted as documents which still spoke to man about the deepest problems of his personal existence. In short, it provided a method of historical understanding that at one and the same time bridged past and present and permitted the recovery of the Protestant Reformers' conception of Scripture as the Word of God addressed to the consciences of men. But this mode of interpretation also opened up a new possibility for recovering the unity in diversity of the New Testament, because, as James M. Robinson has pointed out, the "*kerygma* came gradually to be recognized as the centre not only of the Gospels, but also of primitive Christianity itself,"[46] and this *kerygma,* although expressed in various mythological concepts, was precisely the proclamation which called men to faith in God.

This conception of the unity of the New Testament proclamation also had another advantage. It constituted an alternative to the centrality that had been given to the historical Jesus in liberal Protestantism and to dogmatic beliefs—whether theological or historical—in orthodoxy. The Gospel, or *kerygma,* Barth and others discovered, is not about the miraculous deeds of Jesus, nor is it about his superior religious self-consciousness. It is, rather, the proclamation that in the lowly and despised man Jesus, whose historical life was as ambiguous as any other historical life, God had disclosed his own righteousness and the futility of trusting in the righteousness of men. "All human activity is a cry for forgiveness," wrote Barth, "and it is precisely this that is proclaimed by Jesus and that appears concretely in Him."[47]

This new position had its own internal problems, one of which I noted in the section above dealing with the historical Jesus, namely, how paradoxical it seems both to insist on the revelation of God in Jesus Christ and to argue that the historical Jesus was as ambiguous a person as any other. Another of these problems, however, had to do with the nature of historical interpretation itself. Barth had insisted that the interpreter must be utterly loyal to the text, confident that the author knew what he was doing. Bultmann, who to Barth's surprise came to the defense of his commentary, expressed some reservations about this "utter loyalty."[48] While it is true that the interpreter of a text must try to see the issues through the eyes of its author, he cannot be so loyal that he fails to see where that author himself failed to do justice to his subject matter. One must, to be sure, listen to and wrestle with Paul, but that also means to see where Paul himself sometimes failed to communicate properly his vision. One must, in other words, determine the degree to which the subject matter really has achieved adequate expression in the words and statements of the author. One cannot assume that even Paul spoke only in the spirit of Christ, for other spirits also come to expression through him. Consequently, historical criticism can never be radical enough.

Bultmann himself, consequently, turned to making clear the presuppositions of the understanding of any text, a task made even the more urgent because of the growing interest on the part of philosophers in the whole problem of hermeneutics. It is in this context, in fact, that Bultmann's proposal to demythologize the New Testament must be understood. It actually represented the attempt (1) to do full justice to the culturally conditioned character of the New Testament language, (2) to wrestle with the subject matter of the New Testament in such a fashion that it becomes intelligible to the present, and (3) to preserve the "psychic distance" between the interpreter and the author so that the interpreter could criticize the author if the latter did not do justice to his own intention.

(1) The attempt to do full justice to the culturally conditioned character of the New Testament language required, Bultmann insisted, that one must recognize the gulf separating the first century and our own. This means quite specifically that in the reconstruction of the Biblical "world-picture," a reconstruction which is necessary before one can fully understand the crucial ideas, one must realize that, from the standpoint of the present, the first-century "world-picture" was a mythological one.

(2) The fact that the language and thought-forms are mythological requires that they be translated into contemporary terms. But a translation is only possible if the interpreter has some point of contact, something in common, with the past, some present understanding of that of which the text is speaking.[49] The interpreter of a text, Bultmann argued, must have what he called an *existentiell* life-relation with a subject matter before he can understand how a given author deals with it, for it is out of his own life-relation to the subject matter that the interpreter is able to address productive questions to the text and so discover what answers are given there. It is, to illustrate, impossible for a man unacquainted with the problems of musical composition to understand a text in musicology, just as it is fruitless for a man who refuses to understand the complexities of economics to try to write about the influence of trade on the development of Egyptian civilization. This prior understanding, or life-relationship, need not be a rigid one, for the text may enlarge one's perspective on the matter. Nor need it entail agreement with the author of a text, for the "*existentiell* encounter with the text can lead to a yes as well as to a no, to confessing faith as well as to express unfaith, because in the text the exegete

encounters a claim, i.e., is there offered a self-understanding that he can accept . . . or reject, and therefore is faced with the demand for decision."[50]

(3) Finally, it is in the light of the interpreter's understanding of the subject matter that one judges the adequacy of the author's own handling of it, a judgment which led Bultmann into an extensive treatment of the distortions that are involved in the use of mythological or "objectivizing" language. Unlike liberal or orthodox exegesis, however, this enterprise required that the interpreter take myth seriously. Bultmann argued that it was a prescientific way of expressing man's awareness that he is "not master of the world and of his life, that the world within which he lives is full of riddles and mysteries and that human life also is full of riddles and mysteries. Mythology expresses a certain understanding of existence."[51] Consequently, it is important to analyze carefully the structure of any particular myth in order to discover (1) why the user of it thought it important to employ as a vehicle for his thought, (2) what understanding of existence is conveyed in its use, and (3) what problems arise for the author because of his use of it. Only in this way can one establish what the author intended to convey and whether he was successful in doing so. Only in this way can one understand.

6 · *The Deeper Issues in the Debate Concerning New Testament Interpretation*

In light of the preceding discussion, one can readily see that historical inquiry raises as serious and complex problems for New Testament interpretation as it does for Life-of-Jesus research and that here also Troeltsch's analysis proves haunting.

Consider the problem of historical understanding itself. On the basis of his principle of correlation, Troeltsch argued that no event or text can be understood unless it is seen in terms of its historical context. This meant, he thought, (1) that no critical historian could make use of supernatural intervention as a principle of historical explanation because this shattered the continuity of the causal nexus, and (2) that no event could be regarded as a final re-velation of the absolute spirit, since every manifestation of truth and value was relative and historically conditioned. Troeltsch believed that "history is no place for absolute religion and absolute person-alities."[52]

It is commonly believed that contemporary Protestant theology, especially dialectical theology, represents a repudiation of this prin-ciple of correlation and the two implications drawn from it. This is only a half-truth and, therefore, misleading. Consider, for ex-ample, the contribution of Barth's *Epistle to the Romans* and Bultmann's efforts to demythologize the New Testament, both of which have been regarded as diametrically opposed to Troeltsch's principle of interpretation. The works of these men actually embody a much more complex relationship to the principle of correlation. Both Barth and Bultmann accepted the view that no event could be explained except in terms of the causal nexus to-gether with the first implication that supernaturalistic modes of explanation were to be rejected. But both theologians rejected the second implication Troeltsch drew from his original principle, namely, that no single event could fully manifest the divine life.

This acceptance of one aspect of Troeltsch's principle and the rejection of the other was possible only because of a new theory of historical understanding. Barth and Bultmann, in effect, distin-guished between "explaining" and "understanding" an event. His-torical understanding, they said, depends to some extent on a reconstruction of the historical context in which an event or a text occurs, but this reconstruction may only be regarded as the first step toward historical understanding. True understanding occurs only when the interpreter comes to terms with the subject matter which is expressed in a text, when he comprehends in a vital way the perennial human questions which moved the author and the an-swers he proposed to them. To penetrate to this level, to under-stand in this sense, means that the interpreter must himself wrestle with the same question. He must, as it were, enter into a dialogue with the past. Only in this way can he make the past intelligible to the present.

To put the matter in this way, however, is also to reject the second implication Troeltsch saw in his principle of correlation, namely, that the divine reason does not choose to manifest itself in fullness in any one individual. Barth and Bultmann argued that this principle obscures the proper understanding of history. History, they said, is the realm in which, from time to time, reality speaks or breaks forth. This, Barth wrote, is precisely what the Christian means when he speaks of revelation in Jesus of Nazareth. The life and death of this man is that point in history in which one perceives "the crimson thread which runs through all history."[53] In Christ, "we have found the standard by which all discovery of God and all being discovered by Him is made known as such . . ."[54] Bultmann made a similar claim, especially in those essays in which he attempted to state the uniqueness of the Christian religion in contrast to others.[55] The truth of the New Testament is that it presents us with the proper understanding of man's situation before God. In short, both Barth and Bultmann agreed with Troeltsch's rejection of supernaturalism but disagreed with his skepticism concerning the possibility of a final revelation.

The position of Barth and Bultmann on this matter, as we shall see in a subsequent chapter, raises interesting theological problems of its own, problems which also have to do with the relationship of faith and historical inquiry. Stated quite crudely, one of the most important of these problems is this: If Jesus embodies the meaning of all history, does this not presuppose that he need not be considered the only and final revelation? Actually, the early Barth did not hesitate in his commentary to say that he was not. "In Jesus," he wrote, "we have discovered and recognized the truth that God is found everywhere and that, both before and after Jesus, men have been discovered by Him."[56] If this statement is true, however, in what sense is Jesus more than the occasion for the realization of some timeless truth which could have been realized had he never existed? In what sense was Jesus metaphysically unique, as Christian belief has always affirmed he was?

The question drives one to a consideration of Troeltsch's second principle, the principle of analogy. Once again, it is interesting to note that Barth and Bultmann affirmed this principle, albeit in a slightly altered form. All true understanding, they argued, rests on the assumption that the interpreter in the present has access to the same reality with which those in the past wrestled. The interpreter must necessarily assume some point of contact with Paul or with Jesus, for it is only on this basis that he can wrestle with the same questions and criticize the answers given in the past. But if this is true, then Christianity is confronted by a dilemma: without the principle of analogy, it seems impossible to understand the past; if, however, one employs the principle of analogy, it seems impossible to do justice to the alleged uniqueness of Jesus Christ. A great deal of the discussion in contemporary Protestant theology over the nature of hermeneutics is, as we shall see, an attempt to deal with this dilemma.

Finally, there is Troeltsch's third principle of criticism, namely, that every historical assertion can only achieve a lesser or a greater degree of probability and that no historical affirmation, therefore, can support the passion of faith. The certitude of faith must be independent of the probabilities of Biblical research. As we have seen, the dialectical theologians agreed with Troeltsch particularly at this point, and they attempted to secure faith against the uncertainties of Biblical criticism. This attempt, as we have also seen, has been severely criticized, not only by conservative theologians but by those who may be considered the heirs of dialectical theology, the proponents of the new quest and the new hermeneutics. Ernst Fuchs, Ernst Käsemann, James M. Robinson, all have argued with Gerhard Ebeling that Christian faith is necessarily exposed to the vulnerability and ambiguity of the historical.

On the surface, at least, this criticism seems just. Even if one ignores for the moment the possibility of historical knowledge about Jesus, it is difficult to see how one could hold, as the dialectical theologians did, that the Biblical *kerygma* is the object of faith and yet insist that faith is absolutely independent of all historical inquiry. How would one even know *what* the *kerygma* is except by an act of historical understanding? How can one grasp *what* Paul or John presents as an object of faith except by means of historical investigation?

To be confronted with this question is, however, to be confronted with the basic issue Troeltsch believed was inherent in his first principle of criticism: If historical inquiry can at best yield only results of a greater or lesser degree of probability, and if faith is said to be dependent on such inquiry, then how does one avoid identifying faith with assent to certain historical propositions and, thereby, corrupting the balance of judgment which is the *sine qua non* of critical historical work?

7 · An Angle of Vision

The preceding discussion makes clear, I hope, how complex and yet how important these issues are for theology. At one level, they may be regarded purely as philosophical problems, for example, the nature of historical explanation and understanding, the relationship of results to presuppositions, the distinction between fact and interpretation, the uses of analogy, the problem of objectivity, and the like. Yet, the resolutions of these philosophical problems obviously have theological implications, just as one's theological judgments impinge on the theory of historical interpretation.

Because these issues are so complex, it seems fruitless to try to solve them all within the pages of a single book. I do not propose to do so. Instead, I wish to create an angle of vision that will enable us to see these problems from a somewhat different standpoint, a standpoint from which it might prove fruitful to attempt a solution. This standpoint is based on the convictions that it is less helpful to talk about the historical method than it is to explore what I shall call the historian's morality of knowledge, or ethic of assent; that it is more confusing to try to define historical understanding than it is to ask how historians go about justifying their claims; that it is more misleading to ask how one can verify a historical assertion than it is to explore the numerous and diverse kinds of judgments historians make and the kinds of assent they solicit from their colleagues and readers.

This angle of vision, to be sure, owes much to the standpoint of Troeltsch who was so concerned with the characteristics of the historian's judgment. But his analysis was formulated in the somewhat ponderous and now unconvincing conceptual framework of German idealism, and it has seemed relatively easy for his critics to dismiss him for that reason. But one can, I believe, reformulate his most important insights in a fashion that is less heavy-handed, less inclined to carry the argument so quickly into the never-never land of metaphysical disputes.

The procedures and techniques of so-called analytic or linguistic philosophy are especially useful in this regard. In the first place, there is some virtue, I think, in discussing the problems of historical understanding in the context of the Anglo-American rather than the Germanic philosophical tradition. Until quite recently, the discussion of the problem of history has proceeded as though no English philosopher, with the exception of R. G. Collingwood, has had anything important to say. But a large and impressive literature dealing with the logic of historical inquiry and the nature of language has been produced in the last decade by American and English philosophers.[57] This literature has not only been unassessed, but does not even seem to be known by those in this country preoccupied with mediating the insights of such Continental scholars as Heidegger and Gadamer. It is assumed, mistakenly I think, that the new frontiers of theology will necessarily have scouts whose reports must first be translated from the German.

In the second place, the literature of the newer linguistic philosophy of history is singularly free from the neologisms and obscurities of so much contemporary German philosophy—especially existentialism—dealing with the subject of historical understanding. This lucidity, oddly enough, seems suspect in the eyes of those who are fascinated by the *Tiefsinningkeit* of that philosophy, as if clarity were necessarily a mark of superficiality and understanding too important to be easily understood. There is, to be sure, some truth in the charge that linguistic philosophy seems to be too preoccupied with questions of logic and meaning, in contrast with the larger issues of metaphysics. But this, I believe, is a superficial judgment. In fact, just because this philosophy has concentrated so heavily on the uses of language and the nature of truth-claims, it has something very important to contribute to the understanding of the relationship of historical judgments to religious beliefs. The linguistic philosophers have shown that these problems are too subtle and complex to lend themselves to high levels of abstraction, that it is far more productive, although a great deal more difficult, to sort out the issues one by one. Troeltsch saw that the crucial issue concerned two types of judgments, and it is unlikely that our opinions about more weighty matters will stand much scrutiny if we are unclear about this one.

NOTES TO CHAPTER ONE

1. Ernst Troeltsch, *Die Absolutheit des Christentums* (Tübingen: J. C. B. Mohr, 1902), p. 1; cf. Herbert Butterfield, *Man On His Past* (Cambridge: Cambridge University Press, 1955), p. 98.

2. Quoted by Ernst Cassirer in *The Problem of Knowledge*, trans. William H. Woglom and Charles W. Hendel (New Haven: Yale University Press, 1950), p. 228.

3. Ernst Troeltsch, *Gesammelte Schriften* (Tübingen: J. C. B. Mohr, 1913), II, 729-753.

4. *Ibid.*, p. 734.

5. *Ibid.*, p. 730.

6. Wilhelm Pauck points out the paradoxical relation in which Protestantism stands to historical criticism in *The Heritage of the Reformation* (rev. ed.; Glencoe, Ill.: The Free Press, 1961), pp. 30 ff; cf. Gerhard Ebeling, *Word and Faith* (Philadelphia: Fortress Press, 1960), chap. i.

7. Emanuel Hirsch, *Geschichte der neuern evangelischen Theologie im Zusammenhang mit den allgemeinen Bewegungen des europäischen Denken* (Gütersloh: C. Bertelsmann Verlag, 1954), V, 491.

8. David F. Strauss, *The Life of Jesus Critically Examined*, trans. George Eliot (5th ed.; London: Swan Sonnenschein & Co., 1906), Sec. 144.

9. Geoffrey Faber, *Oxford Apostles* (Baltimore: Penguin Books, 1954), p. 18.

10. Rudolf Bultmann, *Glauben und Verstehen* (Tübingen: J. C. B. Mohr, 1933), I, 2 f.

11. Hirsch, *op. cit.*, p. 492.

12. Strauss writes concerning his predecessors: "The entrance to the Gospel story was through the decorated portal of mythus, and the exit was similar to it, whilst the intermediate space was still traversed by the crooked and toilsome paths of natural interpretation." *Op. cit.*, Sec. 11.

13. *Ibid.*, Sec. 14.

14. *Ibid.*

15. Elsewhere, I have attempted to show how Strauss' Hegelian presuppositions enabled him to think historically, although they also stultified his judgment at another level. "D. F. Strauss' *Life of Jesus* Revisited," *Church History*, XXX (1961), 191-211.

16. Albert Schweitzer, *The Quest of the Historical Jesus,* trans. W. Montgomery (New York: The Macmillan Co., 1964), p. 96.

17. Quoted by Schweitzer, *op. cit.*, p. 243.

18. See Karl Barth, *The Epistle to the Romans,* trans. Edwyn C. Hoskyns (6th ed.; London: Oxford University Press, 1933), p. 105. Cf. Emil Brunner, *The Mediator,* trans. Olive Wyon (Philadelphia: Westminster Press, 1947), pp. 184 ff.

19. D. M. Baillie, *God Was in Christ* (New York: Charles Scribner's Sons, 1948), p. 28.

20. *Ibid.,* p. 52.

21. I write "alleged" because Bultmann's position is considerably more complex. See Van A. Harvey and Schubert M. Ogden, "How New is the 'New Quest' of the Historical Jesus?" in Carl E. Braaten and Roy A. Harrisville, *The Historical Jesus and the Kerygmatic Christ* (New York: Abingdon Press, 1964), pp. 197-242.

22. James M. Robinson, *A New Quest of the Historical Jesus* (Naperville, Ill.: Alec R. Allenson, Inc., 1959). A revised German edition appeared under the title *Kerygma und historischer Jesus* (Zürich: Zwingli Verlag, 1960) and a second edition of this will be published shortly.

23. See Harvey K. McArthur, "A Survey of Recent Gospel Research" in Martin E. Marty and Dean G. Peerman (eds.), *New Theology No. 2* (New York: The Macmillan Co., 1965), pp. 201-221.

24. Troeltsch, *Gesammelte Schriften,* II, 729-753; cf. his article "Historiography" in James Hastings (ed.), *Encyclopedia of Religion and Ethics* (New York: Charles Scribner's Sons, 1914), VI, 716-723.

25. See H. R. Mackintosh, *Types of Modern Theology* (London: Nisbet & Co., 1937), pp. 201 f.

26. Strauss, *op. cit.,* Sec. 14.

27. Rudolf Bultmann, *Existence and Faith,* ed. Schubert M. Ogden (New York: Meridian Books, Inc., 1960), pp. 291 f.

28. *Ibid.,* p. 292.

29. Richard R. Niebuhr, *Resurrection and Historical Reason* (New York: Charles Scribner's Sons, 1957).

30. Alan Richardson, *History Sacred and Profane* (Philadelphia: Westminster Press, 1964), p. 153.

31. Ebeling, *op. cit.,* pp. 56 f.

32. Rudolf Bultmann, *Die Erforschung der Synoptischen Evangelien* (3d ed.; Berlin: Alfred Topelmann, 1960), p. 15. The reader may confirm Bultmann's impression by perusing a recent anthology of scholarly opinion about Jesus, *Der historische Jesus und der kerygmatische Christus,* ed. Helmut Ristow and Karl Matthiae (Berlin: Evangelische Verlaganstalt, 1960).

33. Ebeling, *op. cit.,* pp. 17-61.

34. It appears that the views of the Protestant Reformers, especially of Luther, were quite radical when measured against the subsequent views of Protestant orthodoxy. Convinced that the sole content of revelation is God's righteousness revealed in Jesus Christ, Luther identified the inspiration of the Holy Spirit with the *proper* witness to God's justifying act. The Word of God, then, became the standard against which the words of the various Biblical writers were measured. This "canon within the canon" enabled Luther to be quite critical of much that was in the Bible. See his prefaces to the New Testament in *Luther's Works: Word and Sacrament, I,* ed.

E. Theodore Bachmann (Philadelphia: Muhlenberg Press, 1960), XXXV, 357-411.

35. Hellenistic modes of thought may have penetrated more deeply into Judaism than hitherto believed by many scholars; nevertheless, the picture I have painted represents something like a consensus among New Testament critics.

36. See Rudolf Bultmann, *Theology of the New Testament*, trans. Kendrick Grobel (New York: Charles Scribner's Sons, 1951), 1, 46 f. For an interesting discussion of the way Jesus' death was interpreted, see Heinz-Dieter Knigge "Erlösung durch Jesus Tod," *Una Sancta*, XVIII (1963), 341-377.

37. See especially Paul's letters to the Thessalonians.

38. Herbert Braun, *Gesammelte Studien zum Neuen Testament und seiner Umwelt* (Tübingen: J. C. B. Mohr, 1962), pp. 243-282.

39. *Ibid.*, pp. 252 ff.

40. See Philipp Vielhauer, "On the 'Paulism' of Acts," *Perkins School of Theology Journal*, XVII, 1 (1963), pp. 5-17.

41. F. C. Grant, *An Introduction to New Testament Thought* (New York: Abingdon Press, 1950), p. 30.

42. Barth, *Epistle to the Romans*, p. 6.

43. *Ibid.*, p. 8.

44. *Ibid.*, p. 10.

45. *Ibid.*, p. 8.

46. Robinson, *op. cit.*, p. 38.

47. Barth, *op. cit.*, pp. 96 ff.

48. See Rudolf Bultmann, "Karl Barth's 'Römerbrief' in zweiter Auflage," *Anfänge der dialektischen Theologie*, ed. Jürgen Moltmann (Munich: Chr. Kaiser Verlag, 1962), I, 119-142.

49. See Bultmann, "Is Exegesis Without Presuppositions Possible?" *Existence and Faith*, pp. 289-296; cf. *Essays*, trans. James C. G. Greig (London: SCM Press Ltd., 1955), pp. 234-261.

50. Bultmann, *Existence and Faith*, p. 296.

51. Rudolf Bultmann, *Jesus Christ and Mythology* (New York: Charles Scribner's Sons, 1958), p. 19.

52. Troeltsch, *Die Absolutheit des Christentums*, p. 41.

53. Barth, *op. cit.*, p. 96.

54. *Ibid.*, p. 97.

55. Bultmann, *Essays*, pp. 209-233.

56. Barth, *op. cit.*, p. 97.

57. In 1961 and 1964, the recently founded journal *History and Theory*, which is devoted entirely to the problems of the philosophy of history, published extensive bibliographies of books and articles in this field between 1945-1961. See Beiheft 1 (1961) and Beiheft 3 (1964). In 1962, the fifth annual Conference of the New York University Institute of Philosophy was devoted entirely to problems in the philosophy of history, and its proceedings were published as *Philosophy and History*, ed. Sidney Hook (New York: New York University Press, 1963). For one of the more recent general introductions to the subject matter, see William H. Dray, *Philosophy of History* (Englewood Cliffs, N.J.: Prentice-Hall, Inc., 1964).

II

Autonomy, Assessment, and Sound Judgment

1 · The Ideal of Sound Judgment

ALTHOUGH Ernst Troeltsch saw that the results of historical inquiry raised serious problems for traditional Christian belief, he was mainly concerned to point out that the crucial issues lay at the deeper level of method and presupposition. He perceived that the historical method is but the expression of a new morality of critical judgment that has seized the imagination of the scholar in the Western world and that it is this ideal which seems incompatible with the ethic of belief that has dominated Christendom for centuries. In this chapter, I shall explore some of the basic elements of this new morality because it is impossible to understand sympathetically the difficulties the critical mind has with Christian belief, or to evaluate the various attempts made by Christian theologians to surmount these difficulties, without some clear conception of the basic elements of this ideal of critical judgment.

Four interrelated aspects of this ideal are especially important: the radical autonomy of the historian; the responsibility he has for making his arguments and statements capable of rational assessment; the need to exercise sound and balanced judgment; the need to use his critically interpreted experience as the background against which sound judgments are made about the past. Because of the close connection between the first three of these elements, I shall discuss them in this chapter and reserve the fourth for the next one.

2 · *The Autonomy of the Historian*

If there is any characteristic of the modern critical spirit readily identifiable, it is the insistence on the right to think for oneself, to be free from any authority that would circumscribe research and inquiry. This elevation of autonomy to the first rank of intellectual virtues is deeply rooted in the Western intellectual tradition, Socrates being its first champion and martyr. Although deeply rooted in this tradition, however, this virtue came to full flower only in the Enlightenment. Indeed, in his famous essay in which he tried to delineate the spirit of this movement, Immanuel Kant identified enlightenment with autonomy.[1] Enlightenment, he wrote, is man's release from all authority that would deprive him of his freedom to think without direction from another.

Contrary to some interpretations of the Enlightenment, it was not characterized by a naive confidence in man's actual rationality. Kant's essay is not devoted to the proposition that men are rational; it is, rather, a revolutionary call for men to throw off the chains of a brutish existence and to dare to think. Kant did not believe that enlightenment was common or even easily achieved among men. We do not live in an enlightened age, he wrote, but in an age of enlightenment.[2] And it was just because he believed men found thinking for themselves difficult and dangerous that he found it necessary to issue a manifesto. "Have the courage to use your own reason"[3] was his declaration of independence against every authority that rests on the dictatorial command, "Obey, don't think."

From the standpoint of the twentieth century, it requires an act of historical imagination to conceive of the magnitude of the revolution Kant called for and that was finally realized. It required nothing less than a transformation of the intellectual ideal that had possessed the heart of Christendom for centuries, the ideal of *belief*. Kant celebrated the will-to-truth more than the will-to-believe, investigation more than certainty, autonomy more than obedience to authority. Some prophetic souls in the nineteenth century, like John Henry Newman and Friedrich Nietzsche, saw the implications of this new revolutionary attitude, and their writings reflect a

sense of the profundity of the transformation of values involved.
Both foresaw that the new ethic of rationalism would, like a tidal
wave, inundate the continent of Christian belief. Newman desperately tried to find a rock of authority against which the floods
could not prevail while Nietzsche preached the emergence of a new
man out of the drowning of the old. But, to change the metaphor,
both were quite aware that a new epoch had been conceived and
that a new culture was coming to birth.

The new spirit of autonomy permeated all aspects of human
culture—philosophy, the sciences, historiography, and finally, government. So far as historiography was concerned, the Copernican
revolution occurred, as R. G. Collingwood notes, with the discovery that

so far from relying on an authority other than himself, to whose
statements his thought must conform, the historian is his own authority and his thought autonomous, self-authorizing, possessed of a
criterion to which his so-called authorities must conform and by
reference to which they are criticized.[4]

This discovery was revolutionary, Collingwood continues, because it contradicted the traditional and widely held view that the
historian's task is one of compiling and synthesizing the testimony
of so-called authorities or eyewitnesses. Formerly, the function of
the historian was regarded essentially as an editorial and harmonizing one. It rested on the assumption that the historian has an
obligation to believe another person's report when that person
claims to have knowledge of or to have observed an event. The
historian is regarded as the believer and the person believed is the
authority. This, however, is not critical but "scissors-and-paste"
history. "In so far as an historian accepts the testimony of an
authority and treats it as historical truth," writes Collingwood, "he
obviously forfeits the name of historian; but we have no other
name by which to call him."[5]

So expressed, this declaration of autonomy may sound extreme,
an overreaction, perhaps, to the naive confidence of a previous
generation concerning the trustworthiness of testimony. Hence,
some may think that it needs to be interpreted largely as a dra-

matic way of warning the historian to be on his guard against error and fraud. There is some truth in this thought. It can scarcely be doubted that the autonomy of the critical history of the eighteenth and nineteenth centuries was occasioned to some degree by the discovery of the widespread occurrence of error, fraud, and forgery that were perpetrated, as often as not, by souls who otherwise deserved to be thought honest and saintly men. Marc Bloch, for example, cites a number of instances from medieval times in which fraud was committed for what must have seemed, at the time, to have been the highest of motives: the false charters and pontifical decrees aimed at securing disputed property for the church, or at supporting the claims of the Roman See, or at defending the monks against the bishop, the bishop against the metropolitan, and the popes against the emperors.[6] So numerous were such frauds that one can only conclude, with Bloch, that "forgeries were hardly offensive to public morality. As for plagiarism, it was at this time universally regarded as the most innocent act in the world."[7] Skepticism of received reports, therefore, became a necessary attitude for the critical historian.

It would be an oversimplification, however, to interpret the radical autonomy of the historian as merely a dramatic warning to be on one's guard against error and fraud. This autonomy is grounded in the nature of historical knowledge itself. The historian has primarily, though not solely, to work with the judgments and inferences of others, and his own conclusions, like theirs, are judgments and inferences. But no witness simply hands down a complete, photograph-like description of an event; rather, he selects, alters, interprets, and rationalizes. Insofar as this is true, an element of judgment is necessarily present. But, as F. H. Bradley once perceptively pointed out,[8] judgments are not mere random inventions or isolated occurrences of thought. They presuppose other judgments, beliefs, and opinions as the background against which they occur and in the light of which they have meaning. What a witness thinks he sees is in large part filtered through the prism of his own individual mode of perception and conception which, in turn, is heavily influenced by the modes of thought of the culture of which he is a part. Men are historical creatures, and their judgments reflect the "world" that they bring with them and to which they appeal in support of those judgments.

It is the function of the historian to assess these judgments and inferences, to establish not only their meaning but their truth. He cannot avoid either task, for to assume that the reports mean what the ordinary reader takes them to mean overlooks the historically conditioned nature of thought. To leave them uncriticized is simply to attribute to the witness a capacity for critical judgment the historian himself lacks or is too timid to exercise.

Insofar then as history aspires to be knowledge, in contrast to belief, the historian must give reasons for what he asserts. As soon as the reasons are forthcoming one ceases to rely on mere authority or testimony. This is why Collingwood can argue that the historian has no right to leave his authorities unchallenged.

If anyone else, no matter who, even a very learned historian, or an eyewitness, or a person in the confidence of the man who did the thing he is inquiring into, or even the man who did it himself, hands him on a plate a ready-made answer to his question, all he can do is to reject it: not because he thinks his informant is trying to deceive him, or is himself deceived, but because if he accepts it he is giving up his autonomy as an historian and allowing someone else to do for him what, if he is a scientific thinker, he can only do for himself.[9]

The historian *confers* authority upon a witness. He reserves the right to judge who or what will be called an authority, and he makes this judgment only after he has subjected the so-called witness to a rigorous cross-examination. Like Bacon's scientist, who does not merely observe nature but puts specific questions to it, the historian calls his witnesses to the stand and extorts information from them "which in their original statements they have withheld, either because they did not wish to give it or because they did not possess it."[10]

The historian, in short, is radically autonomous because of the nature of historical knowledge itself. If the historian permits his authorities to stand uncriticized, he abdicates his role as critical historian. He is no longer a seeker of knowledge but a mediator of past belief; not a thinker but a transmitter of tradition.

3 · The Historian's Judgment and the Assessment of Argument

Although the radical autonomy of the historian is ranked high on the scale of values derived from the critical ideal of judgment, it cannot be isolated from another value that prevents that autonomy from becoming mere subjectivism: the communication of the historian's conclusions to others in such a way that these conclusions can be assessed by those who have competence to do so. The will-to-truth, which requires a protest against all restrictions on inquiry, is a correlate of the will-to-communication. The early defenders of enlightenment were also aware of this. Thus, in the same essay in which Kant eloquently demanded freedom from authority, he made it clear that this was a "freedom to make public use of one's reason at every point."[11] This public use of reason was an obligation Kant laid especially upon the scholar. He conceded that in one's vocational role as, say, a clergyman or civil servant, it might be necessary and proper to make one's utterances conform to the conditions laid down by the community of which he is a representative. But the scholar must enjoy complete freedom, for only if he possesses complete freedom can he fulfill his duty "to communicate to the public all his carefully tested and well-meaning thoughts on that which is erroneous. . . ."[12]

This emphasis on public communication reinforces the demand for rational assessment. It puts the highest priority on logical candor and the giving of reasons for one's claims. For all claims are implicit appeals to other persons. And our respect for persons is directly proportionate to the degree to which we make clear the worthiness of our claims. Consequently, logical candor is not a rationalistic ideal; it is the necessary condition for all responsible dialogue that aims at achieving genuine knowledge.

It was their aspiration to achieve genuine knowledge that partially justified the frequent comparison of history with the physical sciences made by nineteenth-century historians. For them, science provided the paradigm of knowledge. This comparison, as we shall

see, can be misleading, but it is not misleading to say, as Collingwood does say, that

> History has this in common with every other science: that the histo-
> rian is not allowed to claim any single piece of knowledge, except
> where he can justify his claim by exhibiting to himself in the first
> place, and secondly to any one else who is both able and willing to
> follow his demonstration, the grounds upon which it is based.[13]

It is the word "justify" here that must hold our attention
throughout this discussion of the morality of historical knowledge.
For the issue that will concern us in the subsequent pages is not a
theory of historical explanation but the justification of the explanations historians offer when these explanations are challenged.
The hallmark of knowledge, in contrast to emotive expression on
the one hand, and opinion on the other, is, as Stephen Toulmin has
pointed out, that it consists of assertions that are something like
claims to a right or a title.[14] And when these claims are challenged one is able to produce some appropriate justification for
them. But all claims presuppose standards or canons. Whether any
specific claim is to be regarded as a valid one can only be judged
on its merits which, as in all cases where truth is at stake, are
functions of the argument and the evidence brought forward on its
behalf. Without such merits, the assertion can only be considered
as a belief or an opinion. Indeed, to say "I believe" is tantamount
to saying, "I lack sufficient grounds to claim 'I know,' " just as to
say, "I am of the opinion that," immediately apprises our listener,
in most cases, that our assertions do not justify a certain level of
certainty even in our own eyes.

It is in this context that the frequent but too roughhewn question, "Can history be objective?" is best examined.[15] The issue is
not, as we shall see in a later chapter, whether the historian necessarily selects some events to write about rather than others; or
whether the historian writes with bloodless detachment or not; or
whether he can abstract himself from what are loosely called his
presuppositions; or whether judgments about remote events can be
proved absolutely. The issue is, rather, as John Dewey has pointed
out, "Upon what grounds are some judgments about a course of

past events more entitled to credence than are certain other ones?"[16] Just as we can give reasons for our claims about such diverse things as the guilt of a defendant in a murder trial, the superiority of Mozart's Fortieth Symphony to the Third Symphony of Ralph Vaughan Williams, the integrity of one political candidate in contrast to another; so, too, the historian can presumably justify one set of assertions about the past in contrast to others it is possible to make.

What are the grounds upon which some judgments about a course of past events are more entitled to credence than others? The answer to this question serves to divide philosophers of history into roughly two groups: (1) those who have maintained that entitlement to credence is directly proportionate to the degree to which historical explanations approximate scientific explanations; and (2) those who have argued that historical explanations are of a unique sort and require no reference whatever to the hallmark of scientific explanations, the subsumption of a statement under a law.[17]

The first group of philosophers insist that explanations in general and historical explanations in particular are sound only when they utilize laws; that is, when a conclusion is derived deductively from premises that include universal laws together with a certain singular statement or assertion. Although the historian, unlike the scientist, does not *establish* laws, it is argued, he *uses* them explicitly or implicitly, although these laws are usually of such a well-known sort that to state them would be trivial. Nevertheless, it is possible to restate the historian's explanations in the form of a deduction, and it is this possibility that justifies calling these explanations knowledge.

The second group of philosophers have brought this argument under sharp and, perhaps, devastating criticism.[18] Although there are important differences among these critics, they are unified at least in the view that the historian neither uses laws explicitly nor implicitly and that the scientific model is, therefore, fundamentally irrelevant. William Dray, who has written the most extended criticism of what he calls the "covering law model," insists that a covering law is neither a necessary nor a sufficient condition for historical explanations.[19] He argues that historical events are unique and that explanation models useful for prediction in science simply do not apply to history. Furthermore, he maintains, with Collingwood and others, that history has fundamentally to do with the actions of human beings, and to understand such actions, the historian must discover the "thought-side" of them. He must *"penetrate* behind appearances, achieve *insight* into the situation, *identify* himself sympathetically with the protagonist, *project* himself imaginatively into his situation. He must *revive, re-enact, rethink, re-experience* the hopes, fears, plans, desires, views, intentions, etc., of those he seeks to understand."[20] Since he believes that the covering-law theory can be demonstrated to be irrelevant to this process, Dray concludes that it ought to be abandoned as a model for historical explanation.

It is especially tempting for Christian apologists to reject the theory of historical interpretation which appeals to laws and to identify themselves with the view which interprets historiography as the intuitive re-enactment of the "inside" of past human events. Orthodox theologians, especially, have been enamored with Collingwood's argument because it seems to remove the onus of having to justify certain Biblical narratives as history, especially miracles. Other theologians also have seen in this new model of history the "Magna Carta of modern historians" in general and of New Testament historians in particular. Presumably this new view establishes that since there are no facts without interpretation, it is no objection to the New Testament that it continually blends theological interpretation with fact.[21] Still other theologians employ a similar model to justify a new quest of the historical Jesus, a quest that allegedly escapes the defects of the nineteenth-century attempts to write a life of Jesus.

The temptation to embrace any of these views should be resisted, however, because, as will become plain in the following argument, not only do these alternatives fail to do justice to the extraordinary diversity of purpose expressed in historical inquiry and writing but they tend to distract the reader from the real problem that arises between secular historiography and traditional Christian belief. This problem, I will argue, is best seen, not when we focus on the nature of historical explanation as such, but when we ask about the kinds of justifications that are appropriate for certain kinds of historical statements. The problem of justification cannot, to be sure, be isolated completely from the larger problem of explanation. But there are great advantages in concentrating on the former. By concentrating on the problem of the justification of historical assertions, it is possible to throw into relief the subjective process of judgment itself, and only when this process of judgment is understood does it become clear why the basic but unspoken issue between the historian and the believer is a difference concerning intellectual integrity, the morality of knowledge.

There is another advantage in keeping our eye firmly on the justification of assertions. It provides a point of contact with certain movements in modern logic that are concerned not so much with abstract and formal logic or with "laws of thought" as with the examination of arguments that occur in practical discourse, that is, with the inquiry into the soundness of the claims we make in daily life. Convinced that the models of logicians and philosophers of science have become more and more irrelevant, Toulmin, for example, has persuasively argued that the purpose of logic should be the study of the actual forms of argument which appear in all their variety in everyday life: in scientific, political, ethical, theological, and legal discussion. "Logic," he writes, "is concerned with the soundness of the claims we make—with the solidity of the grounds we produce to support them, the firmness of the backing we provide for them—or, to change the metaphor, with the sort of *case* we present in defence of our claims."[22]

My concern with this development in modern logic is based on the conviction that this approach opens up a new series of possibilities for answering our questions about history and belief. It robs the usual models of historical understanding of their seductive power. Once it is seen that the standards in the light of which historical assertions have too often been measured are irrelevant, it becomes possible to see why the counterreactions with which we are tempted to identify ourselves are equally unnecessary. For example, the attempt by some logicians to superimpose standards taken from the sciences or mathematics on all forms of discourse had the inevitable result of consigning great numbers of perfectly good cognitive assertions to the limbo of meaninglessness. The result was skepticism or frantic attempts to redeem the situation by ingenious epistemological theories.[23] This has also happened in the realm of historical knowledge. When it became clear that very few of our assertions about the past can measure up to standards appropriate to the sciences and mathematics, one was driven to embrace skepticism (all history is an act of faith) or its cousin, relativism (every historian necessarily writes from his perspective). Or one was forced to turn to those curious attempts to redeem history by invoking strange and wonderful faculties, like *Erlebnis* and intuition, or by creating brilliantly imaginative but unconvincing arguments concerning the ability of thought to transcend time.

All of these efforts presuppose, first, that there is one unique kind of judgment called historical and, second, that our ordinary assertions about the past need redemption, that it is necessary to vindicate before the bar of a formal logic our assertions about Caesar's purposes in crossing the Rubicon, the causes of the French Revolution, Abraham Lincoln's intention in releasing the slaves, the reasons for Hitler's defeat. But there would be no need to armor ourselves against skepticism or to flee to bizarre epistemological theories if we but moderated our ambitions, if we demanded of our arguments and claims to knowledge in any field *not* that they be scientifically justified but that they achieve whatever cogency or well-foundedness can relevantly be asked for in that field.[24]

Let us turn, then, to a brief examination of the nature of argument in general and of historical argument in particular. We will need to keep in mind whether there is any one model that covers all the diversity of arguments constitutive of history or whether this diversity itself provides us with a clue for dealing with the problem of historical judgment. In what follows the reader will recognize my dependence on the work of Stephen Toulmin, which I gratefully acknowledge, although I will have to bear the responsibility for the use, and possible misuse, of it.

4 · The Structure of Argument

As soon as one turns from textbooks on logic to the actual discourse of men engaged in daily affairs, he will be struck by the incredible diversity of argument that appears there and the correspondingly diverse justifications brought forward in support of claims and assertions. Men dispute whether a certain candidate for public office possesses sufficient maturity to warrant voting for him, whether a man who is accused of being an accomplice in the mass execution of Jews had a fair trial, whether Professor Segre's theory of antimatter is a good scientific hypothesis, whether taxes should be cut to stimulate the economy, whether Bach should be interpreted according to Albert Schweitzer's theories, whether General Eisenhower had the best strategy for bringing the Third Reich to its knees in 1944, or whether smoking is a contributing cause of lung cancer. In all of these cases, we are presented with different logical types of conclusions requiring correspondingly different types of evidence to support them and different types of steps linking the evidence to the conclusions one infers from it.

In order to call attention to the various types of possible arguments, Toulmin employs a somewhat technical term that will prove important in our subsequent discussion about history, namely, a field of argument.[25] By a "field of argument" he does not necessarily mean a field in the sense that word has come to have in scholarly circles, as when we say of a person that his field is nineteenth-century history, or political science, or chemistry. Rather, the word "field" refers to a logical type of assertion that may be delimited from other types, like statements about motives may be distinguished from geometric axioms, or statements about moral guilt may be distinguished from assertions about legal responsibility. This distinction between field in the scholarly sense and field in the logical sense is especially significant because some scholarly fields like, say, law may be, logically speaking, field-encompassing fields, which is to say, various and diverse logical types of argument are necessary to come to a legal conclusion. In order to determine legal guilt in a murder case, for example, the prosecution may have to employ arguments about motives, medical arguments concerning the cause of death, arguments about the physical possibility of traveling between one city and another in a specified length of time, arguments based on handwriting analysis, and legal arguments establishing the jurisdiction of the court or the admissibility of evidence. To say that two arguments belong to the same field, then, is to say that "the data and the conclusions in each of the two arguments are, respectively, of the same logical type. . . ."[26] To say that two arguments are not in the same field is to say that the data and the conclusions in each of the two arguments are not of the same logical type.

Since there are so many different possible types of argument, the question naturally arises whether there are common features shared by all of the various types so that there can be common standards for assessing them. In short, what features vary from field to field and what features remain the same?

Toulmin argues that all justificatory arguments have a similarity of form regardless of the various types of data one brings forward or the steps one takes to arrive at the conclusion. He calls this form the initial phase of an argument.[27] This phase is one we are all familiar with, although it is so habitual we are scarcely aware of it. It involves (1) formulating a question, (2) marshaling the various likely candidates for a solution to the question, (3) searching for a particular candidate that seems indicated by the evidence, and (4) eliminating the alternatives incompatible with the evidence. These are normally the implicit steps taken whether we are justifying a legal decision, the marking of a ballot, the choice of a business partner, a judgment about military strategy, a prediction about the weather, or an opinion about the adequacy of an explanation in a history book. The criteria invoked in each case (field) may vary widely, but this initial phase provides the context within which all our arguments will take place.

If, for the moment, we pass beyond the initial phase of an argument and attend to any particular one, we will notice that it also has a recognizable structure and form.[28] Any assertion that

we might make can be regarded as a conclusion—let us label it
(C)—for which certain data (D) could presumably be brought
forward were the conclusion (C) to be challenged. The most obvious challenge, of course, is the question, "What have you got to go
on?" When confronted with it we naturally appeal to some facts or
data that we think back up our claim. There may be a dispute
about the data, to be sure, but for the purposes of analyzing the
structure of the argument we need only be clear about the formalities of the matter at this point.

It is possible, however, to challenge a conclusion (C) with another kind of question. Suppose the question with which we are
confronted is not "What have you got to go on?" but "How did
you get from those data to that conclusion?" In this case, our
challenger is not asking for more facts or information but for
something that legitimizes the passage from the given data to the
conclusion. He wants to know something about the steps in our
argument. In such cases as these, we need to possess an inference-
license, or what Toulmin prefers to call a warrant (W). Warrants
are bridges, so to speak, that make possible the passage from data
(D) to conclusion (C).[29]

Suppose, then, we schematize the relationships between data
(D), warrant (W), and conclusion (C) as follows, with the arrow
representing the direction of the argument:

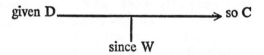

$$\text{given D} \longrightarrow \text{so C}$$
$$|$$
$$\text{since W}$$

A very simple example of such an argument might go something
like this: X claims that Jesus was obviously executed by the
Romans as a political offender. Y asks, "What have you to go
on?" and X replies, "He was crucified, was he not?" X's reply is an
appeal to a fact. But Y is unsatisfied. "Yes, I know," Y says, "but
my problem is how you pass from that fact to your conclusion." X
then appeals to a warrant: "Well, we know that crucifixion was
reserved for political crimes and no other." X's argument, when
diagrammed, is as follows:

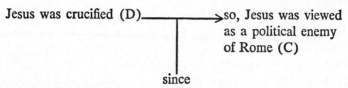

Jesus was crucified (D)⟶ so, Jesus was viewed as a political enemy of Rome (C)

since

crucifixion was reserved for political enemies by Rome (W)

On grammatical grounds alone, it might be said that no sharp distinction can be drawn between data and warrants. But in some cases it is possible to note how each serves a quite different logical function. The appeal to data is direct, while the warrant functions indirectly and in an explanatory fashion, "its task being simply to register explicitly the legitimacy of the step involved and to refer it back to the larger class of steps whose legitimacy is being presupposed."[30] Data are appealed to explicitly, warrants are most often implicit. They certify the soundness of all arguments of a given sort. This, in turn, points to an important fact; namely, warrants in any given field of argument are usually assumed. Indeed, *unless we did tacitly assume some kinds of warrants in any given field, it would be impossible to submit any argument in that field to rational assessment, because the data to which we appeal when challenged depend on just those warrants we are prepared to accept.* "We should not even know what sort of data were of the slightest relevance to a conclusion, if we had not at least a provisional idea of the warrants acceptable in the situation confronting us."[31] Thus, the data to which we explicitly appeal when challenged will depend on the warrants we are prepared to accept, and those warrants are implicit in the steps we are prepared to take from data to conclusion.

This bare framework may seem trivial as it stands, nothing but a modern version of the ancient syllogism. Toulmin insists that it does avoid certain ambiguities in the latter, although it is beyond the scope of my purpose to pursue his reasoning in this respect.[32] But that it is not trivial will become clear, I think, when we add some superstructure and masonry to our basic framework. And the first important addition to it concerns the warrant. Warrants, it will be noted, not only legitimize the step from data to conclusion but also confer *differing degrees of force on a conclusion*. They permit us not merely to assent to a claim but they justify a certain texture of assent.[33] Some warrants authorize us to accept a conclusion unequivocally while others make it necessary to introduce some kind of qualification. Some warrants justify a heavy assent while others require that we indicate some quality of assent ranging from tentativity to near certainty. Thus it is necessary to add still another element to our structure: a model qualifier (Q) that indicates it is appropriate to place a "necessarily" before some claims, a "probably," a "presumably," or a "possibly" before others.

It is also possible, however, to enter two kinds of objections to the use of a warrant: (1) One may insist that the warrant does not apply in the particular case under discussion, that it has, for some reason, no authority, or (2) one may challenge the truth of the warrant itself. In the first case, we have entered a rebuttal (R), and the force of it is to say that the conclusion (C) follows from the data (D) *unless* the rebuttal is true. Thus, if we were to consider the argument that Jesus was executed for political reasons because he was crucified, it might be replied that this is true unless, in this particular case, an exception was made, an exception, say, to appease the Jewish authorities.[34] Our diagram would then look like this:

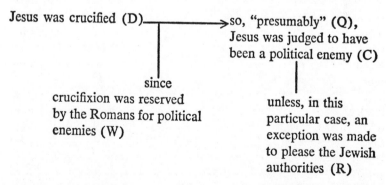

Jesus was crucified (D) ⟶ so, "presumably" (Q), Jesus was judged to have been a political enemy (C)

since
crucifixion was reserved by the Romans for political enemies (W)

unless, in this particular case, an exception was made to please the Jewish authorities (R)

If, however, Y were to reject this warrant, in contrast to questioning its applicability in this case, what then? Then the claimant

X would have to construct another line of defense. He would have to provide a backing (B) for his warrant. In the example above, if Y were to argue that crucifixion was, in fact, not reserved for the political enemies of Rome, it would be necessary for X to settle that issue before any judgment (C) could be made.

When we have added all these elements to our diagram, it will assume this complete form:

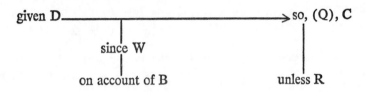

given D————————————————————————→so, (Q), C

| since W

on account of B   unless R

Now, just as data differ from warrants by virtue of their function, so backings, which appear to be like data and warrants, differ from both because of their role in the dynamics of argument.[35] They differ from data in that data are explicitly produced whereas the backing of a warrant will not normally be invoked unless the warrant is challenged. They differ from warrants in that warrants serve the practical function of legitimizing the passage from data to claim, while backings lend authority to this practical function of the warrants.

5 · *The Relevance of the Model: History as a Field-Encompassing Field*

If one holds this model of argument before his mind's eye and at the same time inspects concrete historical arguments, he will be struck by these features. First of all, it will be clear that the reference to historical judgments as such contains an ambiguity and a temptation. The ambiguity is that the term "historical judgments" suggests there is one identifiable class or field of judgments called historical, as there is one class of judgments called, say, mathematical, or chemical, or the like. Assuming there is one such class, the temptation is to think that we can find one identifiable characteristic of such judgments and so discover one single method of verifying them. Or, to use our model of argument, we will be tempted to look for one peculiar field of judgments (and one identifiable set of warrants) we can label "historical."

Philosophers of history have time and again succumbed to this temptation. They have sought to equate history with some unique subject matter, like human intention and action, and then have had to argue (1) that no other type of judgment properly qualifies as historical, and (2) that there is one and only one mode of historical knowledge. Or they have tended to argue that all knowledge, if it is to be called knowledge at all, must conform to the methods appropriate to the sciences and have then arrived at the paradoxical position that most of our confident assertions about the past do not deserve any confidence.

If, however, history is not so much a field as a field-encompassing field, which is to say, made up of diverse kinds of arguments making use of correspondingly diverse data and warrants, then the quest for one theory of historical explanation is seen to be fruitless, creating insoluble paradoxes that paralyze thought.[36] It is possible that some explanations will make use of laws; others will employ "law-like" generalizations; still others will fit neither of these models at all.[37] It follows that there will also be diverse kinds of verification, and no one can anticipate in advance how one can go about ascertaining their truth. To demand that historians should be able to state in advance and in clear and simple terms the criteria for justifying historical claims is naive, and one can only reply to it in such general terms as, "There should be good data and warrants." But this tells us nothing until we know what kind of assertions we have on our hands, for there is no one particular kind of assertion peculiar to history. The real issue is not whether history can be objective or a science but whether, in particular cases, diverse kinds of claims can achieve an appropriate and relevant justification. Just as we do not ask in a sweeping fashion whether legal judgments can be objective or not but attend to the more productive task of sorting out those that are adjudicable, so, too, we ought to forsake the wholesale questions about history and attend to the retail standards by which we can realistically hope to measure diverse claims.

The diversity of claims is perhaps the most striking characteristic of historical writing. This diversity can be seen at all levels of historiography: at the levels of criticism, reconstruction, and interpretation. Consider briefly, for example, the development of the diverse sciences which have been created to handle the problems arising at the level of historical criticism. The science of epigraphy was developed to solve the difficulties encountered in interpreting inscriptions; paleography, to decipher ancient writing. The study of charters and deeds has created diplomatics; the analysis of monuments and artifacts, archaeology; the classification of seals and armorial bearings, sigilography and heraldry. The historian is in many cases dependent on these sciences, and the results in each of them reflect a background of argument. Consequently, it seems arbitrary to reject these as historical judgments on the grounds that they are concerned with external facts or that they are preliminary to the problem of reconstruction and interpretation. One might as well say that the lawyer's attempt to establish the integrity of a witness is not a legal argument because it is only preliminary to the weightier matter of evaluating the bearing of his testimony on the case at hand.

The diversity of historical argument, its field-encompassing character, is even more apparent at the level of reconstruction. Consider, for example, the complexity of Chester Wilmot's discussion of the strategic debate between Generals Eisenhower and Montgomery in 1944 in *The Struggle for Europe*.[38] The question facing the Allied powers at the time was how to bring the war to its quickest and most decisive resolution. Eisenhower's strategy was to advance the Allied armies along a broad front, the entire length of the Rhine, before attacking the heartland of the Third Reich. Montgomery favored a bold, concerted, knifelike thrust at the Ruhr-Aachen area, which was producing 51.7 per cent of the hard coal and 50.5 percent of the crude oil for the German war machine. Montgomery's solution was, as we know, rejected. In order to ascertain the situation and to explain why Eisenhower acted as he did, the historian must perform at least two tasks: (1) he must try to imagine how the situation then looked to Eisenhower, and (2) he must determine, by hindsight, how accurate Eisenhower's assessment was. If we consider the second task first, it is clear the critical historian must first assess the authenticity and truthfulness of the diaries of the relevant German and American generals, the testimony taken at the Nuremberg trials, the minutes of the conferences between Hitler and his naval commanders, the files of the German ministries of Armaments and War Production, telephone and battle logs, interrogation reports of prisoners, and the U.S. Army and Navy files. The multiplicity of types of judgment required here is extraordinarily great: economic estimates of the importance of the Ruhr area for Hitler's armies and economy, military estimates of the vulnerability of the area, which, in turn, require an assessment of the reserves and mobility of the *Wehrmacht,* the significance of the shortage of oil, the almost incredible lack of motorization in Hitler's armies, the existent state of the railways after Allied bombings, the great losses of motor lorries in France since D-Day, etc. If we turn to the first task, i.e., reconstructing the situation as it looked to Eisenhower at the time, this necessitates another series of judgments of the most diverse types. What information did he have at his disposal? Was it accurate? Whose advice and counsel played the weightiest role in influencing his mind?

We can see such questions arise in Wilmot's own mind as he seeks to explain Eisenhower's final decision; and they force Wilmot finally to consider the characters and personalities of the figures involved. Montgomery's plan, for example, would have required Eisenhower to restrain General Patton on the south and, probably, to have called him back to protect Montgomery's flank, for Montgomery was already in the most advantageous position to spearhead the attack. This decision would have incurred the displeasure of both General Bradley, Eisenhower's friend, and Patton, whose temper and independence sometimes approximated insubordination. Both of them disliked Montgomery and distrusted his advice. Furthermore, President Roosevelt, at the time, was eager to point to American victories in the field, faced as he was with an election and anxious not to have the conduct of the war interjected into the political campaign. Could the American people accept the restraint of the most popular and victorious American commander, Patton, and his employment as a mere support for the first entry into Germany by British troops? Wilmot concludes Eisenhower's personality was such that Montgomery's solution could scarcely appear possible to him, although this solution was feasible and would have shortened the war by as much as a year. Eisenhower's great capacity to distill counsel from many sources into one grand compromise solution, a capacity that made him an ideal supreme commander, was the very thing that handicapped him in battle generally, and in this situation, particularly, where it was necessary to "impose his strategic ideas without regard for personalities or public opinion."[39]

Whether Wilmot's reconstruction is correct I am in no position to judge. It is clear, however, that the reader is confronted by a number of arguments, so marshaled together as to constitute something like a case. No one of these arguments deserves to be called historical while another does not, and there can be no one standard, therefore, for judging them. Nor is any one model—rethinking Eisenhower's thought—necessarily illuminating. The data are various, the warrants vary from field to field, and different claims are entertained with fluctuating degrees of assent. In some cases, the argument makes use of very technical data which themselves presuppose laws; in other cases, the argument turns on certain truisms of human nature and conduct. No one field of argument is more uniquely historical than another. The issue in each case is simply the assessment of the argument in terms of its relevant data, warrants, and backings.

Even though these arguments are extremely diverse, and many of them can hardly be called scientific, is there any need for skepticism concerning the possibility of assessment at all? There seems to be no more reason for skepticism here than in cases of law where the reasoning and argument are equally field-encompassing. In fact, the legal process, in some respects, provides a helpful analogy for understanding history. In such a process the court has the responsibility for assessing a number of different types of arguments before a specifically legal conclusion—this act must be judged murder in the first degree—is possible. The court will have to weigh many types of questions: Is a handwriting expert's judgment correct when he claims that the signature on the threatening letter is the defendant's? Does the letter indicate the defendant had a malicious purpose or was he merely the perpetrator of a joke in bad taste? Do tests establish that the stains on the knife are of the same blood type as the deceased? Did the knife belong to the defendant? Was it in his possession at the time of the crime? In each field, there will be pertinent data and assumed warrants and both will confer upon the claims of the prosecution a certain force. And, presumably, there will be relevant rebuttals, "Yes, this is the defendant's knife but it was stolen shortly before the crime." Or, occasionally, a warrant will be challenged: "Can handwriting analysis be trusted?" Courts, in contrast to philosophers, will not be overly concerned about the presuppositions of the inquiry, or whether the explanations conform to scientific models, or whether it is possible to rethink the agent's thought, or whether some special gift of intuition is necessary on the part of the jurors.

6 · The Relevance of the Model: The Levels of Judgment

This model of argument illumines the somewhat vague appeal to soundness of judgment. Although vague, it can scarcely be doubted that this is a standard that historians invoke when judging one another formally and informally. They frequently argue that "such-and-such a historian is learned but lacks judgment" or that "so-and-so knows a lot of facts but he cannot be trusted." It is this judgmental sense which Theodor Mommsen was, in part, noting when he insisted that historians, unlike mathematicians, cannot be trained directly.[40]

Although it is difficult to define what is meant by sound judgment, some idea of its nature can be gained by observing its various operations. One can see how important its role is, for example, in the initial phase of an argument, in sorting out the relevant possibilities for a solution to a problem. It is at work when the historian asks, "What right does this possible claim for my attention have?" To ask whether a solution is a possible one is not to ask, as I shall point out in the succeeding chapter, whether a particular solution is logically possible; it is, rather, to ask whether the candidate has something to be said for it, that is, whether it accounts for or saves some data, given some accepted warrants. This judgment is necessarily a very context-bound affair, and the historian can only rely on his knowledge of that particular past he is studying and his own critically interpreted present experience.

The historian's sense of judgment, his balance and maturity, can be seen in his estimates of the dynamics of argument. Not only must he have a sense concerning what warrants can be accepted without question, so that he will be able to call upon the relevant data, but he must know what argument has the presumption of evidence in its favor, so that he can anticipate certain rebuttals and ignore possible other objections as being too specious to deserve answering. Once again the analogy of law is illuminating. An important aspect of all legal cases in Anglo-Saxon courts is the presumption of the innocence of the defendant. The prosecution must assume the burden of establishing guilt "beyond all reasonable doubt." This presumption, as any good defense lawyer knows, often alters the entire dynamics of argument. It dictates that certain lines of argument will have a greater weight placed on them than others and that the modal qualifiers of the prosecution's claims must be stronger than those of the defense, since the defense has only to preserve the state of reasonable doubt. Indeed, in some cases, it means that if the defense can erode the strength of a single positive modal qualifier of the prosecution, he can get the case thrown out of court. Hence the high drama in court cases often hinges on the collision between the defense and the prosecution over the importance attached to a rebuttal argument in contrast to conflicts over data or warrants. Frequently, there is no way of anticipating in advance what questions and issues will become crucial; but that the lawyers in question must always be sensitive to which issues become crucial in the course of the trial can scarcely be denied. And this is what I mean by sound judgment.

Although there is no neatly specifiable presumption that can be said to operate in history as it does in Anglo-Saxon law, there is a sense in which the historian must acknowledge the consensus that has been formed by the prior work of others in his field, especially if this consensus has been influenced by a great historical writer. Anyone, for example, who would responsibly advocate a new interpretation of Aristotle's work must take account of the views of Sir David Ross, Thomas Case, and Werner Jaeger. By virtue of their exhaustive work, certain presumptions have been established, and these presumptions cast something like the "burden of proof" of legal argument on those who would establish a different thesis. This burden alters the dynamics of argument in subtle ways, conveying a certain weight to this or that argument and lending special importance to this or that rebuttal. The skill of the historian is manifested in his degree of sensitivity to these dynamics. He must know what the crucial questions are, where the weak links in other interpretations lie, which data need to be challenged, and which have been misinterpreted.

Although there is this almost intangible personal element in historical argument, it does not follow that these judgments cannot be justified, or that it is meaningless to ask for evidence and warrants in each case. There is no reason, in other words, for skepticism concerning the possibility of assessment. In justifying his exception to prevailing consensus, the historian can, if he believes it necessary, give reasons for his own individual judgment, and if these reasons are cogent enough, they can alter the reader's entire perspective on the issue. Just as a defense lawyer may give good reasons why a certain point in the prosecutor's case is crucial if that case is to be maintained, a historian can give reasons for his judgmental sense that if a previous hypothesis about Aristotle's work has been decisive and if this hypothesis is untenable, then another one (his own) should be entertained. There may be no abstract rules for advising either lawyers or historians how to sense the dynamics of argument, but this is not to say that one cannot give reasons for justifying his sense of the matter.

This brings us to a final consideration concerning the nature of critical judgment, the quality of assent in historical work. As we have seen in our description of the structure of argument, the claims or conclusions one makes in ordinary discourse are necessarily qualified, and these qualifications are functions of the data, warrants, and the absence or presence of appropriate rebuttals.

Our assertions and claims, in other words, cannot simply be classified as either true or false, but have a certain degree of probability attached to them. This degree of probability need not be
understood in a mathematical or statistical sense; rather, it can
best be viewed as a way of talking about the degree of force a
conclusion is believed to have by virtue of the given data and
warrants. It reflects the trained judgment of the historian, the degree to which he is prepared to stake his authority on a certain
utterance.[41] He communicates his own estimate of the matter, the
quality of assent it deserves, by a careful and judicious placement
of qualifications. He indicates what he believes can be affirmed
with practical certainty, what can be asserted only with caution
or guardedly, and what is to be asserted as possible, given the
present state of his knowledge. The historian's assent, so to speak,
possesses a texture. He does not traffic in mere claims but in qualified claims ranging from tentativity to certitude.

This texture of assent is easier to illustrate than to describe
abstractly, for, as we have seen, it is, in large part, a function of
the warrants ingredient in any argument, and these warrants vary
from field to field. Consider a murder case in which the court hears
the testimony of a psychiatrist called by the defense as well as the
testimony of a biochemist called by the prosecution. The burden of
the psychiatrist's testimony is that the defendant was psychologi-
cally unable to commit the crime he was alleged to have committed. The burden of the biochemist's testimony is that the blood
stains on the jacket of the defendant were undoubtedly human and,
moreover, of the same blood type as the deceased. A clever prosecuting attorney will take full advantage of the fact that since psy-
chiatry is not a science, the warrants employed are open to a kind
of doubt in a way that those of the biochemist are not.[42] Indeed,
the point of the prosecution's cross-examination of the psychiatrist
may be just to demonstrate to the court the extremely uncertain
character of these warrants and, hence, to deprive the claims of
any great force. The defense, on the other hand, will recognize
the unquestioned backing of the biochemist's warrants and will
seek to minimize its importance in some other way.

This point is extremely important to keep in mind; otherwise, one will fail to grasp the significance of the fact that two historians may agree at one level of argument but disagree at another. They may agree that such and such an event occurred but disagree as to the causes of the event or its subsequent influence. That this often occurs cannot be denied, and it is possible because two historians may share data and warrants in one field but disagree in another. Or, it may not be so much a disagreement over data and warrants as it is that in some fields the warrants are not sufficiently tight to justify a hard assent to the conclusion. The latter is often the case just by virtue of some kinds of history, especially those concerned with the rise and decline of civilizations or those which describe national characteristics or cultural epochs (the Renaissance, the Enlightenment, the "Victorian Mind"). These terms are necessarily vague or "open-textured"[43] and the warrants, therefore, will be necessarily loose and more imprecise. The level of generality and the subject matter necessarily make it possible to bring forward exceptions and rebuttals, and the qualifiers, therefore, must somehow indicate that the claims must be made with a kind of tentativity.

This diversity of argument presupposing differing warrants that convey differing weights to conclusions explains why generalizations about the presuppositions of historians can be made only with the greatest caution. On the one hand, it is obvious that every historian must assume certain warrants to be true in certain fields or no argument in that field would be possible. On the other hand, it is misleading to assume that every presupposition or warrant is as arbitrary as every other. Hence, it is not conducive to clarity to talk about presuppositions in general; rather, one must ask in each particular case what the warrant is and to what degree it has adequate backing. I shall discuss this matter at greater length in a subsequent chapter, because it bears directly on the degree to which the historian assumes established knowledge.

Although historical arguments often employ language that is vague and open-textured, it does not follow that assessment of these arguments is impossible. Just because generalizations about the Renaissance, the Victorian mind, the spirit of Protestantism cannot achieve the kind of precision that some assertions about

Petrarch, Benjamin Jowett, or Calvin can, it is not true the historian cannot give reasons for his generalizations and claims.[44] It simply means that the claims need to be qualified to the proper degree. It is not necessary, for example, to banish all generalizations about national character from historical discourse because they are unscientific, nor is it necessary to say that the historian's claims in this area are mere expressions of belief. One need only point out that the balanced historian will indicate in a number of ways how loose such generalizations are and indicate this with the appropriate sorts of qualifications. And this is just what occurs in practice. To the extent a historian dogmatizes about matters of national character and solicits hard assent, other historians begin to distrust his judgment and consider him uncritical.

This discussion is not intended to exhaust the entire complex matter of the presuppositions of historiography but rather to indicate how closely associated the judgmental sense of the historian is related to the matter of assessment. This, in turn, reveals that although it is irrelevant to look for any one model of historical explanation, it is not irrelevant to insist that all responsible claims be candid and that reasons be given for them, reasons commensurate with the degree of assent they solicit from us. We honor this principle in daily life, in law courts, politics, and newspapers, and we praise and blame men for their responsibility or irresponsibility in conforming to it. The same holds true of history, and it is just because this critical ideal has grasped the modern imagination that historical thinking is one of the most impressive triumphs of the human spirit.

NOTES TO CHAPTER TWO

1. Immanuel Kant, "What is Enlightenment?" in Lewis W. Beck (ed.), *Critique of Practical Reason and Other Writings in Moral Philosophy* (Chicago: University of Chicago Press, 1949), pp. 286-292.
2. *Ibid.*, p. 290.
3. *Ibid.*, p. 286.
4. R. G. Collingwood, *The Idea of History* (Oxford: Oxford Universitv Press, 1946), p. 236.
5. *Ibid.*, p. 256.

6. Marc Bloch, *The Historian's Craft,* trans. Peter Putnam (Manchester: Manchester University Press, 1954), pp. 90-137.

7. *Ibid.,* p. 95.

8. See his perceptive but neglected essay "The Presuppositions of Critical History" in *Collected Essays* (Oxford: Oxford University Press, 1935), I, 1-53.

9. Collingwood, *op. cit.,* p. 256.

10. *Ibid.,* p. 237.

11. Kant, *op. cit.,* p. 287.

12. *Ibid.,* p. 288.

13. Collingwood, *op. cit.,* p. 252.

14. Stephen Toulmin, *The Uses of Argument* (New York: Cambridge University Press, 1958), p. 11.

15. I write "roughhewn" because the question has several meanings, as Christopher Blake has shown in his essay "Can History Be Objective?" in *Theories of History,* ed. Patrick Gardiner (Glencoe, Ill.: The Free Press, 1959), pp. 329-343.

16. John Dewey, "Historical Judgments" in Hans Meyerhoff (ed.), *The Philosophy of History in Our Time* (Garden City, N.Y.: Doubleday Anchor Books, 1959), p. 163.

17. The classic statements of the former view are to be found in Karl Popper's *The Open Society and Its Enemies* (Princeton: Princeton University Press, 1950) and Carl G. Hempel's "The Function of General Laws in History," reprinted in *Theories of History,* ed. Patrick Gardiner. See also Patrick Gardiner, *The Nature of Historical Explanation* (Oxford: Oxford University Press, 1952). The latter view was first advocated by R. G. Collingwood in *The Idea of History,* and a modified version of it has been formulated by William H. Dray in *Laws and Explanations in History* (Oxford: Oxford University Press, 1957). Cf. the lively exchange between Dray and Hempel in Sidney Hook (ed.), *Philosophy and History* (New York: New York University Press, 1963). For still another view see Alan Donagan, "Historical Explanation: The Popper-Hempel Theory Reconsidered" in *History and Theory,* IV (1964), 1-26. For a recent and lucid discussion of the matter see William H. Dray, *Philosophy of History* (Engelwood Cliffs, N.J.: Prentice-Hall, 1964).

18. In addition to Dray and Donagan above, see Michael Scriven, "Truisms as the Grounds for Historical Explanations" in Patrick Gardiner (ed.), *Theories of History,* pp. 443-475.

19. Dray, *Laws and Explanations in History,* chaps. ii and iii.

20. *Ibid.,* p. 119.

21. This is the argument of Norman Sykes in "Some Recent Conceptions of Historiography and Their Significance for Christian Apologetic," in *Journal of Theological Studies,* L (1949), 24-37. Sykes' interpretation of Collingwood has been sharply criticized by T. A. Roberts in *History and Christian Apologetic* (London: S.P.C.K., 1960), pp. 11-21.

22. Toulmin, *op. cit.,* p. 7.

23. *Ibid.,* pp. 223-252.

24. *Ibid.,* pp. 217 ff.

25. *Ibid.,* chap. i.

26. *Ibid.*, p. 14.

27. *Ibid.*, pp. 15-22.

28. *Ibid.*, chap. iii.

29. *Ibid.*, pp. 97-103. Michael Scriven in his essay in Gardiner (ed.), *Theories of History,* has a somewhat different but overlapping analysis. He argues that our justificatory arguments may be considered as answers to three kinds of questions: "Is your explanation accurate?" "Is your explanation adequate?" and "Is your explanation relevant?"

30. Toulmin, *op. cit.*, p. 100.

31. *Ibid.*, p. 106.

32. *Ibid.*, pp. 107-122.

33. *Ibid.*, pp. 100 f.

34. It might be asked whether any additional information brought forward in rebuttal, such as the lack of any known crucifixions for religious apostasy, could not be considered as additional data rather than as a factor confirming or disconfirming the warrant. Toulmin argues that the distinction is to be made in terms of function. The fact that Jesus was crucified and the further fact that crucifixion was not used for crimes other than political ones are, it is true, both relevant to the conclusion; but they are relevant in different ways. The one fact is a datum that establishes a presumption; the other, by setting aside one possible rebuttal, tends to confirm the presumption thereby created. See *ibid.*, p. 102.

35. *Ibid.*, pp. 103-107.

36. Patrick Gardiner observes: "The question: 'What is the nature of historical explanation?' is, I suggest, dangerous . . . . For it implies that, provided a careful enough search is conducted, a 'clear and distinct idea' of what historical explanation really *is* may somewhere be found, and, with labour, brought to light. And yet, when philosophers have claimed to have brought it to light their discoveries have been as unsatisfying as they have been various." *The Nature of Historical Explanation,* pp. xi f.

37. See Samuel H. Beer, "Causal Explanation and Imaginative Re-enactment" in *History and Theory,* III (1963), 6-29.

38. Chester Wilmot, *The Struggle for Europe* (New York: Harper & Brothers, 1952).

39. *Ibid.*, p. 468.

40. Theodor Mommsen, "Rectorial Address" in *The Varieties of History from Voltaire to the Present,* ed. Fritz Stern (New York: Meridian Books, Inc., 1956), p. 193.

41. Toulmin, *op. cit.*, chap. ii.

42. One is reminded of the court-martial proceedings against the mutineers in Herman Wouk's *The Caine Mutiny* (Garden City, N.Y.: Doubleday & Co., 1952) in which the success of the defense rests on the extent to which he demonstrates how the claims of the psychiatrist can be differently interpreted.

43. The term is Professor F. Waismann's. See his "Language Strata" in *Logic and Language: First and Second Series,* ed. Antony Flew (Garden City, N.Y.: Doubleday Anchor Books, 1965), pp. 226-247.

44. See Patrick Gardiner's observation in *The Nature of Historical Explanation:* "Generalizations about revolutions, class-struggles, civilizations,

must *inevitably* be vague, open to a multitude of exceptions and saving clauses, because of the looseness of the terms they employ. . . . But this is not to criticize such generalizations provided that they are not expected to do more work than they are fitted for. The scientific model of precise correlation is misleading in any attempt to comprehend the role of these generalizations in history, where they function frequently as *guides to understanding*" (p. 61).

III

The Historian's Standpoint

1 · The Scientific Revolution and the Writing of History

THE three aspects of the critical ideal of historical judgment discussed in the previous chapter are extremely formal in nature. Taken by themselves, they could hardly have accounted for the intellectual revolution wrought by modern historiography. That revolution came about only when these criteria were informed by the new way of looking at the world created by the sciences: when thinking for oneself meant thinking in terms of the new world-picture; when rational assessment meant appealing to the known structures of present experience; when the quality of one's assent was seen to be a function of the warrants grounded in various areas of knowledge. Historical thinking only became revolutionary when it was saturated by what we now call the common-sense view of the world, a misnomer insofar as it conceals how much this common-sense view is really the absorption into our natural habits of thought of an earlier and revolutionary thinking.[1]

The purpose of this chapter is to explore the relationship between this common-sense view of the world and our judgments about the past. As in the previous chapter, I shall be less concerned with a theory of historical explanation than with how historians seek to justify their claims when they are challenged. I am interested in what one has a right to demand before he gives his assent to a conclusion about the past. There is, to be sure, a close relationship between explanations and their justifications, but these are by no means the same things. One can, for example, recognize a faulty justification of an explanation and withhold assent to it without being able to construct the proper explanation. The importance of this distinction will, I hope, become clearer in what follows.

2 · The Debate Concerning the Uses of the Present

It is truistic to say that the historian has no direct access to the past and that his knowledge of it is, therefore, inferential. He has, so to speak, only the tracks of the past, some of which were left intentionally but most of which constitute that greater unconscious residue of life that remains long after life itself has run its course— the spent oil lamp, the rusted weapon, the faded document, the mutilated coin, the moldering ruin. Like a detective who undertakes to reconstruct a crime on the basis of a few clues, the historian patiently seeks to construct a sequence of events that will account for these tracks. Indeed, it is just this characteristic of historical knowledge, Collingwood insists, that defines it as historical.

If he . . . [the historian] or somebody else could have the very same knowledge of the very same events by way of memory, or second sight, or some Wellsian machine for looking backwards through time, this would not be historical knowledge; and the proof would be that he could not produce, either to himself or to any other critic of his claims, the evidence from which he had derived it.[2]

The inferential nature of historical knowledge is most evident where the historian is working with artifacts: from a ruin containing large urns, lamps, coins, household goods of many kinds, the historian infers that he has come upon a dwelling of some sort. The nature and importance of inference can also be seen, however, when we consider the historian's reliance on the reports of witnesses. Here it is not merely that the historian infers what happened by taking the reports and harmonizing them with other reports but that the reports themselves are, in large measure, a texture of inferences and judgments.

The significance of this fact was explored quite perceptively by the philosopher F. H. Bradley in an essay published in the last century entitled "The Presuppositions of Critical History."[3] No one, he pointed out, transmits a literal picture of an event. Rather, this or that aspect is selected and another excluded. An assertion is intellectual and an element of judgment is present. But even the simplest judgment about a so-called fact is far from simple, for it comprehends and presupposes a host of other judgments. Indeed, it must be called a conclusion,

> . . . and a conclusion, however much it may appear so, is never the fiction of a random invention. We bring to its assertion the formed world of existing beliefs, and the new matter of a fresh instance. . . . For everything that we say we think we have reasons, our realities are built up of explicit or hidden inferences; in a single word, our facts are inferential, and their actuality depends on the correctness of the reasoning which makes them what they are.[4]

It is not necessary to agree with Bradley that the actuality of past events *depends* on the correctness of the reasons given for believing in them—a conclusion can be true although the reasons given for it be wrong—in order to appreciate the main line of his argument. For he saw that all narration involves judgment, and judgment implies the possibility of error. Critical history, therefore, requires the rethinking of the judgments of witness according to a canon; otherwise, it is merely the transmission of tradition.

All historical narration, Bradley concluded, has presuppositions. The real difference between uncritical and critical history is whether one has these presuppositions without knowing he has them or whether one "consciously orders and creates from the known foundation of that which for him is the truth. It is when history becomes aware of its presupposition that it first becomes truly critical, and protects itself (so far as is possible) from the caprices of fiction."[5]

What are the presuppositions of critical history? The answer Bradley gave to that question was characteristic of much nineteenth-century philosophy and has found an echo in the twentieth century as well: the uniformity of nature and the causal connection.[6] Thus, the late Marc Bloch wrote that all history assumes that "the universe and society possess sufficient uniformity to exclude the possibility of overly pronounced deviations."[7] So, too, Henri Pirenne suggested that "the eternal identity of human nature" is the postulate on which all history is based, for one "cannot comprehend men's actions at all unless one assumes in the beginning that their physical and moral beings have been at all periods what they are today."[8] In short, the warrants and the backings for historical judgments lie grounded in present knowledge.

Bradley, of course, was aware that some historians, especially the Biblical scholars of his day, did not share this assumption, and so he was forced to state his own canon in the form of an imperative: "The view I have put forward is this, that every man's present standpoint ought to determine his belief in respect to *all* past events. . . ."[9] To be sure, he went on to add, "to no man do I dictate what his present standpoint ought to be," but this addition can hardly be taken seriously in the light of Bradley's subsequent development of the view that the standpoint should be the verifiable world of science.[10] The universality of law and what he called loosely "the causal connexion" were the ultimate presuppositions in the light of which the critical historian judges his so-called witnesses.

Given this premise, Bradley was faced with a problem confronted by every philosopher who argues in this vein, a problem of such magnitude that it constitutes, for many other philosophers, the chief objection to the view of historical inquiry Bradley represents: If one uses present experience as a basis for judging reports about the past, does this not prejudice the possibility of understanding genuinely unique events? Does not this criterion prevent genuine knowledge of the past by forcing the witnesses' experience to conform to our own? The report of an alleged miracle is an interesting case in point, for as Collingwood has shown, a miracle is merely the extreme case of what is true in principle of any historical event, because history is the realm of the unique and unrepeatable.[11] The use of present experience, then, as a limitation on what could have happened, it is argued, is the opposite of the spirit of true scientific inquiry.

Bradley, to be sure, anticipated this criticism, and he urged that no report should be believed unless the evidence for it be of the strongest possible sort. He took this to mean that no witness should be believed unless the historian can be assured that the witness brought practically the same systematized world (critical consciousness) to the observation that the historian would have brought had he been there. "We thus are certain that the men can see for us, because we know that they are able to think for us."[12] But there has been increasing dissatisfaction among philosophers with this kind of answer, especially when it has been coupled with the appeal to immutable natural laws and the "eternal identity of human nature" (Pirenne). It has been pointed out by some that modern science no longer employs the idea of immutable laws but speaks, rather, of probabilities and statistical generalizations. More important, it is not at all clear how relevant the idea of law is for historiography. Historians rarely employ laws or appeal to them or discover them, and as for the "eternal identity of human nature," it is precisely history itself, it is alleged, that has forced us to discard such a notion. We have learned how radically the consciousness of man varies from culture to culture and age to age, and if, as some would say, consciousness constitutes the essence of man, then there is truth in the aphorism, "man has no 'nature'; he only has history."[13]

Collingwood, especially, has come to be associated with this line of criticism. Although very appreciative of Bradley's insistence on the autonomy of the historian and the necessity of rethinking the thought of the witness, Collingwood believed that Bradley's view makes true historical thinking impossible. He insists, first of all, that Bradley's criterion is useful only for checking negatively the statements of authorities. Laws enable us to tell only what could happen, not what did happen.[14] Moreover, they are applicable only to nature, "which has no history," and are useless in historical inquiry where the object is the reconstruction of human experience.

The laws of nature have always been the same, and what is against nature now was against nature two thousand years ago; but the historical as distinct from the natural conditions of man's life differ so much at different times that no argument from analogy will hold. That the Greeks and Romans exposed their new-born children in order to control the numbers of their population is no less true for being unlike anything that happens in the experience of contributors to the *Cambridge Ancient History*.[15]

Secondly, Collingwood charged that Bradley's criterion is positivistic, that is, that it makes history dependent on science.[16] But, on the contrary, "history is its own criterion; it does not depend for its validity on something outside itself, it is an autonomous form of thought with its own principles and its own methods."[17]

Both of these criticisms amount to saying that Bradley's criterion is irrelevant for the historian. This is particularly clear, Collingwood pointed out, when Bradley argued that no witness should be believed unless the historian can be sure that he brought the same critical consciousness to the event as the historian himself would have brought. On these terms, Collingwood concluded, no past witness could ever be believed, for this condition cannot in the nature of the case be fulfilled. Every "witness is always a son of his time, and the mere progress of human knowledge makes it impossible that his point of view and standard of accuracy should be identical with my own."[18]

These criticisms of Collingwood's are important, not only because they go to the heart of the issue before us but also because they have found an echo, albeit a distorted one, among certain Christian apologists.[19] For in Collingwood's assertion that "history is its own criterion" and makes no use of laws, these apologists have found the charter for a new defense of the actuality of the events attested to by the New Testament. These occurrences, it is alleged, are unique and have always been suspect only to the degree that the standard by which they were judged was natural law or present experience. But Collingwood has shown that *all* truly historical events are unique and that neither law nor present experience can constitute such a standard. In short, the so-called miraculous events of the New Testament, particularly the resurrection of Jesus, simply share "in the arbitrariness, irrationality and independence which characterize all events to some degree.

. . ."[20] One might go so far as to say that the resurrection exemplifies the very nature of a unique historical event, and that it is the rationalist's dogmatic and a priori canon which has made it seem otherwise. But even the appeal to science, it is sometimes added, is invalid. The new science, for example, no longer talks about a hard-and-fast determinism of events, of immutable laws of nature. Rather, it appeals to statistical probabilities. Hence, it is no longer scientific to reject miracles, concludes the *Oxford Dictionary of the Christian Church,* and the new science now makes possible "an approaching reconciliation between the Christian tradition and modern scientific research."[21]

Because these issues are so crucial for understanding the relationship between the historian's critical interpretation of present experience and his judgments about the past and because Bradley and Collingwood so clearly represent the options for conceiving that relationship, I shall explore the matter by using their debate as a foil. To anticipate, I shall attempt to show that although Collingwood's criticisms are important, they are not devastating and do not require a basic revision of Bradley's view that the historian's present standpoint should determine his belief about all past events. Collingwood's own theory of historical understanding either affirms what he seems to deny or has recourse to a dubious metaphysical expedient (the ability of thought to transcend time). Moreover, his general views are quite misunderstood if they are taken to mean that the historian has a license to resurrect miracle as a tool of historical interpretation. Nevertheless, Collingwood's criticisms are so important that they require a reformulation of Bradley's view, particularly Bradley's appeal to the world of science as a criterion for testing the reports of witnesses who are sons of their time.

3 · Historical Judgment and the Negative Function of Laws

Collingwood argued that laws play only a negative role in historical judgment; they enable the historian to judge only what could have happened, not what did happen. Furthermore, he insisted that this negative role is confined entirely to judgments about natural, in contrast to human, events, because the terms "possible" and "impossible" have a different meaning in discourse about human thoughts and actions than in discourse about events in nature.

There is some truth in this charge, although I believe it too easily minimizes the importance of such negative judgments, especially in Biblical criticism. Indeed, it was just the assessment of fantastic reports—reports about the "impossible"—in the light of knowledge produced by the science that accounts for the emergence of the very important categories of myth and legend which play such a crucial role in modern historical inquiry. Without the absorption of the concepts of possibility and impossibility into the common-sense world-view of the historian, these categories, as well as the revolutionary and skeptical attitude toward past reports, would never have been forthcoming. This attitude, as well as the terms "myth" and "legend," is a function of a new intellectual standpoint, a standpoint that was centuries in the making and that separates the eighteenth and nineteenth centuries more radically from the fifteenth than the fifteenth from the first. For with the recognition of the gulf separating certain periods, it became clear to what degree every witness was, in fact, a son of his time, how deeply his ideas of possibility and actuality and the relation of one event to another were a function of his world-picture.

Bloch makes this vividly clear in his book *The Historian's Craft*. It was not long ago, he notes, that three-fourths of all reports of alleged eyewitnesses were accepted as fact. At that time if it was related that an animal spoke or that a stick turned into a snake or that blood rained from heaven, there was no question of fact believed to be involved; the question was rather, "What significance should be attributed to these events?" And not even the steadiest minds of our predecessors, Bloch shows, escaped this credulity.

If Montaigne read in his beloved ancients this or that nonsense about a land whose people were born without heads or about the miraculous strength of the little fish known as the remora, he set them down among his serious arguments without raising an eyebrow. For all his ingenuity in dismantling the machinery of a false rumor, he was far more suspicious of prevailing ideas than of so-called attested facts. In this way, as in the Rabelaisian myth, old man Hearsay ruled over the physical as well as the human world. Perhaps even more over the physical world than the human. For, having a more direct experience, men sooner doubted a human event than a meteor or an alleged irregularity of organic life.[22]

Bloch concludes that if so many fictitious events have been swept from our horizon of possibility, it is only because "of the idea of a natural order governed by immutable laws."[23]

It may be that this appeal to immutable natural laws jangles in the sophisticated ear. But one should not overlook how fruitful the idea has been, especially in history. The notion could scarcely have been established so firmly and the observations which contradict it eliminated so surely, Bloch rightly points out, "except by the patient labor of an experiment performed upon man himself as a witness. . . . We have acquired the right of disbelief, because we understand, better than in the past, when and why we ought to disbelieve."[24] It is difficult, therefore, to conceive, as some Christian apologists argue, of the new physics precipitating an agonizing reappraisal of reports of blood raining from heaven, or of sticks turning into snakes, or of animals speaking, or of men in chariots ascending bodily into heaven. Nature, to be sure, may be far more refractory to mathematical description at the subatomic level than hitherto believed, but this does not warrant a return to the credulity once characteristic of a majority of the human race. The new physics, however much it may raise questions about a mechanical model for the universe, can hardly be utilized by a religious apologetic eager to find some small justification for believing in miracles; indeed, it could be argued that the new physics raises more problems in this connection than it solves.[25]

The fact is we tend to reject or suspect such fantastic reports immediately, although more readily, interestingly enough, when they occur in religions other than our own. The problem is how one can account for this. Collingwood, as I have noted, did not dispute the validity of the appeal to laws of nature in this regard; he merely noted that they serve a negative function and are of no use when trying to rethink the thoughts of past agents. His position, then, gives no real support to those who would resurrect miracle as a principle of historical explanation.

4 · *Historical Judgment and Present Knowledge*

Even though Collingwood does not do full justice to the importance of the negative and indirect role of science in historical inquiry, there is truth in his criticism that the use of laws is practically irrelevant so far as rethinking past thought is concerned. For, as he put it, the mind is what the mind does, and there are no known laws of thought in the sense that there are known laws of nature. Consequently, the idea of possibility has a different use in this connection. But to what extent does this criticism seriously undermine Bradley's main thesis that the basis for the historian's judgments, whether about nature or human nature, must be the historian's own critically interpreted present standpoint? Granted Bradley's tendency to equate the term "present standpoint" with scientific knowledge, is it not possible to insist on his main thesis without making that equation, although without denying that scientific knowledge is *an important ingredient* in the historian's standpoint? And if it is possible, is this thesis trivial so far as historical thinking is concerned? My answer shall be that Bradley's main thesis is true, that the equation with law is not necessary but contains, nevertheless, a significant point overlooked by Collingwood and others, and, finally, that it is not trivial so far as Biblical research is concerned. The clue to understanding these matters, I shall suggest, is the complex nature of historical argument, and it is upon this that we must keep our eyes firmly fixed.

As I have tried to show in the previous chapter, historical judgments may be compared to judgments in law courts or in everyday life. To be sure, the analogy is not a strict one because the procedures of law courts are very formalized, and the overall aim is to bring a conclusion under a prior definition laid down by law.

Nevertheless, there is a sense in which arguments in law and in history are analogous. As A. O. Lovejoy notes:

> though the inquiries of the historiographer, especially if they relate to events remote in time, are often more difficult, and sometimes at a lower level of probability, than the inquiries of courts, they have the same implicit logical structure, which is simply the structure of all inquiry about the not-now-presented; and, if they *are* historical inquiries, and not criticism or evaluation, their objective is the same—to know whether, by the canons of empirical probability, certain events, or sequences of events, happened at certain past times, and what, within the existential limits of those times, the characters of those events were.[26]

We think historically, in other words, when as parents we try to determine which one of the children is telling the truth about the crayon marks on the bedroom walls, or when, as friends, we try to discover the root of a misunderstanding, or when, as citizens, we try to make out the real meaning of a public pronouncement on a civic crisis. Historical thinking is an ingredient in all of our thinking.

One of the characteristic features of ordinary thinking is that the assertions we make, the arguments we present, and the grounds we use to support them are those of common-sense, which is to say, they solicit the assent of minds like our own with the same general understanding of reality. For the most part we make no use of technical terms, except those that have become a part of our language, and our causal explanations are pragmatic and unscientific.[27] For example, we say that the cause of an air tragedy was the failure of one of the engines and make no explicit references to the laws of combustion or aerodynamics. This assertion, like so many others, is perfectly intelligible and, it should be added, a good explanation, although, precisely speaking, it is not a scientific explanation at all. Historical narrative, for the most part, has these same general characteristics, as has frequently been noted. It is written for the intelligent man in the street, and its language and explanations differ in no essential respect from the language and explanations given in novels and newspapers. Thus, a historian can explain General Lee's brilliant victory at Chancellorsville in terms of the characters of two men, Generals Lee and Hooker, and no puzzles arise. There are no technical terms peculiar to history as there are, say, to low temperature physics or biochemistry and, most significantly, perhaps, there is no overarching theory.[28]

Philosophers have occasionally deplored these characteristics of historical narrative and have sought, from time to time, to bring some theory to bear on it, theory replete with a special terminology, categories, and laws. These philosophers rightly see that ordinary language is, when measured by the canons of science, notoriously vague and loose. But they wrongly conclude that this vagueness is a disease and can only be cured with a prescription taken from the pharmacy of the exact sciences. It is just the "open-textured" nature of ordinary language that makes it suitable for everyday life and historical inquiry. Over the course of centuries, our language has become a very delicate instrument enabling us to communicate with one another about the richness and complexity of life or to talk about such necessary things as character, the "spirit of the age," the pathos of friendship and love, political responsibility, cultural epochs, and the feeling of men on the morning of battle:

There was a fog that morning, and for several hours the plain was invisible while many divisions of Federal troops got into position, steeples and chimney tops of Fredericksburg just visible above the banked mist to the waiting Confederates on the hills. Then the sun burned away the fog, and all of a sudden the whole panorama was in the open—a breath-taking sight, one hundred thousand men, fighting men ready for work, an army with banners uncoiling in the sunlight, gun barrels gleaming. Lee watched from the highest point on the ridge, and the sight took hold of him—this strong warrior who held himself under such iron control—so that he burst out with something like a cry of exultation: It is well (he said) that we know how terrible war really is, else we would grow too fond of it. . . . Then the moment of high drama passed (unforgettable moment, hanging suspended in the memories of that war forever after) and the fighting began.[29]

The attempt to superimpose the language of the sciences upon such a description as this is a peculiar manifestation of a humorlessness that has not only led to the impoverishment of historical narrative but has been the source of a number of useless philosphical puzzles.

Even though our ordinary language is not scientific, this is not to say that it does not presuppose or imply the sciences, just as our common-sense view of the world presupposes and implies a highly refined "uncommon" sense. The sciences have not only affected our vocabularies, but these, in turn, reflect a way of organizing and of relating things to one another that is the complex product of a development stretching back to the farthest horizons of our known past. The question one reads in the science section of a weekly newsmagazine, "Will a high altitude thermonuclear explosion seriously disturb the Van Allen radiation belt and later the earth's magnetic field?" not only contains words that our more distant forebears could not have understood but presupposes a fabric of beliefs so different from theirs that we could not even begin to explain to them what we mean. So true is this, that it requires a highly disciplined historical imagination to reconstruct how the world must have appeared to them, how they could so intimately, at one and the same time, relate, as they did, the movements of sun, moon, and stars to fits of madness, the menstrual cycle of women, and the rise and fall of dynasties.[30]

It might be argued that ordinary explanations do not even imply laws because the same phenomenon could be explained to a savage and a scientist alike in terms that both would understand and which makes no use of the laws.[31] Of course, it is true that savages know that a fall from a great height can cause physical death, and an explanation for such an unfortunate happening would be as intelligible were it given by a witch doctor as by a modern newspaperman explaining the death of a tribal chief. But no savage, so far as we are aware, understands why bodies fall and why, therefore, it is impossible for us, in contrast to the savage, to entertain his story about the hero who, having stepped off a cliff, rose bodily into the heavens, or why the explanation the savage might give for this alleged fact (the spirits of the air blinded for a moment the spirits of the earth) not only makes no sense to us but is dismissed as fanciful and legendary.

Many ordinary explanations make no use of laws, to be sure,

but they presuppose structures and relationships which laws as parts of theories both describe and explain; and these, in turn, are so much a part of the furniture of our minds that we scarcely recognize how ingredient they are in our thinking. This accounts for why we can take the children out into the yard at night to see the latest comet and why our forebears dropped to their knees in prayer or hid in their houses; why we explain our dreams to a psychiatrist and why some of our ancestors thought they had been spoken to by a spirit.

However difficult it is to analyze precisely, there is truth in the observation frequently made that history presupposes all the sciences. It presupposes physics, for example, insofar as the historian makes judgments about the capabilities of weapons in the battle of Waterloo; it presupposes astronomy, insofar as the historian evaluates reports about the sun having stood still; and it presupposes biology, insofar as the historian assesses the report about a saint who picked up his head after his execution and marched into a cathedral to sing the *Te Deum*. As Morton White has noted, "It seems almost impossible to put a limit on the number of sciences history does presuppose."[32]

But history, like ordinary discourse, presupposes much more than the sciences, for the historian makes judgments about men's motives and values, national character, political trends, institutional capabilities, revolutions—none of which, precisely speaking, can be said to be the subject matter of a science. It is for this reason that Toulmin's reference to fields of argument is helpful, for it makes clear that, while most historical judgments are not scientific, it does not follow that there are not appropriate data and warrants for them, which is to say, data and warrants of the highest relevant sort. We can and do reason about and assess arguments of numerous kinds in contemporary life, and in many of them we can have practical certainty. The problem, in any given argument, is not whether the argument makes use of scientific laws, but whether the warrants and backings for it achieve the highest possible standards.

History, as I have suggested, is not so much itself a field as a field-encompassing field. The historian, like the judge, must make many logically different kinds of judgments, and the backings for them are peculiar to their respective fields. Indeed, as Toulmin points out, unless we are prepared to accept the warrants in any particular field it is impossible to set an argument in that field in motion. In some historical arguments these warrants may be scientific; more often they will not be. Some warrants, although not scientific, may be indubitable; others may be vague and open. But taken together, they constitute the background of the historian's inferences and, if they elicit assent, the background also of his reader.

The literature of the philosophy of history is filled with attempts to account for a strange but significant fact: many of our historical explanations are practically certain and still more of them have a high degree of probability, yet these same explanations make no apparent use of deductive laws. One of the most suggestive of these attempts to account for this fact has been made in an article by Michael Scriven entitled "Truisms as the Grounds for Historical Explanations."[33] Scriven's article is too complex to permit more than noting some of those points that relate to my own views. But he describes the extraordinary variety of explanations historians use and shows the futility of identifying historical explanations with any one type. Historians have not only been preoccupied with Collingwood's "why" questions, but with "what," "which," "how," and "where" questions as well.

The problem, Scriven believes, is whether one can give any enlightening characterization of this variety of explanations at all. After an analysis and rejection of the view that all causal explanations make use of laws, he suggests that the principles underlying historical judgments are truisms, statements, and principles so obvious that no historian would bring them forward as laws, but which, nevertheless, are not empty. The point is that these truisms, which serve as grounds for explanations, "can only be denied by someone who is prepared to deny such an obviously true statement. . . . The truism tells us nothing *new* at all; but it says *something* and it says something *true,* even if vague and dull."[34]

Scriven suggests that good explanations for individual events make use of general statements that are a hybrid of some universal features and some statistical features. These justify the adequacy of our explanations and we appeal to them when called upon to do so. This category of general statements includes truisms, many natural laws, some tendency and probability statements and, in other areas not directly relevant to historical explanations, rules, definitions, and certain normative statements in ethics.[35] The important thing about statements of this type is that they have what Scriven calls a "selective immunity against counter-examples," which is to say, we believe they would hold true unless some other exceptional conditions obtained. They are approximations but, depending on the field of argument, they function so that the burden of proof lies on the one who denies them. Indeed, if in any particular case the generalization is denied, our minds are puzzled and an explanation is called for as to why the generalization does not apply. To argue that these are not sufficient bases for conclusions because they are not as tight as laws overlooks the fact that the only value laws have is to enable us to predict. In history, we need only the level of certainty the context requires. There, we appeal to gross observable behavioral descriptions, and truisms are the best we can expect; and "step for step, level for level, the explanations based on truisms can match those based on laws. . . ."[36] The tighter the generalization, the more force a conclusion will have; the looser it is, the more need for a proper and delicate qualifier. In any case, there is no substitute for our trained knowledge of exceptions.

The significance of Scriven's analysis is twofold: it draws our attention once again to the extraordinary variety of historical judgments, and it explains in what sense it is legitimate to appeal to our present knowledge as the basis for our judgments about the past without equating that knowledge with scientific knowledge. We are not forced to choose between the false alternatives: no generalizations in history or laws. There are generalizations and they give force to our arguments, but they need not be laws. The error of Bradley and others was that they identified present knowledge with scientific knowledge. This error was understandable, however, because in their battle against those who arbitrarily appealed to supernatural causes the scientific model alone seemed to exclude such an appeal. The consequence, however, was that philosophers of history embarked on the misguided attempt to defend the objectivity of history in terms of an irrelevant standard and left themselves open to an inevitable counterreaction.

Given the extraordinary diversity of judgments that constitute history, it should be evident why the assertion, "Every historian has his presuppositions" is both true and misleading. It is true because, as we have seen, every historian's inferences about the past do reflect a background of belief, opinion, value-judgment, and, it is important to add, knowledge. It could not be otherwise, since no argument could elicit assent were this not true. It is misleading, however, because the too-roughhewn term "presuppositions" obscures the plurality of fields and the correspondingly different types of warrants which are implicit in our various claims. It suggests, like the too-monolithic term "historical explanation," that there is but one kind of presupposition and that all are equally arbitrary or well-founded.[37]

The situation is actually more complex and difficult to describe abstractly. The historian's presuppositions are relative to given fields and may be more adequate in some rather than in others. This accounts for an ordinary but commonly ignored fact: that historians rarely disagree with one another wholesale, as we might expect them to if they each had a completely different set of presuppositions. Historians agree and disagree with one another at various overlapping levels. They may agree, for example, that a certain policy was put in writing but disagree as to the motives of the policy-makers. They may agree that a certain event actually happened and concur on the details but differ as to the significance of the causal factors at work in it. The arguments in the one field will employ data and warrants that are agreed upon; those in the other will not reflect a consensus. Both employ presuppositions, to be sure, but it is the difference in type of presupposition that is crucial for understanding both the agreements and the disagreements.

It follows also, as we shall see in a later chapter, that it is far too sweeping to talk about Christian presuppositions. Such talk implies that Christian belief has some direct and equal bearing on every conceivable field in which a historian has to make judgments, so that a Christian will appeal to some other warrants than, say, the atheist does in deciding about the capability of Lee's weapons at Gettysburg or in judging whether the Donation of Constantine was a forgery. Lawyers are wise enough to know that it is too crude to say that every person has his presuppositions, as can be seen in their practice of impaneling juries. They know that atheists and Christians, pragmatists and idealists will, on the whole, all agree that if a defendant pleads in a murder case that an angel came down from heaven, pressed a revolver in his hand, and pulled the trigger, the plea will not be taken seriously. There still may be disagreement, to be sure, as to why the defendant killed his father, but at one level the appeal to sweeping metaphysical presuppositions is irrelevant. Consequently, the lawyer will rarely ask about a juror's presuppositions concerning miracles or the existence of angels. He will be far more interested in a specific field judgment: To what extent does the Christian feel so strongly about capital punishment that this will affect his judgment concerning guilt? But, then, the lawyer may discover that many Christians believe in capital punishment while many idealists and atheists do not. He soon learns that the relationship between one's presuppositions and his concrete and specific judgments is too complex to warrant any sweeping generalization.

This analysis may also illumine why miracle has all but disappeared from the working vocabulary of historians, even in the cases of those who insist that it cannot be excluded.[38] The reason lies in the nature of historical argument and the grounding of most of our warrants in present knowledge. For a historian confronted with a conclusion to the effect that a miracle took place is immediately confronted with a conundrum, and he asks, "Is this conclusion, given the data, a possible one?" Now the concept of possibility is a slippery one, but I think it can be shown that the historian is not asking, "Can one come to this conclusion?" for obviously someone has; nor is he asking, "Is this conclusion logically possible?" for it may be. Rather he is asking, "Is this solution to be taken seriously?" "Is it a likely candidate as an explanation?"[39]

There are very few historical reports that are, in principle, impossible, if by that we mean logically self-contradictory, whether it be blood raining from heaven or a group of monkeys being able to produce Shakespeare's *Hamlet* by playing haphazardly with a typewriter. As Toulmin has shown, pure logical possibility is merely a precondition of possibility in the second sense (Is it a likely candidate?). The logical possibility of an assertion merely puts the claim in the position of being judged possible in a more practical sense.

> . . . logical possibility—if by this we mean meaningfulness—is not so much a sub-species of possibility as a *prerequisite* of either possibility or impossibility; while logical impossibility, inconceivability or meaninglessness, far from being a sub-species of impossibility, *precludes* either possibility or impossibility. Can a proposition expressed in an unintelligible form even be dismissed from consideration as impossible?[40]

It follows, therefore, that the mere logical possibility of an event in no sense constitutes a *prima facie* case in its favor; it merely puts the statement in a form in which we can ask whether there is anything in its favor.

To ask whether an explanation is possible in the practical sense is to ask whether it is a relevant possibility, a likely candidate to account for certain data. It is at this point that an analysis of the matter becomes extraordinarily complex, for relevance or likelihood in historical research is a very context-bound affair. For example, it is not likely that Lincoln was stabbed while he was in Southern Florida instead of being shot in Washington, D. C., or that Jesus was crucified in Persia rather than in Jerusalem, or that General Lee was in California investigating some real estate when the battle of Gettysburg was being fought. Nothing logical rules out any of these possibilities, nor can they be said to be empirical impossibilities; the fact is, they are excluded simply because nothing can be said in their favor and a great deal counts against them. They are not, given what we do know, likely candidates.

In the case of an alleged miracle, i.e., an event that contradicts our present knowledge in a specific scientific field, like blood raining from heaven, the historian will first ask, "What am I being asked to believe?" and then, "What is to be said in its favor?" It is at this point that present knowledge plays such an important role, for if the report contradicts a well-established warrant, the burden of evidence and argument suddenly falls on the one who alleges the report to be true, which is another way of saying that a *prima facie* case exists for the report *not* being considered a likely candidate.[41] The fact that the alleged event cannot be reconciled with what we know about blood and rainfall activates a warning light, so to speak, which alters the dynamics of argument. The one who defends the report as true either must build a far stronger rebuttal than he otherwise might have had to do or attack the warrants upon which we usually base our judgments about blood and rain. He has, if we remember the structure of argument set forward in the previous chapter, to change the qualifier from an "it is highly unlikely that" to an "it is very probable that."

This is extremely difficult to do. If he attacks our usual warrants, then the issue has changed from a historical to a scientific one. But by what right does the historian speak on this issue? As historian, he has no more right to do this than a prosecuting attorney has who in a disputed case of paternity argues with an expert biochemist that no matter what the evidence is concerning blood types, the child *must* be the child of the defendant. The law must assume the existence and validity of certain knowledge; it is no part of its purpose as law to challenge that. So, too, the historian makes his judgments against the background of present knowledge. He has no expertise in the light of which he can enter an objection against that knowledge. Unless certain warrants in any particular field are accepted, no rational assessment of an argument in that field is even possible.

The other alternative for the defender of a miracle is to argue that our usual warrants do not apply in this specific case, to enter a rebuttal (R). This is a sounder argument, but the price paid for it is that conclusions in such cases can never achieve a very high degree of force. For unless some other firm warrant is brought forward, the only possible response is tentativeness or skepticism. Consequently, one cannot elicit the qualification "it is very probable that" in contrast to "it may have been that."

Actually, the skepticism regarding miracles is not based merely on the conviction that they are incompatible with known laws. It is, rather, that the very existence of miracle stories has itself come to be regarded as a normal and expected occurrence. The contemporary historian expects to find miracle stories in certain kinds of literature, which is to say he has more reason for being puzzled when he does not find such stories than when he does. Not only is he aware of the fallibility of human testimony but also of the tendency of the human mind to create myths and legends, especially in the realm of the religious. Indeed, if anything has been learned from the comparative study of religion it is that myth and legend are the almost natural forms of expression for the veneration of extraordinary founders, teachers, and saints of religion.

The knowledge of this deeply rooted tendency of the human spirit is complicated by another fact of extraordinary significance for historiography, namely, the wide discrepancy which exists between men's ideas in one cultural epoch and those in another concerning what is actual and therefore what is possible. While every age, including our own, creates its myths, there is a sense in which myth and miracle are natural in some cultures in a way they are not in our own—so natural, in fact, that the very notion of an event that "breaks known laws" (miracle) itself presupposes our own world-view.[42] In some cultures myth is simply a normal way of explaining certain phenomena, like the course of the stars, insanity, and the weather. It is a kind of primitive science.

The significance of this fact is twofold. On the one hand it underscores Bradley's insistence that since all historical narration presupposes a world of existing belief, no report can be taken at face value; on the other hand it points to the extraordinary methodological problem of rethinking the thoughts of past witnesses, since these thought processes themselves may differ quite sharply from those of the historian. In short, together with modern historiography's discovery that the thought-forms of one age often differ radically from another, the question has arisen whether this difference does not make historical understanding itself impossible.

To raise this question is to come back full circle to Collingwood's objection against Bradley with which this chapter began. For if the historian uses his own present standpoint and will only accept the report of a witness whose consciousness corresponds with his own, how can this test ever be applied? The witness is, in the very nature of the case, a son of his time, and it is impossible that his standpoint and standard of truth be identical with that of a later historian. Although we have come back to Collingwood's question, it is important to understand that we are not in the same position as when we first posed it. For we have seen that present knowledge cannot be identified with scientific knowledge, although, as I have pointed out, scientific knowledge is an ingredient in our present knowledge—so important an ingredient that the concepts of possibility and probability are unintelligible without it. But as soon as present knowledge is given this wider field-encompassing meaning, it becomes clear that the issue between Collingwood and Bradley is not whether the historian must use his own present experience as a canon but whether Bradley's formula for the treatment of witnesses is the best one. Collingwood also presupposes the normative character of present experience; indeed, his own argument against Bradley *turns on the assumption that the historian is also a son of his time*. His real difficulty with Bradley is that Bradley has advocated an irrelevant standard for handling witnesses, namely, that no witness will be believed unless his consciousness corresponds to the historian's.

5 · *Present Knowledge and Rethinking Past Thought*

It is important to understand, because some interpreters of Collingwood have not, that his criticism of Bradley presupposes a very special conception of the task of historiography. In Collingwood's view, the historian does not merely reconstruct a course of past external events, i.e., the facts. Rather, he rethinks the thoughts lying in and behind those events. The historian, in other words, is not concerned merely to know *that* Caesar crossed the Rubicon or that Brutus later stabbed him; he wants to know *why* they did these things. The historian is not merely interested in what happened but

in why it happened as it did. The cause of the event, in Collingwood's view, is "the thought in the mind of the person by whose
agency the event came about: and this is not something other than
the event, it is the inside of the event itself."[43]

Given this special conception of the historian's task, it becomes
clear why Collingwood and some who share this general view believe that the historian not only makes no use of laws but cannot
even use analogies taken from present experience, because the use
of analogies presupposes that our thought processes are like those
of past human beings. But this presupposition is not always true,
Collingwood argues; hence his sarcastic observation that "the
Greeks and Romans exposed their new-born children in order to
control the numbers of their population is no less true for being
unlike anything that happens in the experience of the contributors
to the *Cambridge Ancient History*."[44] Some men in other cultures
and times have thought in a fashion that makes it difficult to think
their thoughts after them, and this is a highly significant fact. We
learn from it that human nature is not fixed or static, that human
consciousness is itself a changing thing. "Thus the historical
process is a process in which man creates for himself this or that
kind of human nature by re-creating in his own thought the past to
which he is heir."[45]

It must be said in Bradley's defense, first of all, that he did not
mean that the historian is limited to analogies drawn from his own
personal experience. He was quite aware that the words "present
experience" are ambiguous, because that experience includes a
knowledge of the past and, moreover, embraces experiences and
knowledge far beyond the limits of the historian's own immediate
experience. Bradley meant that the sole justification for accepting
any reports, past or present, must be a critical one and consistent
with our present critically informed beliefs about the world. He
believed that this doctrine is not a skeptical or limiting one; on the
contrary, "the present experience, which is open to our research, is
so wide in its extent, is so infinitely rich in its manifold details, that
to expect an event in the past to which nothing analogous now
corresponds may fairly be considered a mere extravagance."[46] A
person need not have been to the moon to know that there are

craters on the far side or have been a member of a society that exposed its children to know that there have been—and still are— societies that practice this custom. Collingwood's reference to the writers of the *Cambridge Ancient History* is better sarcasm than it is rational argument.

Nevertheless, after Bradley's case has been properly made, Collingwood's objection does point up a peculiar set of problems that Bradley's position does not adequately handle—nor can it, so long as a sweeping appeal is made to the "eternal identity of human nature" (Pirenne). How do we come to know the thoughts, desires, motives, and purposes of past agents? What kind of status do assertions about them have? What kinds of justifications can one give for them? What is the relationship of these justifications to our present knowledge?

It is impossible within the limits of this inquiry to do justice to these complex problems. I shall focus, therefore, on the ways in which we go about assessing statements about the motives, purposes, and desires of other persons, past and present. For it is obvious that we do discuss such matters in daily life and that we bring forward grounds and reasons and evidence for what we say.

It is important, first of all, to call attention to the basic distinction I have made between how we come to know something and how we go about justifying what we have come to know.[47] Coming to know something, getting in the position of being able to know something, may involve procedures and activities that do not themselves figure in our justifications for that knowledge. A detective, for example, may, in trying to solve a crime, attempt to put himself in the position of the criminal and ask, "What would I have done had I been the accused?" and come to a conclusion that accounts for the evidence. But when, in the courtroom, the detective is asked by the defense attorney to justify his conclusions he had best not appeal to how he came to the conclusion. He had better not say, "I simply imagined what I would have done had I been the accused." Rather, he will, if he wishes to convince the jury, appeal to the evidence, to a fingerprint found on the weapon, to the impression of a shoe in the mud outside the deceased's

window matching that of the defendant. He will try to show that
his reconstruction is the most likely candidate for saving the evidence. The imaginative reconstruction of the crime is only a hypothesis, and whether it is right or wrong can only be justified by
its accounting for what is certainly known.

This distinction is important, because some historians who insist
that history is the re-enactment of past thought or experience
sometimes talk as if the historian had some special intuitive
powers by virtue of which he could "get inside" other minds in a
self-authenticating fashion. They argue that the historian does not
infer what the agent is thinking or feeling but grasps it immediately
and directly. Moreover, these historians sometimes insist that the
historian does not have merely a thought or experience similar to
the subject he is investigating, but an identical one. He does not
only rethink the thought of a past agent but has the identical
thought.[48]

I think it has been shown that this view leads to insuperable
problems.[49] The truth in it consists in the emphasis it places on
(1) the unique task of the historian to recover the reasons why an
agent did such and such, and (2) the importance and function of
the imagination in performing this task. But it is wrong insofar as
it confuses a highly useful and perhaps indescribable method for
arriving at a hypothesis about the "inside" of an event with the
ways in which one would go about confirming that hypothesis. As
Patrick Gardiner points out, the way in which a historian decides
whether his hypothesis concerning, say, Hitler's thoughts is true,
does not consist in getting even closer to those thoughts but in
seeing how far other facts, such as Hitler's behavior, his diaries,
and letters, corroborate such an interpretation.[50]

To understand why an actor did this or that is not as simple a
question as may appear on the face of it, for the answer to it
depends on the level at which we are asking the question. To ask,
for example, why General Lee attacked the very center of the
Union line on the third day at Gettysburg can, of course, be answered, "Because he wanted to win the war," but this does not
take the military historian very far. Given that banality, the historian wants to know why Lee made the particular decision he did in

the face of the strength and position of the Union forces. So, too, to ask why General Eisenhower did not accept General Montgomery's plan to strike a knifelike blow at the heart of industrial Germany is hardly answered, "Because he didn't think it was a very good plan." We want to know why at another level he did not think it a good plan. Frequently, we can and do dispense with these deeper "why" questions because they take us away from the path we are pursuing on the original plain of inquiry. But the historian or the biographer might, in individual cases, need to pursue them and, when he does, interesting problems arise.

What is involved in trying to re-enact the motives and purposes of an agent? In the first place, it will be necessary to re-create the situation he faced. What was Lee's peculiar situation at Gettysburg on the third day of the battle? With what problems was Eisenhower peculiarly confronted as he stood poised on the threshold of Germany? These are the questions the historian must ask, and to reconstruct the situation he must, as we have seen, make countless types of judgment. In the second place, the historian has to establish how the situation must have looked at that time, given the limitations of the particular agent in question. For it is not enough to know what was, from our standpoint, the case; we must know how, given the specific vantage point of, say, Lee, he must have seen the matter. Did he suspect that Meade had reinforced the center of the Union line? If so, was he so overconfident that it made no important difference? Or was his decision influenced by his reasoning that the attacks of the previous days had been unsuccessful only because of lack of coordination?

When one asks how any past agent must have seen a situation, he perhaps relies too heavily on a visual metaphor, as if the problem was simply one of reconstructing an angle of vision, so to speak. But more is involved than this, because persons in both past and present do more than merely see a situation; they evaluate it and interpret it. They attach importance to this fact and to that appearance; they fear the failure of this line of action more than the failure of that; they assess, weigh, hope, fear, suspect, distort. The actual situation is filtered through the prism of an individual character—his ways of thinking, his values, and his disvalues. In order, therefore, for a historian to see through the eyes of his subject, in order to identify himself with his subject's problems, the historian must not only imaginatively disengage himself from his own peculiar point of view, but he must try to identify himself with his subject.

The latter process is not a mystical one; it requires a great deal of concrete knowledge about the subject in question—how he characteristically responded to situations, whether he was clear-eyed and cool, given to disciplining his urge to action, or whether he tended to act without thinking or without weighing alternatives. Unless the historian has an intimate sense of the individual style of perception and thought of his subject, he has no guidelines for his own attempts to re-create that perception and rethink that thought. Without such knowledge, the historian has no check against possible error and no way of disciplining his own imagination.

The historian, then, must have enough firm evidence to reconstruct a relatively unified picture of a person before he can begin to think as that person once thought. The more information the historian has, the firmer the picture will normally be, just as in ordinary life an intimate friend is more likely to be in the position of knowing how another friend will respond to a given situation than a stranger would.

This entire process seems to presuppose that human beings, past and present, have enough in common that this re-enactment is possible, that certain types of thoughts are usually connected with certain types of actions. And yet, if human consciousness varies so much from age to age, to what degree is this presupposition justified?

There have been on the whole two ways in which philosophers have tended to handle this problem. On the one hand some have tried to show that however differently men have thought and believed, one can discern an underlying human nature. On the other hand others have argued that we can really rethink the thoughts only of those who share in some way our own presuppositions, that is, of those who stand in historical and cultural continuity with us. The former view insists on some sort of common essence shared by all human beings, the latter on the radical relativity of human thought-forms.

It is impossible to pursue this problem here. But it is not really necessary, for both views basically assume that we must use analogies taken from our present understanding of human nature in order to understand the past. They differ only in their view as to how far these analogies can be extended, whether they can guide us in attempting to understand an African witch doctor, as well as a member of our own cultural past, or whether they are helpful only in dealing with the latter.

The difficulty consists in describing how these analogies do, in fact, guide our thinking, for just as the relation between our accumulated knowledge of the world and ordinary language is extraordinarily difficult to specify, so, also, is the relation between our inferences about human activity and our assumptions about human nature. Consider, for example, the historian of science at work in reconstructing Babylonian astronomy.[51] With imagination, a mind working over the extant evidence can infer that the chief problem that occupied the Babylonians was the forecasting of the movements of the heavenly bodies. This seems evident because recent excavations have unearthed in the archives of the great cities of Mesopotamia an extraordinary number of baked clay tablets upon which are transcribed detailed planetary observations extending over the course of four centuries. Together with these are tablets predicting the motions and the eclipses of the moon. In addition there are elaborate procedure tables for calculating the daily positions of the planets. Horoscopes were also discovered which were concerned with affairs of state, as well as with the times and places of earthquakes, plagues, famines, and other natural disasters.

If the historian asks what all these things meant, what purpose they served, several obvious answers come to mind. Since the Babylonians, like many other peoples, believed that the movements of the stars had a direct influence on the destiny of the state, the tracing of these stars was a curious combination of piety and the desire for anticipating and avoiding individual and social disasters. This is supported by the fact that one tablet has long columns headed by the names of gods, which also are names of the heavenly bodies. There are also horoscopes and the apparent correlation of natural disasters with the positions of the stars. Compounded with this pious and magical motive were doubtless others. It is well known, for example, that agricultural societies are necessarily preoccupied with the weather and the seasons. In addition, a large land and commercial empire, such as the Babylonian, would have needed, if at all possible, a unified calendar, since every society in that ancient world had a different way of reckoning time, and this would have led to confusion. This hypothesis seems borne out because the documents reveal that the Babylonians were, in fact, preoccupied with the problems associated with predicting lunar and solar eclipses and calculating the evenings on which the new moon would first be visible on the horizon, the latter being an important problem for a society with a lunar calendar.

There is no need to pursue this illustration at length; it is only important to indicate what is involved in this rethinking of past thought. There is, first of all, no mystical intuition called for. The historian infers from evidence what it must have been used for and, given his own knowledge of the heavens and the observations the Babylonians themselves had made (and were limited to), the historian can envisage their problems, how they went about solving them, and even why they were unable in certain cases to solve them; for example, why they were unable to predict solar eclipses, since solar eclipses are visible only from a small part of the earth's surface. Secondly, the historian is guided throughout his investigations by a number of implicit assumptions about human nature and intelligence that lead him to relate types of events to one another. He assumes, among other things, that the tablets are calculations and that the rules of procedure were conscious ones, that the detail and precision with which they were made testify to great carefulness and must have involved a whole class of trained personnel who were highly valued by the state. In short, however different the thought-patterns themselves were, the Babylonian standpoint, given certain beliefs and assumptions, is quite intelligible. It may no longer be our own world-view but we can imagine how it could have been. We can recognize our own humanity in the Babylonian, and only on this presupposition is it possible to make the evidence intelligible at all.

The same imaginative reasoning can be employed in understanding the so-called mythical mind, and has been, in fact, by certain anthropologists. For myth and legend have more than the negative significance that they falsify fact. They have a positive significance as well. They provide a clue to the values, thoughts, purposes, and modes of perception of a people. Thus, Branislaw Malinowski used the myths of the Melanesians as the key to understanding their mentality.[52] By carefully observing how their myths of origin, of death, of the cycle of life, and of magic actually function, it was possible to reconstruct their basic self-understanding. He noted, for instance, the difference between magic and science. In the normal economic and agricultural pursuits, the islander relies for success not upon magic but upon his knowledge of cultivation, and if it were suggested to him that he depend upon an incantation rather than the irrigation of his crops, he would, Malinowski reported, only smile. "He knows as well as you do that there are natural conditions and causes, and by these observations he knows also that he is able to control these natural forces by mental and physical effort."[53] The islander turns to magic only when confronted by fortuitous elements in nature over which he has no control. When he fishes in the safety of the inner lagoon, there are no prefatory magical rites, but when he fishes in the highly dangerous outer lagoon, his preparations are accompanied by an elaborate magic. Magic, Malinowski concluded, is found wherever there is a high degree of contingency.

The anthropologist and historian, in both of these cases of reconstruction, did not insist, as Bradley did, that their subjects have the same critical consciousness as the scientists before accepting any of their reports. Rather, they imaginatively assumed the point of view of their subjects (which is reconstructed from the evidence) in order to see how the world and their experience must have appeared to them. In this sense, Collingwood is correct in criticizing Bradley for insisting that no report should be believed unless the historian can be certain that the witness brought the same consciousness to the event as the historian would if he had been there. This is impossible. It is only by trying to see and to think the way the witness thought that the historian can understand at all. But it does not follow from this that the historian merely accepts the mythical report or narrative. Rather, it is only after the historian understands that there may be a great difference between his own thought and that of a former time that he can begin to rethink the thought of the past and make it intelligible. But in the process of this rethinking, the historian must assume that the world of his witness is the same world as the historian's own, and only on this assumption can he reconstruct the witness's world. Only because we now know how the stars do behave is it possible to understand and not merely repeat the Babylonian's thoughts, to grasp how and why they succeeded and where they failed. And the historian must also assume, however vaguely it must be stated, that there are certain generalizations about human nature that can guide him in his re-enactment of past experience. And although these generalizations are so truistic as to seem scarcely worth stating, they are the indispensable background against which our thinking about other selves takes place. In this sense, Dilthey was correct in stressing that historical understanding is, in a sense, the discovery of the I in the Thou:

If I am to see [a past human] . . . as a person, to understand his mental life in its continuity and coherence, I must trace in his experience the lines of connection with which I am familiar in my own. I can do this in proportion as the consciousness of my own mental structure is present in and governs my understanding of his.[54]

The lines of connection are, to be sure, delicate and complex, but so are the lines of connection between the sciences and our common-sense view of the world. That there is a relationship seems clear, and all attempts to deny that we understand the past in the light of the present usually pay the price of presupposing just what is denied.

In summary, then, the historian's canon for judgments about the past is the same canon he uses in making judgments about the present. It presupposes his present, critically interpreted experience, and this experience is constituted by many diverse kinds of knowledge and belief—different fields—and the warrants for the conclusions in these respective spheres will be correspondingly various. To the extent that our attitude toward received reports is unintelligible without the modern sciences, the historian presupposes the sciences. But our world-view contains much more than knowledge derived from the sciences and, in this sense, to equate present knowledge with scientific knowledge is an error. The historian makes use of many other types of knowledge which are the basis for his truisms and generalizations and which, in turn, aid him in his explanations of individual events. The historian, like his witness, is also the son of his time, and his present standpoint may appear to subsequent generations also to be relative. But he cannot "jump out of his skull" or return to the standpoint of a former time, for his explanations and language inevitably reflect this one. Moreover it is only by taking responsibility for this present standpoint that a better, future one can responsibly emerge. The historian, to paraphrase Bradley, not only does presuppose present knowledge, he ought to do so.

The use of the imperative in this connection brings us to the crucial point in any discussion of these matters—what I have called the morality of knowledge or ethic of assent which is characteristic of the modern mind. For any analysis of the problem of Biblical criticism which ignores this facet of the problem can never appreciate the pathos of the modern mind and its problems with traditional Christian belief.

NOTES TO CHAPTER THREE

1. Stephen Toulmin and June Goodfield, *The Fabric of the Heavens* (London: Hutchinson & Co., 1961), pp. 17 f.

2. R. G. Collingwood, *The Idea of History* (Oxford: Oxford University Press, 1946), p. 252.

3. F. H. Bradley, *Collected Essays,* (Oxford: Oxford University Press, 1935), I, 1-53.

4. *Ibid.,* pp. 14 f.

5. *Ibid.,* pp. 20 f.

6. *Ibid.,* p. 21.

7. Marc Bloch, *The Historian's Craft,* trans. Peter Putnam (Manchester: Manchester University Press, 1954), p. 115.

8. Henri Pirenne, "What are Historians Trying to Do?" in Hans Meyerhoff (ed.), *The Philosophy of History in Our Time* (Garden City, N.Y.: Doubleday Anchor Books, 1959), p. 95.

9. Bradley, *op. cit.,* p. 2. Bradley did not explicitly criticize the Biblical scholarship of his day in this essay but Collingwood tells us that it was directed to the controversy created by the Biblical critics of the Tübingen School; see Collingwood, *op. cit.,* p. 135.

10. Bradley, *op. cit.,* pp. 21 ff.
11. Collingwood, *op. cit.,* p. 139.
12. Bradley, *op. cit.,* p. 29.
13. Jose Ortega y Gasset, *Concord and Liberty* (New York: W. W. Norton & Co., 1946), p. 148.
14. Collingwood, *op. cit.,* p. 239.
15. *Ibid.,* pp. 239 f.
16. *Ibid.,* pp. 139 f.
17. *Ibid.,* p. 140.
18. *Ibid.,* p. 138.
19. See chap. ii, note 21.
20. Richard R. Niebuhr, *Resurrection and Historical Reason* (New York: Charles Scribner's Sons, 1957), p. 171.
21. See "Miracles" in *The Oxford Dictionary of the Christian Church,* ed. F. L. Cross (London: Oxford University Press, 1958), p. 905.
22. Bloch, *op. cit.,* pp. 134 f.
23. *Ibid.,* p. 135.
24. *Ibid.,* p. 136.
25. See F. R. Tennant, *Miracle and Its Philosophical Presuppositions* (Cambridge: Cambridge University Press, 1925). Tennant's analysis of miracle is still worth reading. He notes that the apparent gain for theology consequent upon the discovery by science that the dogma of the impossibility of miracle was untenable was accompanied by equally important loss: "that of a criterion by which any given marvel may be recognized as a miracle in such a sense as to warrant for it evidential value for proving supernatural intervention" (p. 23).
26. Arthur O. Lovejoy, "Present Standpoints and Past History" in Meyerhoff (ed.), *op. cit.,* p. 186.
27. See John Passmore's article "Explanation in Everyday Life, in Science, and in History" in *History and Theory,* II (1962), 106-123.
28. It is significant that the two principal attempts of the last century to rely on a theory about the whole of history both foundered badly on fact: Hegelianism and Marxism.
29. Bruce Catton, *This Hallowed Ground* (New York: Pocket Books, Inc., 1960), p. 231.
30. Toulmin and Goodfield, *op. cit.,* chap. i.
31. Michael Scriven tends to argue in this fashion in Patrick Gardiner (ed.), *Theories of History* (Glencoe, Ill.: The Free Press, 1959), p. 446.
32. Morton White, "Historical Explanation" in Gardiner (ed.), *op. cit.,* p. 368.
33. In Gardiner (ed.), *op. cit.,* pp. 443-475.
34. *Ibid.,* p. 458.
35. *Ibid.,* p. 464.
36. *Ibid.,* p. 463.
37. Cf. Toulmin's observation in *The Uses of Argument* (New York: Cambridge University Press, 1958), p. 176: "When we ask how far the authority of the Court of Reason extends, therefore, we must put on one side the question how far in any field it is possible for arguments to be analytic: we must focus our attention instead on the rather different question, to what extent there are already established warrants in science, in

ethics or morality, in law, art-criticism, character-judging, or whatever it may be; and how far the procedures for deciding what principles are sound, and what warrants are acceptable, are generally understood and agreed."

38. See Schweitzer's acidic judgment in *The Quest of the Historical Jesus*, trans. W. Montgomery (New York: The Macmillan Co., 1964), p. 110 f: "What has been gained is only that the exclusion of miracle from our view of history has been universally recognised as a principle of criticism, so that miracle no longer concerns the historian either positively or negatively. Scientific theologians of the present day who desire to show their 'sensibility,' ask no more than that two or three little miracles may be left to them—in the stories of the childhood, perhaps, or in the narratives of the resurrection. And these miracles are, moreover, so far scientific that they have at least no relation to those in the text, but are merely spiritless, miserable little toy-dogs of criticism, flea-bitten by rationalism, too insignificant to do historical science any harm, especially as their owners honestly pay the tax upon them by the way in which they speak, write, and are silent about Strauss."

39. Toulmin, *The Uses of Argument*, pp. 18 ff.

40. *Ibid.*, p. 170.

41. Cf., *ibid.*, p. 37: "In order for a suggestion to be a 'possibility' in any context, therefore, it must 'have what it takes' in order to be entitled to genuine consideration *in that context*. To say, in any field, 'Such-and-such is a possible answer to our question,' is to say that, bearing in mind the nature of the problem concerned, such-and-such an answer deserves to be considered. This much of the meaning of the term 'possible' is field-invariant. The criteria of possibility, on the other hand, are field-dependent, like the criteria of impossibility and goodness."

42. See Rudolf Bultmann, *Glauben und Verstehen* (Tübingen: J. C. B. Mohr, 1933) I, 214-228.

43. Collingwood, *op. cit.*, pp. 214 f.

44. *Ibid.*, p. 240.

45. *Ibid.*, p. 226.

46. Bradley, *op. cit.*, p. 43.

47. I am indebted to Patrick Gardiner for this line of argument; see *The Nature of Historical Explanation* (Oxford: Oxford University Press, 1952), pp. 127 ff.

48. See Collingwood, *op. cit.*, p. 301, where he writes concerning the rethinking of Plato's thought: "Yet if I not only read his argument but understand it, follow it in my own mind by re-arguing it with and for myself, the process of argument which I go through is not a process resembling Plato's, it actually is Plato's, so far as I understand him rightly."

49. Gardiner, *The Nature of Historical Explanation*, pp. 120-133.

50. *Ibid.*, pp. 129 ff.

51. See Toulmin and Goodfield, *The Fabric of the Heavens*, pp. 23-51.

52. Bronislaw Malinowski, *Magic, Science and Religion and Other Essays* (Garden City, N.Y.: Doubleday Anchor Books, 1954).

53. *Ibid.*, p. 28.

54. Wilhelm Dilthey, *Gesammelte Schriften* (Stuttgart & Göttingen: B. C. Teubner Verlagsgesellschaft and Vandenhoeck & Ruprecht, 1958), VII, 214.

I V

The Morality of
Historical Knowledge
and Traditional Belief

1 · The Pathos of Modern Unbelief

ABOUT the turn of the century, the evangelical theologian Martin Kähler related this experience:

A young man from a long believing home came to me deeply moved inwardly and unsatisfied with modern rationalism. In a discussion with Tholuck, he had been told that if it could be demonstrated that the Fourth Gospel had not been written by John the son of Zebedee, then Christendom would have suffered a blow from which it would be very difficult to survive. This judgment profoundly shook the youth. The clarity with which I might have helped him through the matter escaped me at that time, and he climbed from that point on down the ladder of doubt, rung by rung, passing, I hope, from an intense longing for certainty to sight. That which caused him to stumble in his quest for a firm foundation was the linking of certainty, so far as Christian conviction is concerned, with the results of historical criticism of the sources, results that cannot be anticipated in advance. He was skeptical of all so-called positive results, which is to say, results favorable to the tradition, because he was troubled by the falsifying influence of the demand for belief lying behind them. Tholuck could hardly have calculated the magnitude of his utterance. Since that time it has become progressively more certain to me that my Christian conviction can have no causal connection with the "genuineness" the Gospels may have.[1]

This story reveals a great deal concerning the pathos of the modern mind. The pathos does not consist primarily in the conflict between the student's craving for certainty and his realization that historical inquiry could never, in the nature of the case, gratify it. It consists, rather, in his awareness of the falsifying influence belief frequently exercises on critical judgment, so that he is most distrustful of just those answers he would most like to believe. Indeed, it is just because he is aware that he would like to believe them that he distrusts any tendency in himself to do so.

This pathos is intelligible only if we realize that the revolution in consciousness, which came about with the emergence of historical thinking, is fundamentally a revolution in the morality of knowledge. A new ideal of judgment has gripped the intellect of Western man, and the student sensed that this ideal is incompatible with the ethic of belief that has so long been implicit in Christendom. The old morality celebrated faith and belief as virtues and regarded doubt as sin. The new morality celebrates methodological skepticism and is distrustful of passion in matters of inquiry. If Pascal's belief that the heart has its reasons which the reason cannot know can be said to represent the old ethic, then Nietzsche's conviction that integrity in matters of the mind requires that one be severe against one's heart may be regarded as symbolic of the new one.[2] The old morality was fond of the slogan "faith seeking understanding"; the new morality believes that every yes and no must be a matter of conscience.

The appeal to conscience is in itself quite empty, however, unless that conscience is informed by principles of some sort. Intellectual integrity presupposes not only the will-to-truth but also those standards that provide safeguards against the whims of desire and sentiment. The revolution in historical method occurred only when integrity was identified with loyalty to the methodological procedures of the intellectual community, when historians agreed on general canons of inquiry.

In matters of knowledge, as in matters of politics, the appeal to morality is a delicate affair. It always threatens to blanket discussion with a humorless and moralistic fog. It is no less artificial, however, to assume that the pursuit of knowledge is an autonomous and neutral enterprise and in no way related to conscience and responsibility. The problem of faith and history is not merely a problem of two logics or two methodologies. It is a problem, as Kähler's story reveals, of two ethics of judgment. Otherwise, it is impossible to account for the fierce sense of honesty, the suspicion of one's desire to believe, the sense of resentment against obscurantism, which underlie so much unbelief. Furthermore, only in this way is it possible to account for the character of much Protestant theology in the last century, because a great deal of that theology, as the closing sentences of Martin Kähler's story reveal, is an attempt so to formulate the faith that it escapes the accusation of being intellectually irresponsible. From liberal Protestantism to the new hermeneutic, Protestant theology may be regarded as a series of salvage operations, attempts to show how one can still believe in Jesus Christ and not violate an ideal of intellectual integrity.

2 · *Autonomy and Traditional Belief*

The first great conflict between the new morality of historical knowledge and traditional Christian belief[3] quite naturally occurred over the problem whether the Bible was to be subjected to the same methodological canons that were applied to other ancient and religious traditions and scriptures. The critic insisted on the right to be free and autonomous; the traditionalist insisted that the Bible was a holy and infallible book.

The story of that conflict, which raged through the nineteenth century, is now a familiar one and requires no rehearsal here. At first, Protestant and Catholic theologians alike were outraged at what they regarded to be the stiff-necked and arrogant pride of the "higher critics" who dared to lay such rude hands on Holy Writ. Still, the critics' arguments could not be ignored, and the traditionalists had to say something to their own flocks about them. They had several courses of action open to them: (1) they could appeal to the state to repress the new and dangerous doctrines; (2) they could retreat from discussion and hold up to ridicule the occasional inconsistencies and extravagances of the new science; and (3) they could step into the arena of debate and attempt to vindicate their own views.

The first possibility was still a live one in many parts of Europe at the beginning of the nineteenth century. But the days of the ancient regime were numbered, and kings and magistrates had more pressing problems to deal with than the suppression of Biblical scholarship of a certain kind, although some reprisals were taken in the universities. Besides, there were those Christian theologians who, although they did not agree with the new views, were devoted to freedom of inquiry and charity[4] and, not incidentally, were aware of the dangers involved in tying the destiny of the Christian faith too closely to the crumbling political order.

The second possibility only begged the crucial issues and could not long satisfy any inquiring mind. And more minds were inquiring each day as the new teachings were published and discussed.[5] Furthermore, it became increasingly evident that this possibility presupposed a visible consensus of belief among the traditionalists. For how could one convincingly argue that the Bible was infallible if there were so many varieties of opinion among those who so argued? The progressive development of Protestantism in Europe and in America revealed that there was no such visible consensus. The proliferation of sects and parties, all of which appealed to the authority of the Bible, made it quite evident that this appeal was largely ideological. And what was one to make of the fact that the entire history of conservative Biblical scholarship in the nineteenth century represented a retreat from one announced last-ditch stand to another? If Tholuck claimed that the very last bastion of Christian faith was the apostolic authorship of the Fourth Gospel, a succeeding generation believed this to be obviously indefensible and fell back on what they regarded as a more adequate barricade, only to evacuate that for still another which would also be overrun.

The only really viable alternative was to enter the lists of the debate and to attempt to vindicate the truth of the sacred narratives. To do this, however, it was necessary to pay a costly price: it was necessary to accept the general canons and criteria of just those one desired to refute. One had, so to speak, to step onto the ground that the critics occupied. This was fatal to the traditionalist's cause, because he could no longer appeal to the eye of faith or to any special warrants. The arguments had to stand or fall on their own merits.

The long-range effects of this gradual acceptance of the canons of historical inquiry were complex. A great number of scholars flourished under the new freedom, and Biblical research made extraordinary progress in the subsequent decades. For the most part, the appeal to miracle or to any supernatural intervention dropped from sight. Indeed, Biblical critics sometimes analyzed the texts with a greater degree of ruthlessness than was displayed by their secular colleagues. There were others, however, who could not go this far. They engaged in a less consistent practice. They examined some of the New Testament traditions with the aid of accepted principles of criticism while they left others alone or handled them quite gingerly.

There is a sense in which it can be said that the battle on behalf of the independence of the Biblical historian has been largely won. There are, to be sure, just enough of the remnants of the old authoritarianism around to justify the suspicion that the churches still nourish the nostalgic wish that the lid on this particular Pandora's box had never been lifted. The sporadic occurrence of heresy trials in Protestantism, trials having to do with matters of historical judgment, reveal that the principle of autonomy has won only a shaky victory in many Protestant quarters. And the very existence of the Roman Catholic Biblical Commission bears mute testimony that the church still recognizes the right to censor historical inquiry on dogmatic grounds. Nevertheless, the notion that the results of historical inquiry must conform in any way to the dictates of some authority is abhorrent to most Biblical scholars as well as secular historians.

But freedom from authority only touches one aspect of the historian's autonomy. As we have seen in the second chapter, there is another feature of historical judgment that is also an integral part of autonomy, although it is less easy to define. It has to do with a certain toughness of mind and is very closely connected with the process of historical reasoning itself. We saw that the historian's witnesses and sources are themselves a web of inferences and that the historian must, in the nature of the case, be able to justify those inferences unless, that is, he is willing to settle for the mere transmission of tradition. No witness can be permitted to go unexamined and no authority unquestioned. The historian does not accept the authority of his witnesses; rather, he confers authority upon them, and he does this only after subjecting them to a rigorous and skeptical cross-examination.

Now it is at this point that there is still a great deal of justified suspicion of Christian Biblical scholarship. For one cannot peruse the literature without gaining the impression that there is a notable lack of rigor evident in the handling of certain kinds of traditions: there is too hasty an appeal to the apostolic eyewitnesses; too quick an identification of the earliest traditions with the truth; too narrow a delimitation of the province of the secular historian when dealing with matters of faith; too ready an interjection of quasi-philosophical arguments concerning the nature of fact and its relationship to interpretation.

Consider, for example, an argument concerning the resurrection of Jesus that appears in a recent book by Heinz Zahrnt.[6] This book is especially interesting because it draws heavily upon the views of scholars like Hans von Campenhausen and Gerhard Ebeling, who can scarcely be called fundamentalists. Zahrnt employs the familiar argument that Christianity stands or falls with the resurrection of Jesus. This event, he notes, has a completely different status in the New Testament than does the virgin birth, the descent into Hell, or the ascension. If one tries to ascertain what Zahrnt means by the resurrection, however, certain problems arise. On the one hand, he argues that it "is not an historical event that we can observe in the same way as other events in space and time. It cannot be 'grasped.' "[7] Indeed, strictly speaking, the resurrection, it turns out, is not a historical event at all because it "transcends the bounds of history."[8] On the other hand, even though this event transcends the bounds of history, faith necessarily is interested in what really happened.[9] And any unprejudiced approach to the question must, it is alleged, conclude two things: (1) something happened to account for a remarkable change in the disciples, and (2) their unanimous testimony is that this something was Jesus' resurrection from the dead.[10]

Zahrnt is too sophisticated to argue that one can prove historically that Jesus was raised from the dead. All one can verify, he notes, is that Peter and the other disciples maintained that he was. Then, with that testimony assured, the historian can turn to the Gospel accounts and look for other evidence—the empty-tomb stories, for example—for indirect confirmation of their testimony.

Following with approval the general lines of an argument advanced by von Campenhausen and Ebeling, Zahrnt turns to what is generally regarded as the earliest account of the resurrection appearances, that given by Paul in I Corinthians 15. It is important to note that Paul there assures his readers he is passing on a tradition he has received. Furthermore, Paul actually mentions the names of some witnesses who were still alive. Zahrnt concludes from this that the events Paul relates are "clear, definite, historical facts," and he concurs with von Campenhausen that "anyone who despite this still doubts its reliability might just as well doubt everything that the New Testament contains—and more."[11]

Zahrnt believes that the historical reliability of this report can be further substantiated by the fact that the earliest Christian prayer, Marantha (Our Lord, come), points back to an Aramaic-speaking community and, thus, "we can with some certainty fix the origin of the Easter faith in Jerusalem."[12]

Zahrnt then turns to a consideration of the Gospel accounts. He concedes that these narratives are much later and contain many "legendary features, contradictions, absurdities, and discrepancies."[13] Nevertheless, he insists, this should not occasion doubt in our minds; on the contrary, the contradictions may be indirect testimony to the truth of the resurrection, because they indicate a lack of collusion on the part of the witnesses.[14] Furthermore, Zahrnt believes that the empty-tomb stories should be taken quite seriously. With von Campenhausen, he suggests that the very simplicity of the Marcan account, for example, argues for its nonlegendary character. Its most characteristic feature, in fact, is the lack of any resurrection appearance, although von Campenhausen, to be sure, does admit that the angel is "doubtless a legendary figure."[15] The Marcan account simply registers the experience of joy. We can conclude with von Campenhausen, then, that

> If we examine everything which is open to examination, we cannot in my view avoid coming to the conclusion that the report of the empty tomb itself and of its early discovery must be allowed to stand. There is much to be said in support of it and little definite and convincing evidence against it; it is therefore probably historical.[16]

Now this last statement is sufficiently uncritical to force us to reappraise the entire argument. When dealing with an event so initially improbable as the resurrection of a dead man, the two-thousand-year-old narratives of which are limited to the community dedicated to propagating the belief and admittedly full of "legendary features, contradictions, absurdities, and discrepancies," how could a critical historian argue that since much can be said for it and no convincing evidence exists against it, it is probably historical? Would one expect the only existing reports to contain any negative evidence given the fact that they come from the believing community? And what exactly would count as negative evidence? This is the crucial issue, because Zahrnt's argument has been so constructed that the lack of positive evidence as well as the admitted contradictions and absurdities *count for its validity.* On the one hand, we are told that because the accounts do not report an actual resurrection this testifies to its nonlegendary character. On the other hand, if there had been a report of seeing the event, this surely could have been cited as evidence for the fact that we are dealing with eyewitnesses. Or again, if there are contradictions and absurdities, we are told this indicates lack of collusion. Yet if there had been agreement, this could have been taken to mean the event was practically certain.

In addition to this, a methodological fog drifts over the entire discussion. We are never told, for example, why an angelic appearance is obviously legendary while the story of an empty grave is obviously not. What is the warrant that excludes the one judgment but permits the other? More seriously, we are not even told whether we are dealing with an event at all. On the one hand, the resurrection "transcends history"; on the other hand, historians ought to be interested in ascertaining what literally happened. But if the resurrection transcends history, it is impossible to assess the probability of the account, because we do not know what would constitute data for it or against it. Yet the historian requires just such data if he is interested in ascertaining what literally happened.

What strikes the reader as characteristic of the entire argument is the uncritical attitude toward eyewitnesses. Even if we grant that Paul's report is the earliest one—although that thicket has far more thorns in it than Zahrnt has permitted us to see—this does not mean that the tradition he passed on was a true one. It may be true as an account of what the earliest community believed, but whether what they believed may be called "clear, definite historical facts" is quite a different question. Zahrnt and von Campenhausen cannot be unaware of this, and yet they do everything to reinforce the uncritical passage from "the tradition is the earliest" to "the tradition is true." Indeed, von Campenhausen goes further and apparently tries to coerce the reader's judgment with his remark to the effect that anyone who doubts this report might as well doubt everything in the New Testament—and more. The point is that the critical historian has a duty to doubt it, and, moreover, to reject the all-or-nothing-at-all approach to testimony that is expressed in von Campenhausen's statement. No historian, as Collingwood observed, is under any obligation to consider an alleged eyewitness to be an authority. And no critical historian will reject all statements in a text because some of them appear to be doubtful.

One may observe a similar reluctance to assume responsibility for critical judgment in the works of other highly respected New Testament scholars. T. A. Roberts has done just this in a much neglected book that examines the historical methodology of F. C. Burkitt, C. H. Dodd, and Austin Farrer.[17] In the case of Dodd, Roberts notes that he repeatedly appeals to the earliest tradition about Jesus without raising any question at all about the validity of that tradition. Dodd collects, for example, a group of pericopes of a certain type to show that Jesus was friendly to outcasts. But, as Roberts points out, Dodd also argues that this fact "stands independently of the historical status of the several stories in detail."[18] This is a somewhat peculiar argument, especially in the light of Dodd's inclusion of the story of the woman taken in adultery, which is widely regarded as an interpolation into the text of the Fourth Gospel. Or again, in attempting to document the early tradition of Jesus' power over evil, Dodd appeals to two miracle stories that he admits resemble very closely "popular stories of wonder workers current in the Hellenistic world. . . ."[19] Or still again, Dodd, in discussing the miracle stories as a whole, simply argues that they exist in the tradition and assigns some of them a "superior historical status" just by virtue of their proximity to the central core of that tradition. Roberts concludes that Dodd's argument boils down to this: "Because primitive and original, the tradition is historical."[20]

What is all too frequently lacking in New Testament scholarship practiced by Christians is not scholarship but a certain toughness of mind, and it is this lack that occasions the kind of distrust that Kähler's student exemplifies. The falsifying influence of the demand for belief is so clearly behind it all. It is far more important, writes Allan Nevins in commenting on Lord Acton's praise of skepticism,

to possess the historical spirit—a doubting, critical mind, which demands proofs and verification—than to have a mass of historical learning. The beginning of wisdom in history is doubt. Its votaries should be imbued with the mental toughness of Bret Harte's M'liss, who, told in school that Joshua had bidden the sun stand still and it had obeyed him, shut her text with a loud snap and defiantly asserted: "It's a damn lie. I don't believe it." The true historical scholar is not the man who spills facts out of every pocket. . . . It is the man who, confronted with facts, assertions, and testimony offered with varying degrees of authority, knows how to test them, discard what seems false, and evaluate what seems true.[21]

3 · Assessment, Present Knowledge, and Traditional Belief

The problem of autonomy, it is clear, cannot be separated from the problem of rational assessment, for both are but aspects of one activity aspiring to be knowledge. Such an aspiration requires methodical skepticism, on the one hand, and a vigorous adherence to rational procedures on the other. The *sine qua non* of these procedures is the giving of reasons for one's conclusions. All rational claims are, as we have seen, appeals to other persons' minds, and one's respect for these persons is proportionate to the degree that he gives them to understand what it would mean to accept or to reject these claims. Candor is not a rationalistic ideal; it is the necessary condition for all responsible dialogue. This is not to say, as some positivists have said, that all meaningful utterances must be capable of being verified by sense experience. It is to say that the claims we make in various fields ought to have the most relevant reasons brought forward on their behalf that we can bring. The problem, as I have pointed out repeatedly, is not how to make our assertions scientific, but how to make them so that they can be appropriately assessed.

There is a deep suspicion in the minds of many people—even in the minds of those who, like Kähler's student, would like to believe—that traditional belief is obscurantist. It either appeals to faith, in the last resort, or it permits faith to tip the balance between two possibilities. Now it is important to note that the charge here is not that all faith is illegitimate but only that faith has no function in the justification of historical arguments respecting fact. When faith is used as a justification for believing historical claims that otherwise could not be justified by our normal warrants and backings, the machinery of rational assessment comes to a shuddering halt.

Our now familiar distinction between a claim and the justification of it is of crucial importance here. A lawyer may have faith that his client is innocent, but his arguments in court are logically independent of this trust. The lawyer will have to show why his inner trust is justified, and he will have to appeal to data and warrants that are acceptable to those who remain to be convinced. So, also, a scientist may believe that a certain type of cancer is caused by a specific virus, but the justification of his conviction will not be his confidence but the reasons supporting that confidence. It is precisely this distinction between an assertion and its justification that the appeal to faith most often obscures. If one says, for example, that he has faith that Jesus was born of a virgin, and this statement is challenged, the only rational response to the challenge is to bring forward reasons justifying the claim. But all too often the appeal to faith is but another way of saying that there need be no such reasons or that the reasons, lacking any weight, are still to be taken as good reasons. Faith is used to justify faith.

The force of the word "faith" in traditional belief has usually been to set aside the warrants we commonly use, and since it is impossible to know what would constitute data to back up a claim unless we can assume such warrants, the appeal to faith in matters of fact shatters the possibility of assessment. For this reason, the arguments between traditional believers and others inevitably become arguments not about facts (data) but about warrants. The believer says that ordinary warrants do not apply and his opponent argues that the believer is credulous and living in the past. The believer claims that his opponent takes the modern world-view too seriously, and the opponent protests that the believer is obscurantist.

At this point, the insights of F. H. Bradley are especially instructive. Although he can be criticized for sometimes invoking the authority of the scientific world-view in a heavy-handed way, he actually was making a more subtle point. Bradley's criticism of the conservative New Testament scholars of his time was not that they did not share modern warrants, but that they relied on these warrants in their day-by-day claims and in some of their historical inquiries only to suspend them when they dealt with their most treasured beliefs. His argument was that they were inconsistent men, half-modern and half-primitive, and that, in every case, whether they were one or the other was a direct function of their antecedent traditional beliefs. Consequently, Bradley formulated his standard of critical history in the form of an ethical imperative: One ought to make his interpretation of the past consistent with his interpretation of the present. "Our difficulty is this," Bradley wrote,

—we are asked to affirm the existence in history of causes such as we can find nothing analogous to now in our present experience. On the other hand, it is only from our knowledge of what is that we can conclude to that which has been; and, this being so, how can we first infer from the world to the existence of historical evidence within the world, and then, starting from that, proceed out of the world, when all the time we are unable to stand except upon the basis of the world?[22]

Bradley's criticism has special force for those who believe that it is impossible to escape from the categories and presuppositions of the intellectual culture of which one is a part, the common sense of one's own time. For what we call common sense really consists of beliefs and knowledge that are the result of a long historical development. These necessarily condition the perception and conception of all those who live in a culture. We are, it is argued, social and historical beings whose reasons are qualified by our inheritance and history. We are in history as fish are in water, and our ideas of possibility and actuality are relative to our time.

The attempt, then, to use warrants that are no longer viable in some fields strikes the critical mind as grotesque and anachronistic. This is, no doubt, what Bultmann meant when he wrote that "it is impossible to use electric light and the wireless and to avail ourselves of modern medical and surgical discoveries, and at the same time to believe in the New Testament world of spirits and miracles."[23] He meant that the act of turning a switch, speaking over a microphone, visiting a doctor or a psychiatrist is a *practical* commitment to a host of beliefs foreign to those of the New Testament. It is to say that the world of modern theory—be it electrical, atomic, biological, even psychological—is a part of the furniture of our minds and that we assume this in our reading of the newspapers, in our debates over foreign policy, in our law courts, and, it needs to be added, in our writing of history. In other words, our daily intercourse reveals that we, in fact, *do not* believe in a three-story universe or in the possession of the mind by either angelic or demonic beings.

It is to say more, however. It is to say that we *cannot* see the world as the first century saw it. We can, it is true, imaginatively understand how they could have believed what they believed, but these beliefs are no longer practically possible for us. We have, as it were, bitten of the apple, and our eyes have been opened and our memories are indelibly stamped with the new vision of reality. For all of our judgments and inferences take place, as we have seen, against a background of beliefs. We bring to our perceptions and interpretations a world of existing knowledge, categories, and judgments. Our inferences are but the visible part of an iceberg lying deep below the surface. Our realities are built up of explicit and hidden inferences. We have a new consciousness, and although we can transcend it from time to time in an act of historical imagination, we judge what we understand in the light of our own present knowledge and interpret it in the terms of our own existing "world."

This argument is difficult to make clear because of the very complexity of the matter. What we call our modern world-view or present knowledge is really composed of many different kinds of knowledge. The common sense of any given period, including our own, is field-encompassing. Consequently, the degree of certainty we can have will vary from field to field, just as there are ranges of probability within any given field.

Because our present knowledge is field-encompassing, we should be careful about sweeping appeals to the modern world-view. On the other hand, it is equally fallacious to trade on certain uncertainties in modern knowledge as if that justified a tentativeness toward all of it. Some Christian apologists write as though the fact that scientific theories change justifies not taking present knowledge seriously.

If we recognize the field-encompassing character of our knowledge, we can account, I think, for a phenomenon that traditional belief cannot account for, namely, that we immediately tend to reject some stories as impossible while we entertain other equally strange narratives as possible. Very few historians, for example, would hesitate to apply the category "legend" to the story of the saint who, after being beheaded, walked a few hundred yards to a cathedral with his head under his arm, entered the sanctuary and there sang the *Te Deum*. The historian calls it a legend because it is "impossible"; i.e., knowing what we now know about vocal chords, their relationship to the brain and to the lungs, he can bring forward the strongest warrants in rebuttal of any such conclusion. The warrants are tight, and it is inconceivable how they could be loosened. There are countless other judgments relatively new in the history of thought that one cannot conceive of being altered or relative to the time—the spherical shape of the earth, the circulation of the blood, the necessity of oxygen for the brain, etc. On the other hand, a good historian may be less skeptical of a report of a miraculous cure, not because he believes in miracles, but because psychosomatic medicine is still in its infancy and no tight warrants are forthcoming. This being so, there is considerable room for rebuttal arguments.

The varying degree of tightness of our warrants casts some light on why some alleged miracles are harder to believe than others, a phenomenon that is, on the face of it, quite odd, since in the realm of miracles, no one miracle should be any more difficult to believe than another. Why for example, does the modern mind have more difficulty believing that Jesus could calm a storm or walk on water than that he could heal the sick? The answer, I think, lies in the fact that we know enough about the causes of weather to believe it to be highly unlikely for it to be altered by fiat. So, too, we know enough about weight, specific gravity, and the like to make it difficult to believe that a man could, by exercise of will power, walk on water. On the other hand, we are aware that sickness often has a relationship to the mind, and we are acquainted with stories of strange cures even in the present. To be sure, we make a kind of distinction between the cures of broken bones and the cures of hysterical blindness, but we nevertheless do not think ourselves justified in ruling out a healing miracle. The warrants, in short, are less tight in the latter area than in the former. Not all of our warrants stand on the same level. Some of our modern knowledge is virtually certain; a great deal of it is less so and subject to change.

This observation brings us to another aspect of the ethics of modern knowledge and belief. The morality of scientific knowledge requires that one embrace that knowledge which presently best explains certain phenomena unless one has evidence and reasons of the same logical type for rejecting it. This morality is not arbitrary, moreover, because it springs from the recognition that progress in any field of knowledge is possible only if one builds on present theories and, conversely, that no progress in knowledge is possible if men reject present knowledge for no principled reason. Science proceeds by the judicious correction of past theories. Each new advance in knowledge is possible only by virtue of the criticism of present knowledge.

The history of science provides a number of illustrations of this important truth, but the case of Aristarchos is especially interesting. Aristarchos advanced a heliocentric theory of the universe some seventeen centuries before Copernicus, and he tried very hard to make his view acceptable to his contemporaries without ever convincing them. Aristotle's erroneous view prevailed instead, and men continued to exist in error for one and a half millennia. Should Aristarchos' contemporaries be blamed? Was it merely a misplaced confidence in Aristotle's authority that caused them to dismiss the new (and truer) view? The answer to both questions is no, because Aristarchos' theory was only a speculative hunch and the then known evidence was against it. In a remarkable passage which breathes with the spirit of the critical ethic of belief, the authors of a recent history of science conclude:

So we really need not be surprised that the Greeks remained sceptical about Aristarchos' suggestion: rather, we should congratulate them on their good sense. In judging them as scientists—as rational interpreters of Nature, that is—the important thing, surely, is not to ask how many conclusions they reached which we still accept, but rather how far their conclusions were supported by the evidence then available. In so far as they allowed their judgement to be influenced by the weight of the evidence, they can be said to have thought scientifically.[24]

Now traditional Christian belief seems to its critics to be especially culpable in this respect. The orthodox believer often sets aside the consensus in a given field for no other reason than that this consensus is incompatible with some historical proposition he desires to believe. He is intellectually irresponsible, not so much because he wants certainty, as because he continually enters objections to our normal warrants for no principled reasons. Consequently, his objections are themselves nonassessible and lead to no advance in knowledge. Yet, these same believers are most eager to welcome modern knowledge wherever it seems to support traditional Christian belief in any respect.[25]

The difference between these two moralities of knowledge may be vividly illustrated in the respective attitudes of two nineteenth-century scholars, D. F. Strauss, on the one hand, and the Roman Catholic, Louis Duchesne, on the other. Both were subjected to extreme pressure because of their modernist views on the New Testament. Strauss, however, in defending his work, appealed to a future justification. He completed his *Life of Jesus* with the words: "Time will show whether by the one party or the other, the Church, Mankind, and Truth are best served."[26] Duchesne, teacher and friend of Alfred Loisy, the father of Catholic modernism, also appealed to the future, but not for justification so much as for understanding. He wrote:

The religious authority rests upon its tradition and the members of its personnel who are the most devoted—and also the least intelligent. What is to be done? Are we to hope this will change? Are we to try and effect a reform? But this will not change, and the reform will not be carried through. The only result of attempts of this kind is to get yourself thrown out of the window, with no beneficial results either for others or for yourself. . . . It may be that, in spite of all appearances, the old ecclesiastical edifice is going one day to tumble down, that the gates of Paradise will prevail against it. If it happens so, no one will blame us for having supported the old establishment as long as possible.[27]

4 · Traditional Belief and Sound Judgment

Basically, all of these criticisms of traditional Christian belief are but forms of a more fundamental one, namely, that orthodox belief corrodes the delicate machinery of sound historical judgment. The accusation is not that the traditionalist lacks learning or does not possess the tools of scholarship but that he lacks a certain quality of mind. The failure to criticize his sources rigorously, the ambivalent relationship to present knowledge and rational assessment: these, in the mind of the critic, are but manifestations of a deeper failure. Now this charge must inevitably appear to be vague and even *ad hominem*. In a sense it is, because the ideal by which the historians judge themselves is itself an aesthetic and moral one. Consequently, it is difficult to define abstractly. No concrete rules can be neatly laid out for balanced judgment any more than one can specify exactly what constitutes reasonable doubt in the field of jurisprudence. Just as in any field there can be no general answer to the question, "What makes reasoning adequate in this field?"[28] so, also, no general criteria can be specified for defining what makes historical judgment sound. Yet this is precisely where the problem lies, and to miss this point is to misunderstand the entire issue.

Although the ideal of sound judgment cannot be abstractly defined, one can point out the various ways in which it is often exercised. In the previous chapters, I have attempted to do this. I have tried to show how balanced judgment is called for at many different levels, from the criticism of sources to the final process of narration. In evaluating evidence, it will be exemplified in numerous ways: in the estimation of the importance to be attached to a single document in contrast to others; in the decision concerning the weight to be attributed to the occurrence of error or bias or fraud in a report in which other important and true observations are also contained; in the evaluation of the silence of a witness on certain matters in contrast to what he explicitly says. There are rules of thumb, perhaps, that may guide the fledgling historian in these matters, but these rules are no substitute for that intangible quality that separates the sound historian from the tendentious and undiscriminating one.

So also the historian's judgment is at work in the process of reconstructing what happened. It is exercised in what Toulmin has called the first phase of an argument, that is, in the sorting out of various relevant possibilities that may count as solutions to a problem. These possibilities are necessarily relative to a specific context and, hence, presuppose a great deal of prior knowledge about the event. The range of relevant possibilities for explaining General Hooker's failure and General Lee's success at the battle of Chancellorsville, for example, have already been limited by the historian's knowledge of their respective tactical positions, of the number of men and arms under their command, of their characters and how these generally expressed themselves in strategy. To ask what the possibilities are for explaining Hooker's actions is not to ask, as I have pointed out, what is logically possible to explain these actions, but what commends itself as a likely answer to a question that arises in the mind of a person who already is more or less familiar with the matter. These likely answers are also a function of the historian's knowledge of the pertinent natural and physical laws—the limitations of weapons in the year 1863, the external conditions imposed on observation and movement by terrain and distance, and the like. Furthermore, these possibilities are, as we have seen, functions of certain gross generalizations about human behavior that cannot be called laws but which have a high degree of immunity against exceptions. In short, what makes a candidate for a particular solution a likely one is a function of many kinds of judgments.

The judgment of the historian can also be seen in his decision as to what it is important or not important to argue in any given case. This is often relative to what previous historians have written about the matter or what is popularly believed to have occurred. Like the defense lawyer who must keep a sensitive eye on the dynamics of the prosecutor's argument so that, on behalf of his client, he may challenge an assumed datum or an unwarranted assumption or bring forward a rebuttal to qualify radically an inference drawn from commonly accepted data and warrants, the good historian must know which previously held opinions it is necessary to refute and which can be more or less safely ignored. He must know what it is necessary to explain and what new evidence would alter the entire picture, what rebuttals would be decisive and what counterarguments would require extraordinary and strong support. He will have to anticipate whether the objections to his presentation will take the form of the question, "But is your evidence correct?" or the form "Is your evidence adequate?" or the form "Is your evidence relevant?" Each question will dictate a slightly different kind of argument and presentation.

Finally, the historian's balance of judgment will be manifested in the quality of assent he solicits from his reader. As we have seen, the warrants of an argument convey and license varying degrees of force for a conclusion, a force relative to the strength of the warrants, their backings and to the lack of possible rebuttals, or in some cases, the successful refutation of actual ones. Hence, the conclusions of the historian cannot be classified simply in terms of the disjunctive categories true or false. Rather, they must be distinguished by reference to the degree of probability they possess. The historian, unlike the mathematician, finds it necessary to qualify his judgments in different and significant ways. He does not solicit mere assent but a quality of assent, not mere judgment but a properly qualified type of judgment ranging from tentativeness to practical assurance. Thus, historical narrative is filled with implicit or explicit qualifications such as "it is possible that," "it may have been that," "it is probable that," "it can scarcely be doubted that," or "it is certain that." These qualifications are, as it were, signposts by means of which the historian informs his reader concerning the quality of assent he believes to be fitting and appropriate. He flags, so to speak, those judgments which are controversial and which can be legitimately debated and those conclusions about which only an eccentric or a pedant would quarrel. In short, the historian's ideal is not mere judgment but balance of judgment; his finest tool is not assertion but properly qualified assertion.

The corruption of historical judgment by traditional Christian belief occurs, the critic charges, on all of these levels of which I

have written. In the first phase of an argument, the critical mind
will necessarily assess the likely candidates in the light of his concrete knowledge about the first-century world, gross observations
about human behavior as well as his present knowledge of nature
and the world. In the realm of traditional belief, however, it is
impossible even to formulate a standard for estimating what is
likely or unlikely. The events with which belief is concerned are,
by definition, unique, which is to say, none of our warrants or
analogies apply. Was Jesus born of a virgin? Did he walk on
water? calm the storm? cast out demons? talk with Satan? raise
Lazarus from the dead? turn water into wine? How is it possible
even to get into the position of asking whether these are candidates
for being historical solutions to historical problems?

This initial eccentricity of judgment manifests itself further in
the estimation of the dynamics of argument. For there to be a
productive argument, there will also have to be some agreement as
to what constitutes data as well as warrants. Just as in a courtroom, judge, jury, and attorneys will have to have some common
standards which make it possible to submit evidence, assume warrants, and offer rebuttals, so also in history the development of an
explanation necessarily presupposes some agreement as to what
counts for and what against a conclusion or assertion. But it is just
this that traditional belief makes difficult if not impossible. Consequently, the historian who does not believe in traditional fashion is
basically perplexed by the inner dynamics of argument among the
believing historians. He sees laborious efforts made to harmonize
accounts which he believes cannot be harmonized, given the type
of document or narrative with which one is dealing; or he observes
appeals being made to possibilities that in the nature of the case he
interprets to be highly unlikely and even impossible. Logical possibilities—"miracles are not impossible"—are converted into practical possibilities. The hypothesis of one paragraph becomes the
basis for further inferences soliciting heavy assent in another. Consequently, rebuttals that the critic would consider decisive are put
aside as manifestations of rationalism or "an outdated view of
nature," and warrants and backings are accepted to which he can
attribute no merit. Hence, the critic sees no way of entering the

argument or the realm of discourse, and the ideal of judgment which he has come to prize plays no role whatsoever.

All of these objections come to focus in the critical ideal of assent, and this ideal, like the other ideals of autonomy and assessment, finds characteristic expression in this counsel of perfection of the Enlightenment:

> He that would seriously set upon the search of truth ought, in the first place, to prepare his mind with a love of it. For he that loves it not, will not take much pains to get it; nor be much concerned when he misses it. There is nobody in the commonwealth of learning who does not profess himself a lover of truth; and there is not a rational creature that would not take it amiss to be thought otherwise of. And yet, for all this, one may truly say, there are very few lovers of truth for truth's sake, even amongst those who persuade themselves that they are so. How a man may know whether he be so in earnest, is worth enquiry: and I think there is this one unerring mark of it, viz., the not entertaining any proposition with greater assurance than the proofs it is built upon will warrant. Whoever goes beyond this measure of assent, it is plain, receives not truth in the love of it; loves not truth for truth's sake, but for some other by-end.[29]

The crucial thought here *is the duty of* "not entertaining any proposition with greater assurance than the proofs it is built upon will warrant." For it is believed that it is somehow irresponsible to give a heavy assent to a proposition that properly deserves a soft one or to convert a conclusion in one paragraph into the dogmatic basis of an argument in the next. This ideal of the Enlightenment has its own limitations, to be sure, for it also obscures the difference of fields so far as our judgments are concerned. There are many sorts of judgments—for example, ethical ones—in which we recognize the incommensurability between an assertion and its justification. But most of our contingent historical judgments are not of this sort, and adjudicable arguments can be given for them.

At this point also, traditional Christian belief seems to undermine judgment, because it seems to require, in the nature of the case, that heavy assents be given to propositions that properly elicit soft assents, that assertions with a very low degree of probability be converted into statements possessing a high degree of probability, that mere logical possibilities be confused with likely probabilities. This, in turn, seems to be a function of the fact that the passion of faith is tied indissolubly to certain specific historical assertions of a unique kind.

There have been those who argue that this counsel of perfection is nothing but rationalism and that most of our knowledge is rooted in a "leap of faith." This argument has especially been popular in the writings of those Christian apologists influenced by Sören Kierkegaard and existentialism. But this is a dubious reading of Kierkegaard; indeed, some of his writings, at least, can be read as making the opposite point. In his *Concluding Unscientific Post-script,* for example, Kierkegaard argues not that history rests on faithlike presuppositions but, on the contrary, that faith and history do not mix because history is an "approximation process" in which it is necessary to be "objectively light." What is true of history, he argues, is true in philosophy.

In sawing wood it is important not to press down too hard on the saw; the lighter the pressure exerted by the sawyer, the better the saw operates. If a man were to press down with all his strength, he would no longer be able to saw at all. In the same way it is necessary for the philosopher to make himself objectively light; but everyone who is in passion infinitely interested in his eternal happiness makes himself subjectively as heavy as possible. Precisely for this reason he prevents himself from speculating.[30]

Just as it is comic for a philosopher to be passionately interested in the outcome of his speculations, so it leads to fanaticism for a historian to attach ultimate concern to the results of historical inquiry.

It is a self-contradiction and therefore comical, to be infinitely interested in that which in its maximum still always remains an approximation. If in spite of this, passion is nevertheless imported, we get fanaticism. For an infinitely interested passion every iota will be of infinite value. The fault is not in the infinitely interested passion, but in the fact that its object has become an approximation-object.[31]

There is nothing in these observations by Kierkegaard with which the young man in Kähler's story could not agree. The difference lies in the fact that Kierkegaard was willing to take refuge in the absurd, whereas for the young man it was a matter of the deepest concern to discover whether the Christian faith had some basis in reasonable belief. It would not have helped him simply to claim that Christianity is based on faith. His problem was what to have faith in, and how this faith is related to the morality of knowledge.

NOTES TO CHAPTER FOUR

1. Martin Kähler, *Der sogenannte historische Jesus und der geschichtliche, biblische Christus* (2d ed.; Leipzig: Deichert'sche Verlagsbuchhandlung, 1896), p. 8, n. 1.

2. See Blaise Pascal, *Pensées and The Provincial Letters* (New York: The Modern Library, 1941), p. 95. Cf. Walter Kaufmann (ed.), *The Portable Nietzsche* (New York: The Viking Press, 1954), p. 632.

3. I am aware that "traditional belief" is also a field-encompassing term and that my use of it may appear to be too sweeping. I obviously intend to refer to traditional belief only as it pertains to historical propositions. But since it seemed cumbersome to write "traditional Christian historical belief" I have used this terminological shorthand.

4. As Schweitzer points out, Neander, especially, exemplified a splendid attitude. See *The Quest of the Historical Jesus* (New York: The Macmillan Co., 1964), pp. 101 f.

5. Schweitzer ironically notes how the fear of Strauss inspired some Protestant theologians with catholicizing tendencies. They wished Strauss had written his *Life of Jesus* in Latin so that the common people might not have read it. (*Ibid.*, chap. ix.)

6. Heinz Zahrnt, *The Historical Jesus*, trans. J. S. Bowden (New York: Harper & Row, 1963).

7. *Ibid.*, p. 121.

8. *Ibid.*

9. *Ibid.*, pp. 122 f.

10. *Ibid.*, pp. 123 ff.

11. Quoted by Zahrnt, *op. cit.*, p. 127.

12. *Ibid.*, p. 128.

13. *Ibid.*, p. 129.

14. *Ibid.*

15. *Ibid.*, p. 131.

16. *Ibid.*, p. 132.

17. T. A. Roberts, *History and Christian Apologetic* (London: S.P.C.K., 1960).

18. Quoted by Roberts, *op. cit.*, p. 103.

19. Quoted by Roberts, *op. cit.*, p. 103.

20. *Ibid.*, p. 105.

21. Allan Nevins, *The Gateway to History* (rev. ed.; Garden City, N.Y.: Doubleday Anchor Books, 1962), p. 67.

22. F. H. Bradley, *Collected Essays* (Oxford: Oxford University Press, 1935), I, 25.

23. Rudolf Bultmann in Hans W. Bartsch (ed.), *Kerygma and Myth*, trans. Reginald H. Fuller (New York: Harper Torchbooks, 1961), p. 5.

24. Stephen Toulmin and June Goodfield, *The Fabric of the Heavens* (London: Hutchinson & Co., 1961), p. 126.

25. Merrill Tenney appeals to the concepts of atomic interchange and of "a fourth dimension" as aids in understanding how the resurrected body of Jesus could penetrate other matter without itself becoming disarranged. See *The Reality of the Resurrection* (New York: Harper & Row, 1963), p. 122.

26. David F. Strauss, *The Life of Jesus Critically Examined*, trans. George Eliot (5th ed.; London: Swan Sonnenschein & Co., 1906), Sec. 152.

27. Quoted by Alec Vidler, *The Modernist Movement in the Roman Church, Its Origins and Outcome* (Cambridge: Cambridge University Press, 1934), p. 78.

28. See Stephen Toulmin, *An Examination of the Place of Reason in Ethics* (Cambridge: Cambridge University Press, 1961), p. 161.

29. John Locke, *An Essay Concerning Human Understanding*, abr. and ed. A. S. Pringle-Pattison (Oxford: Oxford University Press, 1934), Book IV, chap. xix. A powerful statement of the same ethic may be found in William Kingdon Clifford, *Lectures and Essays* (2d ed.; London: Macmillan & Co., 1886), pp. 339-363.

30. Sören Kierkegaard, *Concluding Unscientific Postscript*, trans. David Swenson (Princeton: Princeton University Press, 1941), p. 55.

31. *Ibid.*, p. 32.

V

The Morality of Historical Knowledge and the Dialectical Theology

I · Is the Morality of Knowledge a Secular One?

As we have seen in the previous chapter, the heart of the issue before us is the collision of two moralities of knowledge, the one characteristic of the scholarly world since the Enlightenment, the other characteristic of traditional Christian belief. As soon as the issue is posed in this fashion, one possible way of resolving it comes immediately to mind. One might say:

If, as you have argued, the issue is an ethical one, and if moral decisions are themselves but an aspect of one's faith and commitments, then surely it is simply a matter of choice whether one wishes to be a child of the Enlightenment or of the church. The real question is whether one wants to be accepted by the scholarly establishment or whether he wills to remain loyal to the Word of God. And if moralities are judged by their fruits, is there really more to be said in favor of rationalism than of belief?

Some Christian theologians have cast the issue in precisely those terms. In an essay published in 1947 on the conception of revelation and its relation to historical science, Erwin Reisner, for example, argues that the acceptance of revelation requires one to surrender everything that belongs to the godless world, including "the whole superstition that calls itself science, above all historical science."[1] This science is founded on a sinful autonomous act, the presumed right of man to sit in judgment on sacred traditions. Its scholars would rather be right in the eyes of men than in the eyes of God. Men, however, do not judge the Word of God; it judges them. Consequently, "the real call of today . . . is to make a turn of 180 degrees and bring historical science, especially in so far as it has gained a dominant position within theology itself, under the judgment of revelation and mark it plainly as an erroneous path leading to falsehood."[2]

Unfortunately, the matter is not quite as simple as Reisner suggests, as even so convinced an enemy of Christianity as Nietzsche understood. If Reisner believes that the morality of knowledge underlying the sciences is an expression of unbelief, Nietzsche suggested that Christianity has only itself to blame for the revolt of the modern conscience. It was, after all, Christianity which taught the world that God is truth and truth, divine, and it was Christianity which held aloft the ideal that one should be prepared to sacrifice everything in the service of this divinity. If men took seriously this will-to-truth and embraced everything which seemed to safeguard it, then Nietzsche felt it was no exaggeration to say that Christianity as dogma perished of its own morality.[3] Faith and enlightenment, in other words, are not simple antitheses.

It was given to liberal Protestantism, as Christoph Senft has pointed out,[4] to reject this too-easy juxtaposition of enlightenment and faith. Although most of the liberal theologians would have been uncomfortable at the thought of agreeing in any respect with Nietzsche, they saw, nevertheless, that the autonomy and integrity underlying contemporary skepticism could also be interpreted as an expression of something like faith. Consequently, they sought to take the Enlightenment and its ethic seriously without succumbing to rationalism on the one hand, or supernaturalism on the other.

The theology of Wilhelm Herrmann provides a fine illustration of this, and he is particularly interesting because he anticipated in many respects the solution to this problem later proposed by the dialectical theologians. Herrmann was keenly aware that the conditions of belief were quite different for his contemporaries than for men of antiquity. He was, in this respect, a historical thinker. He understood that science and technology have created a new and different world, so that the demand to believe certain things imposes quite a different burden on the modern conscience than that which a person in medieval times had to carry by reason of the same demand. The peculiar pathos of modern man, Herrmann saw, was that "the more sincere . . . [he] is, the more impossible is it thus made for him to become a Christian."[5] Indeed, "one may call those happy who do not see themselves forced out of the traditional forms of Christianity by the duty of sincerity."[6] Such a situation is incredible, Herrmann believed, especially if seen from the standpoint of Protestant faith. He appealed to Luther's view that faith should liberate the conscience, not lay a burden upon it. Faith is joy, release, trust, and no man can be liberated by holding for true something which he does not inwardly understand to be true.

A word can have for men the significance of a word of God only when it brings him to true self-examination under the circumstances in which he stands at the moment. Every religious thought which does not become intelligible to us in this way remains foreign to us, though we may give it out ever so defiantly as the expression of our own convictions and excite our imagination ever so strongly with it.[7]

It is an error, then, to identify faith with assent or belief. Faith cannot be regarded as the making of other men's beliefs our own, even if these other men are called apostles. Faith cannot be identified with the acknowledgment of the Bible as God's Word together with a firm trust in its narratives and doctrines. This, Herrmann argued, is the Roman Catholic conception of faith, the only difference between it and the customary Protestant one being that the Catholic believes both the Bible and the church while the Protestant clings only to the former. Faith is, rather, the finding of God in one's own spiritual life, and it is only this experience, Herrmann insisted, that can provide the ground for an inward joy and the revolution in one's self-understanding. Only this certainty can provide a rock against the floods of doubt.[8]

Such a faith, Herrmann concluded, is made possible only when one person encounters another who inspires this certainty and trust. The person of Jesus serves such a function for the Christian. By virtue of the fullness of his spiritual life, his ability to judge the conscience, and, most of all, his power to mediate the sense of forgiveness, Jesus liberates the self.[9] The picture of his inner life as it is given in the New Testament is so powerful that it can and does become the ground of faith. One cannot demonstrate to everyone that Christ is such a ground, of course, but "in every man the necessary conditions exist for his finding in the tradition about Jesus in the books of the New Testament, the picture of a Man who by the power of His personal life holds us suspended over the abyss."[10]

Herrmann's solution to the problem of faith and history seems basically paradoxical, however. How can he argue that faith does not involve any assent to historical propositions and at the same time insist that faith is dependent on some sort of apprehension of Jesus' character and personality? How can the character and personality of Jesus even be known except through historical inquiry? And if historical inquiry is the final court of appeal regarding the truth of the picture, does this not once more involve faith in the anxiety attendant on the relativities of Biblical research?[11]

Herrmann was never able to solve his problem, and for most of his students even the attempt to do so became increasingly superfluous because of the further development of New Testament criticism. The consensus emerged, as we have seen in the first chapter, that the New Testament did not yield a picture of the inner life and personality of Jesus. Although it could be inferred that he was a charismatic personality, this personality was not, it was argued, the basis of the faith of the first-century disciples. Nor should it be for ours. Then as now, the object of faith is the proclamation that Jesus was resurrected. The Gospels are *kerygmatic* documents, reflecting the faith in the risen Christ. They are not sources for a reconstruction of the personality of the historical Jesus.

The dialectical theologians, especially in their earliest writings, took full advantage of this situation created by Biblical criticism. They argued, in effect, that Herrmann was correct in distinguishing faith from assent, but wrong in trying to relate faith to the inner life of Jesus. The *kerygma,* they insisted, was not about the inner life of Jesus but about God's act of judgment and renewal which was revealed in his life and death. They distinguished between the Jesus of history and the Christ of faith, between the man Jesus and the hidden Word of God. They emphasized the "divine incognito" in contrast to the visible, moral superiority of the historical Jesus. Consequently, the dialectical theologians all insisted that historical inquiry, concerned as it is with a description of the facts of Jesus' life, is irrelevant for Christian faith.

The dialectical theologians interest us for two reasons. They have, first of all, so radicalized the concept of justification by faith that, if one accepts their understanding of it, faith and the morality of historical knowledge cannot be put in simple opposition to one another. Indeed, the dialectical theologians not only see no conflict between faith and the modern ethic of knowledge, they regard them as standing in a very close relationship. They see the morality of knowledge as a secularized version of faith. In this way, the dialectical theology has attempted to solve the problem of the believer who would also be an honest historian.

There is a second reason for looking closely at these theologians. The same radical interpretation of justification by faith, which permitted them to accept the morality of historical knowledge, seems to permit a conclusion about the relationship of faith to history that these theologians seem especially anxious to avoid, namely, that faith has no essential relationship to a past historical event. The doctrine of justification implies that faith is a possibility for man as man. Yet it is precisely this implication the dialectical theologians resist, because it seems to cut the cord between faith and the man Jesus of Nazareth. How, then, can one reconcile this new conception of faith with the church's traditional insistence on the centrality of a historical event? This is the question we must keep in our minds as we examine the dialectical theology.

2 · The New Understanding of Faith

The single name "dialectical theology" tends to obscure the diversity of the theologians usually denoted by it. As any theological student knows, there are significant differences between, say,

Karl Barth and Rudolf Bultmann, or between Reinhold Niebuhr and Paul Tillich. Nevertheless, there are certain common motifs amidst this diversity, and it would be an error to allow the obvious diversity to blind one to an underlying unity. All of them, for example, understood themselves to be engaged in a thorough exploration of the significance of the principle of justification by faith for all aspects of man's life. This was particularly true in the formative stages of the movement. And if there have been ruptures in the movement since those early years when they all battled against the dominant errors of liberalism, these ruptures, I believe, are only intelligible against the backdrop of this basic unity.

The most radical attempt to rethink the contemporary significance of the idea of justification by faith was, of course, made by Barth in *The Epistle to the Romans,* the second edition of which in 1922 may be regarded as the manifesto of the new theological movement. Faith, Barth argued, may not be identified with belief, religious feeling, morality, religion, or any other aspect of man's experience. Faith is, rather, the realization of the abysmal gulf separating man from God. It is the recognition of the "qualitative distinction between time and eternity."[12] Consequently, faith is closely allied to, if it is not identical with, a recognition of the ambiguity and questionableness of life.[13] Faith can only emerge when this all-embracing contrast between man and God is acknowledged. Genuine faith is a void, a not-knowing,[14] the utter dissolution of man and all of the possibilities in which he takes pride.[15] One might say that men love God not when they enjoy the satisfactions of religion but when "veritably and existentially, quite clearly and once for all, without possibility of avoidance or escape, they encounter the question: 'Who then am I?' For the contrasted and inevitable 'Thou' involved in this question is— God."[16]

Grace, in Barth's view, does not bridge the gulf between God and men, but exposes it, and the exposure is such that men are able to accept God as the one they do not know.[17] For only in the awareness of the total ambiguity of the human situation can men experience the gift of God's acceptance and so love the Judge.[18] It follows that revelation is not the communication of truths otherwise inaccessible to the reason, but the precipitation of the *Krisis* in which the negation of all human aspirations is exposed. The Christian perceives this *Krisis* in Jesus of Nazareth; not in the example of his superior piety or morality or sinlessness, but in his ignominious death. His greatest achievement, Barth writes, is a negative achievement, for "he bids farewell to all those achievements by which men obscure the fact of death. . . ."[19] He sacrifices every human possibility. His death is the clue to the meaning of his life.[20] "Herein He is recognized as the Christ. . . . The Messiah is the end of mankind, and here also God is found faithful."[21]

Just because Barth interpreted revelation to mean the exposure of the ambiguity of human righteousness, he could argue, as he could not in his later writings, that this revelation is not confined to the life and death of Jesus of Nazareth. The decisive and once-for-all nature of Christ consists in the fact that "in Jesus we have discovered and recognized the truth that God is found everywhere and that, both before and after Jesus, men have been discovered by Him."[22] The revelation, for example, can be found in the law, which condemns unrighteousness, or in a cry of complete despair, or by a calm, unprejudiced religious contemplation of the triviality of human life, which is to say, that man is not God. And it is just this truth, Barth declared, "which is precisely and in strict agreement with the gospel of the resurrection—His everlasting power and divinity."[23]

This concept of faith inevitably strikes the reader as an unrelieved negativism, a rejection of all that is distinctively human. That criticism is to some extent justified in Barth's case. But the point he is making is this: the way to a genuine and nonidolatrous affirmation of human life is through the way of negation, through the crucifixion of the self. As Edward Thurneysen expressed it in his little book on Dostoevsky, which so influenced Barth in his early years, it is only when man despairs of being able to complete his own tower of Babel that

he has his hands free for joining in the work of building all the smaller towers of the earthly city, which is dear to him in its transitory nature, in its relativity and limitations, because it points to the entirely different heavenly city for which he is waiting. He no longer seeks to make the titanic stride of educating man into a superman, or even into a noble person; therefore he may and can rejoice in the many thousand steps that must be made on earth in the present.[24]

Otherwise expressed, the realization of meaning in history will be more untainted in fact if purity is not prematurely claimed for men's attempts to achieve it.

Barth, as I have indicated, was by no means alone in insisting that this view represents the Biblical understanding of justification. Although the other dialectical theologians may here and there have quarreled with certain aspects of Barth's interpretation, they were all agreed concerning the basic nature of faith. Consequently, a similar analysis permeates the writings of Brunner, Bultmann, Gogarten, and, in this country, Tillich and the two Niebuhr brothers. In *The Protestant Era,* for example, Tillich argues that the Protestant message must necessarily take a threefold form: (1) the destruction of the secret reservations harbored by modern man which prevent him from accepting the ambiguities of his existence, reservations which find expression in all world-views or any absolute claims to truth; (2) the proclamation of the judgment "that brings assurance by depriving us of all security"; (3) the "witness to the 'New Being' through which alone it is able to say its word in power . . . without making this witness again the basis of a wrong security."[25]

All of the dialectical theologians regarded faith as something deeper than mere belief or assent to any type of proposition. Indeed, they argued, as we have seen, not only that faith is compatible with radical intellectual doubt but that it necessarily implies a recognition of the partial and ambiguous character of any claim to truth, especially any religious claim.[26] This is why, incidentally, so many of the dialectical theologians were impressed by existentialism, because existentialism constituted a criticism of all attempts to speak objectively about God and showed that the fundamental problem of man was not what he believed but *how* he believed what he believed. His problem is whether he does or does not believe authentically.

3 · The New Understanding of Faith and the New Morality of Knowledge

Faith, as it was understood by the dialectical theologians, has a structure that, if it is not analogous to the new morality of knowledge, has a close affinity to it at many important points. Gogarten, for example, insisted that the autonomy and responsibility of the sciences, including history, were made possible by the Protestant concept of justification.[27] H. Richard Niebuhr, on the other hand, was more cautious and was content to point out that the Protestant theologian will recognize that there is something like radical faith in the work of the secular communities of learning influenced by the Enlightenment.[28]

Although it can be questioned whether Protestantism stands in a causal relationship to the autonomy exemplified by the modern scientific spirit, Gogarten's thesis is worth rehearsing briefly because of the light it casts on the structural affinities of the new morality with the Protestant conception of faith. He argues that it was the unique contribution of the Protestant Reformation to shatter the *Weltanschauung* of the medieval world and, hence, to free the self for God, on the one hand, and for the world, on the other. By this Gogarten means that the medieval vision of reality was bound to the static categories of classical Greek metaphysics. The actual world, according to this understanding, consists not so much in change, which is to say in history, but in certain unalterable and eternal structures. The will of God is that men conform to these eternal patterns; hence, history is thought to be fulfilled just to the degree that man takes his place within an already existing and eternal framework. "Consequently it is not the historical uniqueness of the life of each individual which constitutes the substance of this medieval history, but the metaphysical and general which is established in advance of the historical and particular, and from which the historical and particular alone derives a significance."[29]

Luther's message shattered this understanding, Gogarten argues.[30] By means of his doctrine of the two kingdoms, Luther repudiated the medieval church's claims to sovereignity over the world and granted a new autonomy to man. Life in the world was entrusted to reason and to government; the salvation of the soul was a matter for God. Although Luther, to be sure, was conservative in worldly matters, the upshot of this distinction between the two realms was to grant complete independence to the sciences. In the name of faith, so to speak, science was free to do its own work. Subsequent Protestantism quickly perverted this understanding by absolutizing the Bible as a new law but, nevertheless, the Protestant principle had its own logical momentum and it was no longer possible to return to the medieval point of view.

Whether there is, as Gogarten argues, some causal relationship between Protestantism and the autonomy of the sciences is a question we may leave for the historians of ideas to decide. The point is that the dialectical theologians believed that the virtues of autonomy and intellectual responsibility are related in an intimate fashion to faith, when faith is understood not as belief in doctrine but as trust in being itself. H. Richard Niebuhr, particularly, was interested in pursuing this theme. There is, he maintains, something like the radical faith of which Protestantism speaks in "the established habit of scientific skepticism toward all claims to absolute significance on the part of any finite being and of the absolute truth of any theory of being."[31] For faith when rightly understood is not so much knowledge as the precondition of knowledge.

It removes the taboos which surround our intellectual life, making some subjects too holy to be inquired into and some too dangerous for us to venture into. . . . So long as we try to maintain faith in the gods, we fear to examine them too closely lest their relativity in goodness and in power become evident, as when Bible worshipers fear Biblical criticism, or democracy worshipers fear objective examination of democracy. But when man's faith is attached to the One, all relative beings may be received at his hands for nurture and for understanding. Understanding is not automatically given with faith; faith makes possible and demands the labor of the intellect that it may understand.[32]

The same motif is expressed in this anecdote related by the late Alexander Miller in his book on the meaning of justification for the twentieth century. In response to a student's question whether he had the right to keep his faith at the price of his intellectual integrity, Miller replied, that the

"faith" which is kept at such a price is no faith at all. The sin that damns is hypocrisy, not atheism, if we are reading the Bible aright. "The situation of doubt, even of doubt about God, need not separate us from God." The really destructive atheism is not the denial of God; for that denial, if it is honest, keeps a man in the company of Job and other men of integrity. The really destructive atheism is fear of facts. For fear of facts, from whatever source they come—whether facts of biblical criticism, of physical science, of Marxist analysis—is the existential denial that the world is God's and that, as the Letter to the Colossians puts it, "all things cohere in Christ."[33]

If the negative aspect of faith has its corollary in the habit of skepticism, there is also a sense, Niebuhr insists, in which certain positive aspects of faith have their analogues in the scientific ethic. Science is not only ruled by a respect for fact but also by a respect for those to whom the facts are communicated, so that we might speak of the "interpersonal faithfulness of the scientific community."[34] For the scientific community more than any other has been noted by the elaborate defense it erects against error and self-deception, a defense that necessarily manifests itself in the disciplines and procedures of rational assessment. And this, in turn, is undergirded by the still more basic confidence that everything is meaningful, that everything is worthy of inquiry. Science, ultimately, is a commitment to a universal knowledge, and in this the theologian recognizes something like the radical faith in being itself.[35]

Gogarten also has made much of this point. Faith, he argues, necessarily demands secular knowledge just as it demands "works," for faith is the inner freedom that permits man to take responsibility for his world. The aim of God's redemption, Gogarten understands Paul to say, is to enable man to see the world as his rightful inheritance.[36] In faith, man is freed from an undue evaluation of the world (mythologically speaking, man's bondage to the world and its powers), and he is given the world as "a gift," a loan. The world is turned over to man. It is given into his care. He is to watch over it, to provide it with form and order, to domesticate it. Since man is responsible for civilizing the world, the world becomes for man a truly historical world in a far more radical sense than medieval man could ever envision.[37]

Both Gogarten and Niebuhr, in effect, view radical faith and enlightenment as correlates, and the two elements of the morality of knowledge, autonomy and assessment, are but secularized versions of the ethic of faith.

But the analogy does not stop there. The idea that the knowledge of the world's structures is a human responsibility necessarily leads to the view that this knowledge is historically conditioned. The scientist and the historian have no option but to accept the best of present knowledge, because it is only by building on present knowledge, relative and incomplete as it is, that any further progress is possible at all. But this is just another way of reaffirming the third element in the morality of historical knowledge: one must be loyal to the warrants that are a part of one's own present and critically interpreted experience.

It can scarcely be denied that a great deal of the appeal of the dialectical theology consists in this radicalization of faith, the interpretation of it as a confidence and loyalty underlying mere belief. Not only is the believer liberated from all concern lest the results of Biblical criticism threaten faith, but the act of criticism itself is regarded as being made possible by faith. The morality of knowledge is not the antithesis to faith but its expression. But this solution is not without its own theological problems: What is the content of faith if it can be said to be distinguishable from all belief? In what sense can Christian faith be called historical if no historical inquiry is relevant to its truth or falsity? If faith, as Barth wrote in his *Epistle to the Romans,* can be found in the question "Who am I?" what essential connection does it have with a unique act of God in Jesus Christ?[38] If faith, as Tillich writes, is consistent with the most radical doubt, what then is the content of faith? Is it accessible to man as man quite apart from the alleged revelation in Christ to which Christendom has always clung?

The curious thing is that many of the dialectical theologians do not appear to want to embrace the consequences of the view that faith is accessible to man as man.[39] On the contrary, they affirm that Christian faith, unlike other types of faith, is faith in Jesus Christ, in an act of God that occurred once-and-for-all two thousand years ago. How, then, are these two apparently contradictory motifs to be reconciled? This is the question I shall pursue in the remainder of this chapter.

4 · Faith and Fact in the Theology of Rudolf Bultmann

The problem of reconciling a radical conception of faith with the traditional emphasis on a unique and saving act of God in Jesus Christ is most evident in the theology of Bultmann. His case is especially interesting because he shares the same understanding of faith that was set forth so starkly by Barth in his *Epistle to the Romans* but has tried to articulate it in the categories of existentialist philosophy. Just because he does translate this conception of faith into secular philosophical terms he is faced with the question whether this faith is possible without reference to Christian revelation.

In general, Bultmann's views are so familiar that they need not be rehearsed here in any great detail. Quite briefly, he argues that the message of the New Testament is couched in a mythological language and that this message can be understood by modern men only if it is interpreted in a conceptual form that illumines their own experience. The reason the mythological terms of the Bible must be translated into more intelligible forms, Bultmann believes, is not simply because modern man is no longer able to believe in a mythical world of supernatural beings who break into the nexus of history, but because the careful analysis of the use of mythology in the New Testament itself reveals that the intention of the Biblical writers is not to win assent to certain objective doctrines but to bring man to an authentic self-understanding, to a radical faith. The New Testament writers were primarily concerned to confront man with the self-destructiveness of trying to secure his existence on his own terms (to justify himself) and to proclaim to him the possibility of a new mode of existence (faith), an existence in which he finds his security in the unseen, in God.

Faith, in short, is an *existentiell* self-understanding and, therefore, something quite different from holding certain objective beliefs to be true. The Bible is distinguished from other literature in that it "becomes a word addressed personally to me, which not only informs me about existence in general, but gives me real existence."[40] It is a proclamation which directs itself immediately to the reader. It precipitates a decision, holding as it does before men's eyes the two possibilities of faith and unfaith, authentic and inauthentic existence. The vehicle for this proclamation is the preaching of the death and resurrection of Jesus Christ. But this preaching does not hold before the hearer a mere historical account of this event and ask him to believe it to be true.[41] Rather, the proclamation is that this event was "for me," that is, that one must identify his own life with Christ, must die to himself, if he would experience new life. The preaching calls for men to participate in a certain pattern of life, to appropriate the event for themselves.

It follows, Bultmann attempts to show, that the christology of Paul and John does not consist in a theory about Christ's divine nature but in a proclamation concerning the significance of his death for the believer. It contains an explication of the new self-understanding of faith. To be sure, this proclamation was necessarily couched in the mythological thought-forms of the time, but the intention of the New Testament writers was not to get intellectual assent to a doctrine but to present the reader with a new possibility of existence. Thus, Bultmann can write that Paul's doctrine of justification (his view that man can only experience new life when he gives up trying to justify himself) could be said to be his real christology, that to know Christ is to know his benefits.[42] Christology is not a speculative belief concerning Christ's divine nature but the articulation of a new understanding of existence. One does not first believe that Jesus was divine and experience a liberation of the self; rather, by grasping the significance of the event one experiences a liberation of the self and calls Christ divine.

It is just because the New Testament writers were so concerned with the appropriation of a new understanding of existence that makes it possible to translate the Gospel into existentialist terms, because existentialist philosophy, Bultmann believes, has developed the most adequate conceptuality for understanding human existence.[43] It makes clear that the basic problem of man is not what he believes but how he responds to life, whether he does so authentically or inauthentically. Existentialism, then, provides the categories for talking about man's "fallenness" (sin) as well as about "openness," "freedom," and "authenticity" (faith). In great detail it shows that man is the kind of being who can win or lose himself. He must choose to become fully human, and he can do this only when he ceases to live anxiously in an attempt to secure his life on his own terms and opens himself up to the possibilities of the present and the future. Existentialist philosophy, to be sure, does not prescribe any one concrete ideal of life, but it does show that man can only achieve authenticity by resolution and decision, and thus it helps to make what the Bible is talking about intelligible.[44]

There are, of course, many possible questions one can raise about Bultmann's position. But the one that concerns us here is this: If faith can be defined as a certain possibility of human existence which takes the form of self-surrender, in what sense is such a faith dependent on a past act of God in Jesus of Nazareth? Granted that the death and resurrection of Jesus provide a symbol embodying the true pattern of authentic existence in which the Christian participates, is it not possible that the same self-understanding might be gained in some other way by someone who had never heard of Jesus? Is not the faith that Bultmann describes a general human possibility? In what sense is the historical truth of the New Testament essential to faith when it is understood in this existentialist fashion?

That Bultmann is quite aware of the legitimacy of this question is indicated by the fact that he raises it himself and deals with it at some length in the essay in which he first proposed the program of demythologization.[45] Is it possible, he asks, to have an authentic self-understanding (faith) without Christ? Can one, as Dilthey proposed, translate all dogmas into universally valid propositions about the "historicity of human life?" Is it possible, as Kamlah suggests, to have a secularized version of Christianity in which there is no reference to Christ?

Bultmann's answer is equivocal. On the one hand, he argues that faith is no mysterious supernatural quality but simply the fulfilment of true human nature. It is a possibility that belongs to a man as man, a possibility for which he is accountable if he forfeits it. So, also, love is not "some mysterious supernatural power, but is man's 'natural' mode of relationship."[46] On the , other hand, Bultmann argues that faith and love are not human possibilities if by this we mean that one has only to know what they are and, then, to actualize them. They are made possible only by prior act of God in Jesus Christ and in the *kerygma* about him. They can be achieved in no other way.[47]

The real issue, Bultmann explains, is not whether the true nature of man can be discovered apart from the New Testament, although, as a matter of fact, it has not been: even existentialism is but a secularized version of Christian anthropology.[48] The real question is whether man can realize his own true nature without the prior initiative of God. It is true that Christianity and existentialism both believe that man is fallen, but the difference between them is that existentialism assumes that man can achieve his authentic being by his own efforts, whereas the New Testament "affirms the total incapacity of man to release himself from his fallen state . . . ;" hence it requires an act of God to make man capable of faith and love and authenticity.[49] And the act whereby God empowers man to this, Bultmann insists, occurred only in Jesus Christ and in the proclamation about him. The philosophers confuse a theoretical possibility (a possibility in principle) with an actual one (a possibility in fact). They do not understand that man lost this actual possibility with the fall.[50] Consequently, the "fallen, natural man" can only know despair, and he can be liberated from this despair only by a redemptive act of God. The mythological language of the New Testament but expresses the insight "how through the appearance of Jesus, the world and man are brought into a new situation and thus are called to a decision for or against the world. . . ."[51]

One would think that this insistence on a unique act of God in

Jesus would pose the same dilemma for Bultmann that it did for his teacher, Wilhelm Herrmann. For if God only acts to redeem man in a past historical event, does this not mean that faith is dependent on some historical knowledge about Jesus? And if it is, in what sense can faith be independent of the only means by which such knowledge could be gained, namely, Biblical criticism? Bultmann's characteristic answer strikes many readers as a curious one. The Christian faith, he argues, is not a historical report that might be critically verified or rejected; rather, it proclaims to man

that in what happened then, however it might have been (*es möge gewesen sein wie es wolle*), God has acted, and that through this act of God the Word of divine judgment and forgiveness which now confronts him is authenticated. The meaning of that act of God is nothing other than the actual establishment of this Word—the proclamation of this Word itself. No historical science can control or confirm or reject this affirmation. For that this Word and this proclamation are God's acts stands on the other side of historical observation.[52]

It is just Bultmann's insistence that radical faith is a universal human possibility coupled with the argument that faith is dependent on an act of God in an event about which little can be known ("however it might have been") which is so perplexing. Insofar as Bultmann insists that faith may be translated into existentialist categories, no reference to Jesus seems necessary. But insofar as there is an essential reference to Jesus, it is difficult to see how faith is completely independent of historical inquiry, as Bultmann claims it is.

This tension in Bultmann's thought manifests itself in an extreme formlessness when he writes about revelation. Since he is committed to the view that God acts only in Jesus Christ and in the proclamation about him but insists that no historical knowledge of that event is relevant to faith, it is difficult to know what he means by an "act of God," or what possible relevance the life of Jesus has for one's self-understanding. In liberal theology and in orthodoxy, the picture of Jesus' life gave some content to such things as self-surrender, obedience, love, and faith. In Bultmann's

theology, the act of revelation is contentless. It is a happening with
no structure and in no way positively informs the pattern of faith.
If one asks what function Bultmann's appeal to Jesus has, the only
answer is that it serves to denote the cause precipitating the passage from unfaith to faith. The content and form of faith, however,
can be gained by a philosophical analysis of human experience.

This formlessness can best be seen in Bultmann's treatment of
the Fourth Gospel. He argues that the author of this Gospel understands that, in the last analysis, Jesus *"reveals nothing but that he
is the Revealer*. And that amounts to saying that it is he for whom
the world is waiting, he who brings in his own person that for
which all the longing of man yearns. . . . John, that is, in his
Gospel presents only the fact (*das Dass*) of the Revelation without
describing its content (*ihr Was*)."[53] Does this mean, then, that
revelation is an empty fact? Bultmann anticipates this question,
and his reply matches point for point Barth's description of faith
given in *The Epistle to the Romans*. Bultmann writes,

> But if the Revelation is to be presented neither as the communica-
> tion of a definite teaching nor as the kindling of a mystical experience
> of the soul, then all that can be presented is the bare fact of it. This
> fact, however, does not remain empty. For the Revelation is repre-
> sented as the shattering and negating of all human self-assertion and all
> human norms and evaluations. And, precisely by virtue of being such
> negation, the Revelation is the affirmation and fulfilment of human
> longing for life, for true reality.[54]

This equation of revelation with the negation of all human self-
assertions and norms, however, merely raises again the question
whether the reference to Jesus is at all necessary in order to account for that kind of faith. Surely the negation of all human self-
assertion, as Barth saw in his commentary on the Romans, is an
insight that is possible to man as man. Furthermore, even if it be
granted that a prior act of God is required for man to come to this
realization, does it follow that this act occurred only in the
event Jesus of Nazareth? Indeed, may we not press the point still
more vigorously? Does not Bultmann's appeal to an act of God
only in Christ constitute a contradiction if one, like Bultmann,

interprets faith as the passage from inauthenticity to authenticity?

Schubert M. Ogden has sustained this objection to Bultmann more thoroughly than any other, and his argument, I believe, constitutes a challenge to all dialectical theology.[55] Ogden, following through the implications of some similar criticisms made by Fritz Buri, insists that the validity of Bultmann's entire project depends on showing how the belief in the cross and the resurrection may be interpreted not as objective events but as ways of expressing an understanding of existence. To believe in the cross is to be crucified with Christ and to believe in the resurrection is to experience new life. But both of these are put forward as possibilities for man as man, and necessarily so. Otherwise, it would be impossible for man to be regarded as guilty for not having faith. To proclaim, as the Gospel does proclaim, that *all* men are sinners is intelligible only if faith is a genuine possibility for all men. But if faith is a possibility for all men, how can Bultmann argue that this possibility is made actual only by an act of God in Christ?

Furthermore, Ogden and Buri reject Bultmann's view of the distinction between existentialism and Christianity. Bultmann, it will be remembered, says that existentialism believes that although man is "fallen," he can liberate himself by his own efforts, while Christianity claims that an enabling act of grace is needed. In the first place, there are some existentialists, Karl Jaspers for example, who also point out that man experiences his freedom as a gift. In the second place, Bultmann's appeal to original sin and the fall is equivocal. When he is debating with orthodoxy, Bultmann insists that the fall cannot refer to an event in the past or a fatelike state which holds man in his grip so that he is helpless. Otherwise, man could not be held responsible for his condition. On the other hand, when Bultmann is debating with the existentialists he presupposes just this orthodox notion of the fall that he argues is mythological. In the third place, Bultmann's claim that man cannot liberate himself argues only for the occurrence of grace; it does not argue that this occurrence may be localized in an event that happened two thousand years ago. Finally, Bultmann's distinction between a "possibility in principle" and a "possibility in fact" is a spurious one. For if authenticity is only made possible "in fact" in Jesus of

Nazareth, what is this but to say that faith was never really an
existential possibility at all for those who have not heard the Christian proclamation? How then can they be held responsible, or
viewed as fallen, if there was nothing they could respond to, or
against which they decided and fell? It seems clear that Bultmann
has not solved the problem of faith and history, and that his attempt to do so falls either into formlessness on the one hand or
into contradiction on the other.

5 · *Faith and Fact in the Theology of Paul Tillich*

A similar ambiguity hovers over the theology of Tillich. On the
one hand, he develops in a powerful way a conception of faith
which has affinities with the morality of knowledge and which,
correspondingly, has little relation to the historical figure of Jesus
of Nazareth or, for that matter, to any traditional Christian symbols. On the other hand, he insists that Christian faith is dependent
on the actual life and death of Jesus of Nazareth. If the former
conception enables Tillich to handle deftly the problems posed by
historical research, the latter insistence brings those problems to
the fore again and forces Tillich to engage in a tortured attempt to
extricate himself from them. This attempt, as I shall seek to show,
is quite unsuccessful.

In many of his writings, especially those that might be called
apologetic,[56] Tillich interprets faith, as both Barth and Bultmann
do, as the experience of grace when all the human securities of
belief and action are shattered. It was this insight, he claims, which
was the essence of the Protestant Reformers' doctrine that man is
justified by faith; hence, it may be called the Protestant Principle.[57] The Reformers, however, explored the significance of this
principle only in the religious-ethical sphere of life, whereas Tillich
is impressed by its importance for the religious-intellectual sphere
as well.[58] Just as the Reformers argued that man is justified by
faith even though a sinner, Tillich insists that man is reconciled to
God even though he exists in the state of doubt, even doubt about
God. "There is," he writes, "faith in every serious doubt, namely,

the faith in the truth as such, even if the only truth we can express is our lack of truth."[59]

Underlying this interpretation of the Protestant Principle is Tillich's conception of faith as "ultimate concern," by which he means that faith has to do with the question of the final meaning of life, man's stance toward being itself.[60] So expressed, this principle seems somewhat formal. But this is precisely Tillich's intention, because he insists that this concern is independent of any particular symbols or beliefs. It follows that whenever an ultimate concern is expressed, the divine is present. Consequently, faith cannot be identified with conscious assent to any truth. In fact, Tillich can affirm this apparent paradox: atheism is literally an impossibility because even "he who seriously denies God, affirms him."[61]

The implications of this view are set forward in Tillich's book *The Courage to Be*. After analyzing the various forms of courage that have been expressed in human history, including that one characteristic of Christian theism (the courage to exist before a divine personal subject), he argues that there is still a higher form, the courage that "transcends theism." This is the courage of "absolute faith," that is, "the accepting of the acceptance *without somebody or something that accepts*. It is the power of being-itself that accepts and gives the courage to be."[62] And this courage can be present even "in the anxiety of fate and death when the traditional symbols, which enable men to stand the vicissitudes of fate and the horror of death have lost their power."[63]

What seems remarkable about the description of absolute faith is its apparent formlessness, although Tillich, like Bultmann and the early Barth, understands it to be a way of talking about the cruciform structure of faith, the self-surrender and negation of everything finite which brings one into confrontation with the Absolute. Be that as it may, the significant point is that this absolute faith has no essential connection with the alleged once-for-all revelation in Jesus Christ, although Tillich believes it found perfect expression in his life.[64] Such an absolute faith is a possibility available to man as man, even a man who has never heard of Jesus of Nazareth. Indeed, if faith is not such a universal possibility,

Tillich's thesis in *The Courage to Be* is meaningless, since his basic point is to demonstrate how faith can appear when all traditional Christian belief and symbolism are rendered unintelligible. It is just this radicalization of faith that constitutes Tillich's power as an apologetic theologian in our times, but it depends on his cutting any essential tie to Christian revelation.

It is quite easy to see how this conception of faith enables Tillich to solve the problem of how one may be both an honest historian and a believer. There are no possible means by which the results of historical inquiry could threaten absolute faith; consequently, the certitude of faith is quite indifferent to the probabilities of Biblical research and criticism. It is, Tillich writes, "a disastrous distortion of the meaning of faith to identify it with the belief in the historical validity of the Biblical stories."[65] It is not, he says "a matter of faith to decide how much legendary, mythological and historical material is amalgamated in the stories about the birth and the resurrection of the Christ. . . . They are questions of historical truth, not of the truth of faith."[66]

On the other hand, Tillich is a Christian theologian who is convinced that the essence of Christian faith is the confession that Jesus is the Christ, a confession which has to do with a historical fact and an interpretation of that fact.[67] This fact is no symbol, although symbols are used to express its significance. It is a historical event, and if this "factual element in the Christian event were denied, the foundation of Christianity would be denied."[68]

But if this is so, how is this factual element preserved (1) without vitiating the radical conception of faith, or (2) without collision with historical research, whose province it is to establish the facts? Does Tillich, like Bultmann, fall into contradiction when he tries to combine his absolute faith and a confession about a past historical event?

At the outset, it must be said that in one respect, Tillich is not quite as vulnerable as Bultmann is on this matter if, at any rate, we confine ourselves to their explicit statements.[69] Whereas Bultmann tends to argue that the form of the life of Jesus is irrelevant for faith, the function of the revelation being to make the transition from inauthenticity to authenticity possible, Tillich, at least, tends to see the picture of Jesus in the New Testament as that which has the power to awaken and to structure faith. The picture of Jesus—his deeds, words, and sufferings—is for Tillich the basic image or parable of faith.[70] Nor does Tillich argue, as Bultmann does, that this revelation occurred *only* in Jesus of Nazareth, although he believes that it appeared perfectly there and, in that sense, is final.[71] The revelation in Jesus of Nazareth illumines and is not discontinuous with the mystery of all being. It presupposes the occurrence of preliminary and adumbrated revelations elsewhere in human experience.[72]

Nevertheless, it still remains a question how this historical revelation may be affirmed as essential to faith without prejudice to the universal possibility of faith on the one hand or without colliding with the morality of historical knowledge on the other. It is the second issue with which we are particularly concerned here. How is it possible to affirm that Jesus is the decisive event for faith while insisting that "historical research can neither give nor take away the foundation of the Christian faith?"[73]

The answer lies, Tillich believes, in understanding both the functions and limits of Biblical criticism and the nature of Christian faith. Historical research, he says, contains two elements, the analogical-critical and the constructive-conjectural.[74] It is this analogical-critical element which, unfortunately, threatens most orthodox belief and which blinds its adherents to the positive functions Biblical criticism also serves, namely, its usefulness in sorting out the historical elements from the legendary and mythological and thus providing a tool for the interpretation of the christological symbols. But the constructive-conjectural aspect of Biblical criticism constitutes the most important element, because it leads to the effort to get at the facts behind the Biblical narratives, the facts about Jesus of Nazareth behind the picture of Jesus as the Christ.

The most significant development in this entire enterprise has been, Tillich goes on, its failure.[75] The upshot of all the various attempts in the last century to recover the facts about the historical Jesus has been the conclusion that "there is no picture behind the biblical one which could be made scientifically probable."[76] And this situation is due not merely to some preliminary shortcoming that might be overcome in the future; it is due to the nature of the sources themselves. The New Testament picture of Jesus is not an objective one but reflects the faith of the early church, and it is impossible to disentangle the facts from the interpretive elements. It is no legitimate solution to this problem to argue that the essentials of the New Testament picture are trustworthy, although some details are open to doubt, because the essentials depend on the particulars.[77] Nor can one escape by arguing that Biblical research reflects secular prejudices and that a genuinely Christian historical method would be less skeptical. Tillich argues that there is no such thing as a Christian historiography. There is only one methodological procedure, and it contains a built-in principle of self-criticism. It follows, then, that historical research cannot provide a foundation for faith by confirming the Biblical picture of Jesus to be a true one.

This argument of Tillich deals with only one aspect of the problem, however. Even if it were granted that Biblical criticism cannot confirm the truth of the New Testament picture of Jesus, it still remains possible, in principle at least, that criticism might *disconfirm* it. Some as yet undisclosed source, for example, might cast legitimate doubt on some crucial aspect of the picture or on the fact that Jesus ever lived at all. Tillich is aware of this and himself raises this question. He also rejects two answers frequently heard in reply to it, namely, that historical research as yet has not supported such skepticism and that faith itself overcomes such skepticism. The answer, he insists, lies in grasping the certitude of faith. Faith is certain of only one thing, namely, "the appearance of that reality which has created the faith."[78] One's own participation in faith "guarantees a personal life in which the New Being has conquered the old being."[79] Faith cannot, of course, guarantee that Jesus was the person who was the New Being, but whatever his name, the New Being occurred. No historical criticism can threaten this immediate awareness of those who have been actually transformed into faith.

Tillich's argument at this point parallels Herrmann's earlier one: faith presupposes a prior personal incarnation of faith. Even if one grants this, however, it will scarcely support what Tillich makes of it. The question is whether the cause of faith was a historical person with just the traits which Tillich pictures Jesus as having. Could historical research, for example, legitimately question whether Jesus' words were of the sort Tillich suggests they were, or that he was a man in whom there were no traces of unbelief, *hubris,* or concupiscence, or that he continuously accepted his cross?[80] Surely it is the province of historical research to raise such questions, and insofar as it is, no faith as such can be said to guarantee the answers. Tillich has already acknowledged that. We must ask then whether he means something like what Bultmann means, namely, that it is the mere fact of Jesus' existence, apart from any concrete historical traits, which must be presupposed in order to account for the transition from unfaith to faith? Or does he mean that the important thing about Jesus was his own faith, which necessarily could not be the object of any historical inquiry?

That Tillich does not wish to adopt Bultmann's solution seems quite clear, for he argues that the newness of the New Being would be empty without concreteness.[81] Nor does he rely on the hiddenness of Jesus' inner life, as Herrmann might have done.[82] His solution, rather, is to claim that

The power which has created and preserved the community of the New Being is not an abstract statement about its appearance; it is the picture of him in whom it has appeared. No special trait of this picture can be verified with certainty. But it can be definitely asserted that through this picture the New Being has power to transform those who are transformed by it. This implies that there is an *analogia imaginis,* namely, an analogy between the picture and the actual personal life from which it has arisen. It was this reality, when encountered by the disciples, which created the picture. And it was, and still is, this picture which mediates the transforming power of the New Being.[83]

This answer, however, hardly lays any serious objection to rest. In the first place, the issue is not whether the picture can be *verified* with certainty but whether historical research can *disconfirm* in principle any of the concrete traits. Secondly, the point is that as soon as one asserts that there is an analogy between the picture and the event, this constitutes a historical judgment which is open, in principle, to disconfirmation. The issue is whether the picture is to be taken on faith as a true picture. If it is to be so taken, then Tillich has violated his own restrictions on the matter, for he has said that "faith cannot guarantee any empirical factuality." If it is not to be so taken, then criticism has the final word, and Tillich's attempts to dissociate faith and criticism fail.

The ambiguity of Tillich's solution can be clearly seen in this statement: "The concrete bibilical material is not guaranteed by faith in respect to empirical factuality; but it is guaranteed as an adequate expression of the transforming power of the New Being in Jesus as the Christ. Only in this sense does faith guarantee the biblical picture of Jesus."[84] But, we may reply, what is an "adequate expression" if it does not have some relation to the concrete, empirical traits manifested by the event it attempts to picture? If it has no such relation, in what sense can it be adequate? If it has such a relation, how can this be immune from historical inspection and judgment?

One suspects that the real reason Tillich believes historical criticism can neither confirm nor deny the foundation of Christian faith is because the weight of his position finally rests on the New Testament picture of Jesus. It is really indifferent to Tillich whether this picture corresponds in any way to a past historical event. It is the picture of Jesus that conveys the power which grasps the religious imagination. One is driven to this conclusion respecting Tillich's position because (1) he admits that we cannot get behind the picture and encounter the historical Jesus, and (2) it is unnecessary to do so because faith is enkindled by the picture. But what does it add to faith, then, to say that the picture bears some analogy to the event if there is no way of verifying it and if the very attempt to do so is to step over the limits of faith? These questions have a special force when we realize that Tillich leaves open the question whether there are "other ways of divine self-manifestations before and after our historical continuum."[85] In short, the picture of Jesus has its power because it represents the cruciform nature of any revelation—"The decisive trait in his picture is the continuous self-surrender of Jesus who is Jesus to Jesus who is the Christ."[86] Once that truth is grasped, nothing is added to faith by the assertion "and it happened in just this way."

If Tillich is not to be interpreted in this fashion, what could the following quotation possibly mean?

All these . . . [historical] questions must be decided, in terms of more or less probability, by historical research. They are questions of historical truth, not of the truth of faith. Faith can say that something of ultimate concern has happened in history because the question of the ultimate in being and meaning is involved. Faith can say that the Old Testament law which is given as the law of Moses has unconditional validity for those who are grasped by it, no matter how much or how little can be traced to a historical figure of that name. Faith can say that the reality which is manifest in the New Testament picture of Jesus as the Christ has saving power for those who are grasped by it, no matter how much or how little can be traced to the historical figure who is called Jesus of Nazareth.[87]

6 · Faith and Fact in the Theology of Karl Barth

Bultmann and Tillich both exemplify the problem that arises when one accepts with utmost seriousness the Protestant principle of justification by faith and identifies faith with the surrender of all attempts at self-justification rather than with doctrinal or historical belief. Such a view of faith contains within it a powerful critique of all intellectual claims to finality, even those of Christian belief itself, and thus releases faith from the anxieties and problems of Biblical research. Indeed, as we have seen, faith, when properly understood, motivates critical work, for such work is regarded as a responsibility of faith. On the other hand, this view seems to cut any line of essential connection between faith and a once-and-for-all revelation in Jesus Christ, so that the Christian dogma, as Nietzsche observed, is threatened by its own essential morality.

Ironically enough, it is Barth, the one who launched the ship of dialectical theology onto these chartless seas, who now seems frightened by its course and who has tried to bring the helm about 180 degrees.[88] Consequently, the understanding of faith, which he propounded so powerfully in his commentary on Romans, has been repudiated in his later writings. The earlier view, he now believes, leads inevitably to what one might call a theological agnosticism, which is to say, it does not take seriously the unique revelation of the knowledge of God in Jesus Christ. Hence, Barth's later works represent the attempt to unfold the objective knowledge of God that he believes is given to man in a real historical event.

It is possible to illustrate this shift in Barth's thought in a number of ways, but the most interesting for our purposes is his treatment of the resurrection, that point at which the problem of fact and faith most clearly emerges. In his earlier writings, Barth explicitly denied that the resurrection was a historical event. "The resurrection of Christ, or his second coming, which is the same thing, is not a historical event; the historians may reassure themselves—unless, of course, they prefer to let it destroy their assurance—that our concern *here* is with an event which, though it is the only real happening *in* is not a real happening *of* history."[89] The resurrection is a symbol for "the non-historical relating of the whole historical life of Jesus to its origin in God."[90] Indeed, it could be said that the resurrection would cease to be resurrection if it were some abnormal event side by side with other events.[91] Resurrection is the " 'non-historical' happening, by which all other events are bounded, and to which events before and on and after Easter Day point."[92] It has nothing to do, then, with miracles, an empty tomb, or the continued personal existence of Jesus. It is, rather, the "disclosing of Jesus as the Christ, the appearing of God, and the apprehending of God in Jesus."[93]

In his later writings, however, Barth characteristically insists on the historicity of the resurrection, and it is no accident therefore that he increasingly finds himself in polemic with Bultmann, who could have written any of the above statements. The trouble with Bultmann, Barth claims, is that he eliminates the objectivity and reality of the resurrection, even though he is to be commended for emphasizing its centrality in the New Testament. This elimination will not do, Barth insists. The point is that whatever was proclaimed in Jesus' name derives from the *fact* that Jesus entrusted it to the disciples *after he was raised from the dead*.[94] This implies, not only that the disciples had an "objective encounter" with Jesus, but that he was raised bodily, which is to say physically.[95] To call a literal resurrection a "nature miracle," as Bultmann does, is "splitting hairs."[96] Such terminology does not help us to understand the event but only discredits it. The event could not have been what it was—God himself manifested in the resurrection— unless it "genuinely and apprehensibly" included nature and, therefore, was physical.[97] To be sure, the event is not merely physical, since the resurrected Jesus appeared to the disciples "in the mode of God." But it was the man Jesus, nevertheless, "who now came and went among them."[98] The Scriptures make clear that it is "the fact that the risen Christ can be touched which puts it beyond all doubt that He is the man Jesus and no one else."[99] The witness of the early church is such that it is impossible to erase this bodily character of the resurrection. This is precisely the point of the tradition of the forty days between resurrection and ascension. "For unless Christ's resurrection was a resurrection of the body, we have no guarantee that it was the decisively acting Subject Jesus Himself, the *man* Jesus, who rose from the dead."[100] For this reason the story of the empty tomb and of the physical appearances are "signs" that cannot be omitted. They are not the *esse* of the belief in the resurrection, to be sure, but they are inferences to be drawn from it and ought not to be omitted.

These assertions about the resurrection in Barth's later works seem to raise all of the same problems that beset orthodoxy and, as we have seen, precipitated its collision with the morality of knowledge, a collision *The Epistle to the Romans* sought to avoid. Such a view seems, on the surface at least, to require a sacrifice of the intellect. Nevertheless, Barth claims that this is not so. First of all, such a belief, he argues, does not require a sacrifice at all but, on the contrary, is something to "be accepted fully and gladly even to-day."[101] Secondly, doubt about the resurrection only arises if one takes with excessive seriousness, as Bultmann has, the finality of the modern world-view. But, "is this modern view so binding as to determine in advance and unconditionally our acceptance or

rejection of the biblical message?"[102] Thirdly, "it is sheer superstition to suppose that only things which are open to 'historical'
verification can have happened in time. There may have been
events which happened far more really in time than the kind of
things Bultmann's scientific historian can prove. There are good
grounds for supposing that the history of the resurrection of Jesus
is a pre-eminent instance of such an event."[103] All that need be
conceded, Barth concludes, is that the resurrection narratives are
not to be taken as history in the scientific sense of the word. The
Matthean, Lukan, or the Synoptic accounts as a whole, not to
mention the Johannine, are obviously contradictory and fragmentary.[104] The forty-day tradition, for example, is linked symbolically with the Old Testament stories of the flood, the Elijah
cycle or, possibly, the conquest of Canaan.[105] The topography
and chronology are vague and there are no independent sources.
The narratives, in short, are legendary. But all one should conclude from this, Barth argues, is that these stories "are describing
an event beyond the reach of historical research or depiction.
Hence we have no right to try to analyze them or harmonize them.
This is to do violence to the whole character of the event in question."[106] But despite the contradictions and vagueness, despite
the imaginative and poetic nature of the legends, they, nevertheless, "are agreed in substance, intention, and interpretation. None
of the authors ever even dreamed, for example, of reducing the
event to 'the rise of the Easter faith of the first disciples.' "[107]

It must be said that there is considerable ambiguity in Barth's
argument at this point. On the one hand, he insists that the resurrection is a physical and bodily fact while, on the other hand, he
claims that the historian can determine nothing about it. This
ambiguity invites criticism, and it has not been lacking. Two of
the most forceful critics have been Christian Hartlich and Walter
Sachs, and their joint criticism is especially interesting because it
has directly to do with the morality of historical knowledge.[108]
They make much of Barth's apparently contradictory claim that
the resurrection is a fact and yet a fact of such a nature that no
historical science could verify or falsify statements about it. They
argue (rightly, I think) that the historian is not interested pri-

marily in an a priori denial that certain events can happen. His function, rather, is to determine the degree of probability an event may claim according to the rules of criticism and to make a judgment concerning it, a judgment the historian should be ready to revise in the light of new evidence.[109] The issue is not whether a resurrection is thinkable or could have happened, but the grounds upon which one claims that it did. Barth, of course, believes he has such grounds. But it is not enough to say this. He is required to state what constitutes the reality of historical events and what would constitute sufficient grounds for believing in a resurrection.[110] So long as Barth asserts that the resurrection is an event in space and time, he must define some sort of conditions for judgments about events in space and time. Nor is Barth's distinction between *Historie* and *Geschichte* more than a verbal solution to this. It merely discloses the weak point in his argument, because to affirm an event in space and time without sufficient reason is either arbitrary or a sacrifice of the intellect. Since Barth says his view does not involve the latter, he must be held responsible for the former. He has, in effect, exempted himself from any possibility of assessing the historical truth of his claims.[111]

Hartlich's and Sach's argument sometimes appears heavy-handed, as when they demand that Barth state in advance his criteria for the reality of historical events. As we have seen in our initial chapters, this is an unreal demand, for the historian actually has no one criterion because he is dealing with a field-encompassing field. Nevertheless, these critics of Barth are close to the heart of the matter, the morality of historical judgment. To say that Barth's view is an arbitrary one is to say, first of all, that he makes historical assertions on the basis of faith which he then claims no historian has the right to assess. He claims that the bodily resurrection is a *guarantee* that it was Jesus who appeared to the disciples and yet insists that no historian can, in the nature of the case, assess this claim. He insists that the resurrection was physical and appeals to the story of Thomas in the Fourth Gospel to prove it but deals with none of the numerous critical questions concerning the historical veracity of that Gospel or the function miracle stories have in it. He appeals to the forty-day tradition and the empty-tomb stories but in no way answers the many questions Biblical critics have raised about these stories. Consequently, Barth uses the stories to argue for the historical nature of the events but concedes that the stories cannot, from a historical standpoint, stand any critical scrutiny. This leaves the believer in the position of accepting an argument the warrants of which are historical in type but which are, at the same time, confessed to be contradictory and "imaginative-poetic." It leaves the inquirer in the position of having to accept the claims of alleged eyewitnesses or risk the state of being a faithless man. Insofar as the believer wants to be historian, or the historian a believer, he has to surrender the autonomy of critical judgment. Barth, in effect, claims all the advantages of history but will assume none of its risks.

This surrender of autonomy is closely linked to two related problems. First of all, it is very difficult, given Barth's treatment of the Biblical sources, to know what we are being asked to believe. Given the fact that there are conflicting types of resurrection stories in the New Testament—nonphysical as well as physical types of appearances—just what are we to believe occurred? What is a resurrection?[112] Barth's argument throws the weight on the physical type of appearance. Yet this is just the type of story that most New Testament historians are inclined to doubt. The appearance of Jesus to Paul, which is the earliest tradition we have, is not of this type, for example. But since Barth refuses to permit the historian to analyze the narratives in an attempt to assess the various levels of tradition and, therefore, the degree of probability appropriate to each, it is impossible even for faith to clarify its own object.

In the second place, even if we could establish what it is the disciples are asking us to believe, Barth's view, if applied to any other religious literature, renders all critical historical inquiry impossible. All arguments about the past—even Barth's own argument—necessarily make implicit use of certain warrants grounded in present knowledge. But Barth, nevertheless, blithely argues against Bultmann that the Christian need not take the modern world-view as binding. In one sense, Barth is correct, because the modern world-view is not a monolithic one; it, too, is field-encompassing. But in another sense Barth is incorrect. For to say that the historian does not depend on a monolithic world-view is not the same thing as saying that there are no (modern) warrants the historian must rely on in judging the possibility or probability of any assertion about the past. The issue is, by what right does Barth in this particular case suspend those warrants he normally uses and which he applies when, say, dealing with the story of Jonah or Joshua? The historian necessarily relies on some present knowledge just as Barth himself does in the very process of trying to establish that the resurrection was, in fact, physical. The issue, as F. H. Bradley saw, is one of consistency. For if Barth's own argument presupposes these warrants, how can one enter into debate with him if he suspends them when his own inferences are questioned?

But even if one grants that a historian should not rule out in advance the possibility of a physical resurrection, or that he might have some special reason for suspending his usual warrants, does the argument justify the passion with which these assertions about a resurrected body are believed? Or does Barth's approach, like that of orthodox belief, entail a corrosion of historical judgment? Here again, Barth's view seems basically contradictory. On the one hand, in order to justify the heavy assent of the believer he appeals to the hearing and seeing of the risen Jesus by the apostles, an appeal that achieves its force just by virtue of its employment of certain familiar common-sense categories like touching, hearing, and seeing. On the other hand, the stories are immediately immunized against assessment by the concession that they are not literal or historical. He offers with his right hand something that he takes away with the left. The result is that the machinery of the argument grinds to a halt as soon as it is taken seriously as an argument. It is no longer clear what would count as data and warrants and backings for, or a legitimate qualification of, the argument. Consequently, it is impossible to give any kind of weighted assent, because it is simply not clear what would be an appropriate one.

NOTES TO CHAPTER FIVE

1. Quoted by Gerhard Ebeling, *Word and Faith*, trans. James Leitch (Philadelphia: Fortress Press, 1963), p. 18.
2. *Ibid.*, p. 19.
3. Friedrich Nietzsche, *Genealogy of Morals*, trans. Horace B. Samuel in *The Philosophy of Nietzsche* (New York: Modern Library, 1927), p. 791. Nietzsche goes on: "After Christian truthfulness has drawn one conclusion after the other, it finally draws its *strongest conclusion*, its conclusion *against* itself; this, however, happens, when it puts the question, '*what is the meaning of every will for truth?*' " See Karl Jaspers, *Nietzsche and Christianity*, trans. E. B. Ashton (Chicago: Henry Regnery, Gateway Edition, 1961), chap. ii; cf. Walter Kaufmann, *Nietzsche: Philosopher, Psychologist, Antichrist* (Princeton: Princeton University Press, 1950), pp. 307-316.
4. See Christoph Senft, *Wahrhaftigkeit und Wahrheit* (Tübingen: J. C. B. Mohr, 1956).
5. Wilhelm Herrmann, *Faith and Morals*, trans. Donald Matheson and Robert W. Stewart (New York: C. P. Putnam's Sons, 1904), p. 29.
6. Wilhelm Herrmann, *The Communion of the Christian with God*, trans. J. Sandys Stanyon, rev. Robert W. Stewart (New York: C. P. Putnam's Sons, 1906), p. 2.
7. Herrmann, *Faith and Morals*, pp. 32 f.
8. Wilhelm Herrmann, *Gesammelte Aufsätze* (Tübingen: J. C. B. Mohr, 1923), pp. 295-335.
9. Herrmann, *The Communion of the Christian with God*, pp. 81-101.
10. Herrmann, *Faith and Morals*, p. 61.
11. Cf. Rudolf Bultmann's criticism in *Glauben und Verstehen* (Tübingen: J. C. B. Mohr, 1933), I, 3 ff.
12. Karl Barth, *The Epistle to the Romans*, trans. Edwyn C. Hoskyns (6th ed.; London: Oxford University Press, 1933), p. 10.
13. *Ibid.*, pp. 42, 82.
14. *Ibid.*, p. 88.
15. *Ibid.*, p. 110.
16. *Ibid.*, p. 319.
17. *Ibid.*, p. 45.
18. *Ibid.*, p. 156.
19. *Ibid.*, p. 159; cf. p. 97.
20. *Ibid.*, p. 202.
21. *Ibid.*, p. 97.
22. *Ibid.*
23. *Ibid.*, pp. 46 f.
24. Eduard Thurneysen, *Dostoevsky*, trans. Keith R. Crim (Richmond: John Knox Press, 1964), p. 73.
25. Paul Tillich, *The Protestant Era*, trans. James Luther Adams (Chicago: University of Chicago Press, 1948), pp. 203 f.
26. Cf. Paul Tillich, *The Courage to Be* (New Haven: Yale University

Press, 1952), pp. 182 ff. Cf. Reinhold Niebuhr, *The Nature and Destiny of Man* (New York: Charles Scribner's Sons, 1948), II, 214 ff.

27. See Friedrich Gogarten, *The Reality of Faith*, trans. Carl Michalson and others (Philadelphia: Westminster Press, 1959), chap. x. Cf. his *Verhängnis und Hoffnung der Neuzeit* (Stuttgart: Friedrich Vorwerk Verlag, 1958), chap. vii.

28. H. Richard Niebuhr, *Radical Monotheism and Western Culture* (New York: Harper & Brothers, 1960), chap. vi.

29. Friedrich Gogarten, *Demythologizing and History* (London: SCM Press Ltd., 1955), p. 23.

30. Gogarten, *The Reality of Faith*, chap. x.

31. H. R. Niebuhr, *op. cit.*, p. 86.

32. *Ibid.*, pp. 125 f.

33. Alexander Miller, *The Renewal of Man* (Garden City, N.Y.: Doubleday and Co., 1956), p. 137.

34. H. R. Niebuhr, *op. cit.*, p. 81; cf. p. 132.

35. *Ibid.*, p. 87.

36. Gogarten, *The Reality of Faith*, p. 58.

37. Gogarten, *Demythologizing and History*, p. 26.

38. Bultmann raises just this question in *Anfänge der dialektischen Theologie*, ed. Jürgen Moltmann (Munich: Chr. Kaiser Verlag, 1962), I, 136 ff.

39. H. Richard Niebuhr is, as we shall see, perhaps the real exception to this generalization.

40. Rudolf Bultmann, *Jesus Christ and Mythology* (New York: Charles Scribner's Sons, 1958), p. 53.

41. Hans W. Bartsch (ed.), *Kerygma and Myth*, trans. Reginald H. Fuller (New York: Harper Torchbooks, 1961), pp. 35-43.

42. Bultmann, *Glauben und Verstehen*, I, 262.

43. Bultmann, *Jesus Christ and Mythology*, p. 55.

44. *Ibid.*, p. 56.

45. Bultmann in *Kerygma and Myth*, pp. 22-33.

46. *Ibid.*, p. 34.

47. Rudolf Bultmann, *Essays*, trans. C. G. Greig (London: SCM Press Ltd., 1955), p. 16.

48. Bultmann in *Kerygma and Myth*, p. 26.

49. *Ibid.*, pp. 27, 33.

50. *Ibid.*, p. 28 f.

51. Rudolf Bultmann, *Glauben und Verstehen* (Tübingen: J. C. B. Mohr, 1961), II, 257. My translation. Cf. *Essays*, p. 285.

52. Bultmann, *Glauben und Verstehen*, II, 16. My translation. Cf. *Essays*, p. 18.

53. Rudolf Bultmann, *Theology of the New Testament*, trans. Kendrick Grobel (New York: Charles Scribner's Sons, 1955), II, 66.

54. *Ibid.*, pp. 67 f.

55. Schubert M. Ogden, *Christ Without Myth* (New York: Harper & Brothers, 1961), pp. 76-94, 105-126.

56. Tillich views all theology as apologetic in the sense of correlating

Christian answers to basic human questions, but I am referring to those writings in which he does not appeal directly to Christian symbols.

57. Tillich, *The Protestant Era*, chaps. xi, xiii-xv.

58. *Ibid.*, p. xiv.

59. *Ibid.*

60. Cf. Paul Tillich, *Dynamics of Faith* (New York: Harper & Brothers, 1957), chap. i. Cf. his *Systematic Theology* (Chicago: University of Chicago Press, 1951), I, 11-15.

61. Tillich, *The Protestant Era*, p. xv.

62. Tillich, *The Courage to Be*, p. 185. Italics mine.

63. *Ibid.*, p. 189.

64. Tillich, *Dynamics of Faith*, p. 98; cf. *Systematic Theology* (Chicago: University of Chicago Press, 1957), II, 155.

65. Tillich, *Dynamics of Faith*, p. 87.

66. *Ibid.*, p. 88.

67. Tillich, *Systematic Theology*, II, 98.

68. *Ibid.*, p. 107.

69. It could be argued that Bultmann relies implicity on the picture of Jesus in the New Testament even if he explicitly seems to deny it.

70. Tillich, *Systematic Theology*, II, 118-138.

71. Tillich, *Systematic Theology*, I, 133.

72. *Ibid.*, pp. 139 ff. Cf. II, 88 f.

73. Tillich, *Systematic Theology*, II, 113.

74. *Ibid.*, p. 101.

75. *Ibid.*, p. 102.

76. *Ibid.*

77. *Ibid.*, p. 103.

78. *Ibid.*, p. 114.

79. *Ibid.*

80. *Ibid.*, pp. 124-135.

81. *Ibid.*, p. 114.

82. *Ibid.*, p. 124.

83. *Ibid.*, pp. 114 f.

84. *Ibid.*, p. 115.

85. *Ibid.*, p. 101.

86. Tillich, *Systematic Theology*, I, 134.

87. Tillich, *Dynamics of Faith*, p. 88.

88. See the essay by Hans W. Frei in *Faith and Ethics*, ed. Paul Ramsey (New York: Harper & Brothers, 1957), pp. 9-116.

89. Karl Barth, *The Word of God and the Word of Man*, trans. Douglas Horton (New York: Harper Torchbooks, 1956), p. 90.

90. Barth, *The Epistle to the Romans*, p. 195.

91. *Ibid.*, p. 115.

92. *Ibid.*, p. 203.

93. *Ibid.*, p. 30.

94. Karl Barth, *Church Dogmatics*, eds. G. W. Bromiley and T. F. Torrance (Edinburgh: T. & T. Clark, 1960), III/2, 442.

95. *Ibid.*, pp. 448 f.

96. *Ibid.*, p. 451.

97. *Ibid.*
98. *Ibid.*, p. 448.
99. *Ibid.*
100. *Ibid.*
101. *Ibid.*, p. 447.
102. *Ibid.*
103. *Ibid.*, p. 446.
104. *Ibid.*, p. 452.
105. *Ibid.*
106. *Ibid.*
107. *Ibid.*
108. Christian Hartlich and Walter Sachs in *Kerygma und Mythos*, ed. Hans W. Bartsch (Hamburg: Herbert Reich Evangelischer Verlag, 1952), II, 113-125. Cf. Bultmann's criticism in *Essays*, pp. 259-261.
109. Hartlich and Sachs, *op. cit.*, p. 117.
110. *Ibid.*, pp. 118 f.
111. *Ibid.*, p. 120.
112. See chap. vii below.

VI

The Morality of Historical Knowledge and the New Quest of the Historical Jesus

1 · The Dissatisfactions with the Dialectical Theology

THE various attempts of the dialectical theologians to reconcile Christian belief with the morality of historical knowledge are, as we have seen, basically unstable. When Bultmann and Tillich emphasize the radical meaning of faith in a way characteristic of the early Barth, their description of faith seems peculiarly empty, uninformed by any Christian symbolism or any reference to Jesus Christ. In fact, it is admittedly compatible with unbelief. On the other hand, when they insist that Christian faith is based on an act of God in Jesus Christ, it is difficult to see how this is compatible with what they have said about justification by faith or how it avoids a collision with Biblical criticism. Bultmann and Tillich only appear to resolve this contradiction: Bultmann, by arguing that Jesus reveals nothing except that he is the revealer; Tillich, by tacitly making certain historical assertions on the basis of faith while claiming this to be illegitimate. Barth escapes this dilemma only by modifying his earlier conception of faith and refusing to take the presuppositions of critical history seriously. None of the three theologians makes clear how it is possible to be both a critical historian and a believer.

[164]

It was inevitable that the general position of dialectical theology would tend to break apart in a subsequent theological generation. On the one hand, there naturally would be those who believe that the tension could only be relaxed by dropping all reference to a unique act of God in Christ. On the other hand, there would be those who argue that the distinctive nature of Christian faith could be preserved only by insisting on the decisive importance of the historical Jesus and by exploring the consequences of this for historical understanding. Such a rupture became clearly evident during the demythologizing debate.

Bultmann, it will be remembered, had called for a thoroughly existentialist interpretation of all the mythological concepts in the New Testament. This was possible, he claimed, because what one finds there is the presentation of two possible modes of human existence, faith and unfaith, with the demand to choose between them. The only theological statement Bultmann did not consistently demythologize was that one referring to a decisive act of God in the cross of Christ, an act that makes the transition from unfaith to faith possible. In this way Bultmann sought to avoid any simple identification of Christian theology with existentialist philosophy. He affirmed the total incapacity of man to save himself, and he insisted that it is only the redemptive act of God in Jesus that first makes possible surrender, faith, love, and the authentic life of men.[1]

As I have argued in the preceding chapter, this reference to a decisive act of God in Jesus Christ seems gratuitous within the framework of Bultmann's theology. For him, Jesus is merely the historical cause (*das Dass*), which initiates faith. The figure of Jesus does not inform in any way the content (*das Was*) of faith. Moreover, this reference to Jesus not only seems unnecessary but contradictory, since it is impossible to reconcile with Bultmann's basic premise that faith is a possibility for man as man. It was this contradiction that became the object of polemic by certain theologians who had otherwise been impressed by the demand for an existentialist interpretation of the New Testament. Fritz Buri, in Europe, and Schubert M. Ogden, in America, maintain that Bultmann's failure to demythologize the New Testament language about a decisive act of God represents a curious failure of nerve and a fundamental inconsistency in his enterprise.[2] Both theologians argue that the incapacity of man to save himself, which Bultmann had regarded as the sole difference between existentialism and Christian theology, implies only that God's grace is prevenient, not that it occurs exclusively in Jesus of Nazareth. Consequently, they conclude, Bultmann's christocentrism must also be eliminated as a remnant of mythology. There is, in fact, no constitutive difference between an existentialist philosophy, which insists that man experiences grace and freedom as a gift, and the Christian message. The New Testament message will be free from mythical elements only when it is recognized to be but one symbolic way of expressing an insight into the nature of authenticity. The entire Christian story is a dramatic and concrete drama (a myth) which expresses "an intense awareness of existence as grace,"[3] an awareness which Christians have, but which is in no sense restricted to them.

However much this alternative so roughly stated may appear to be but a modern version of the old liberal and idealistic view that the incarnation is simply a symbol of some timeless truth, it cannot be so easily dismissed. Buri and Ogden argue, first of all, that the timeless truth to which Christianity witnesses is that God encounters men in history, something idealism could not understand. Secondly, they regard their own position as the logical consequence of the Protestant understanding of justification by faith as it bears on historical belief. Indeed, it is noteworthy that both Buri and Ogden argue that it is Bultmann's view—that God is revealed *only* in Jesus Christ—which is a piece of arrogance and, more seriously, which prejudices the radical and universal character of God's grace.[4] Buri and Ogden rest their case less on an appeal to the unintelligibility of special revelation or to some idealistic philosophy than on the argument that the Christian proclamation of divine forgiveness itself presupposes that all men are "without excuse." All men have rejected God's gift of authentic existence (faith), a possibility presented to the disciples in Jesus Christ, to be sure, but, nonetheless, a universal human possibility.

The possibility of taking this theological option alarmed other theologians also influenced by Bultmann even before the "left wingers," as Buri and Ogden came to be labeled, described it in detail. Was it based on a misinterpretation of Bultmann's theology or was there a basic flaw in the master's position which permits this "left-wing" criticism of it? The evidence indicated the latter, and, consequently, these former students of Bultmann—those on the "right," so to speak—increasingly, but gingerly, began to criticize their teacher and to distance themselves from his views. While acknowledging Bultmann's contribution to form criticism and New Testament interpretation, Fuchs, Ebeling, Käsemann, Bornkamm, to mention a few, made it quite clear that they could not accept his conception of the relation of the historical Jesus to the *kerygma* of the church.[5] They argued that although there are admitted difficulties in reconstructing a reliable historical picture of Jesus, these difficulties need not lead to skepticism. At any rate, skepticism should not be made into a methodological principle, as Barth, Bultmann, and Tillich seem to have done, because this threatens the essence of Christian faith itself. Christian faith, they claimed, is nothing less than the proclamation that God has raised the earthly Jesus from the dead, and unless this proclamation has some continuity with the person and teaching of Jesus, then the church might as well concede that this message is nothing but the symbolic presentation of certain timeless truths that would be just as true even if it turned out that Jesus was a mythical being.

One of the most striking developments in Protestant theology in the past decade, then, has been a new quest for the historical Jesus in just those circles where, one might have thought, skepticism concerning such an enterprise would be the rule. Although there are important differences among these scholars, they have enough in common to justify treating them as variants of one ideal-type of theology. They all suppose it would be fatal to the Christian faith were it to be shown that the *kerygma* is not firmly grounded in the life and teachings of Jesus of Nazareth. Consequently, they assume a different attitude toward the relationship of faith to critical his-tory than did the dialectical theologians. If Bultmann and Tillich claimed that historical research can neither confirm nor deny the truth of the *kerygma,* these men argue that although no historical inquiry could confirm the truth of it, such an inquiry could, in principle, disprove it by casting doubt on its historical kernel. Historical criticism, in short, cannot supply the grounds of faith, but it can give a negative answer to the truth of faith.

2 · *The Presuppositions of the New Quest*

Although there have been a number of articles and books which have contributed to the literature of the new quest, James M. Robinson's *A New Quest of the Historical Jesus,* more than any other single work, delineates the critical issues. He argues that German theology may now be characterized as post-Bultmannian, which is to say, although deeply influenced by Bultmann, it is characterized by a critical restatement of his position, particularly with respect to the significance of the historical Jesus for faith. Although the post-Bultmannians agree with Bultmann that the attempt of Protestant liberalism to discover the Jesus of history, in contrast to the Christ of faith, was naive and illegitimate, they do not agree that the Jesus of history is altogether irrelevant for faith. Indeed, they feel that the new theological situation makes both possible and necessary a new quest of the historical Jesus, although as a *new* quest, it must be different in procedures and objectives from the old.

The old quest, Robinson maintains, was both illegitimate from the standpoint of faith and impossible from the standpoint of historical method. It sprang from the urge to drive a wedge between the Jesus of history and the Christ of dogma. Hoping to free the figure of Jesus from all the orthodox doctrines about him, the nineteenth-century liberals hoped to reconstruct the real Jesus by means of an objective historical method which would at the same time prove Jesus' religious superiority and his absoluteness. Thus, liberal piety could find a firm foundation in historical fact unencumbered by a dogmatic superstructure.

The illegitimacy in all of this, Robinson claims, was its attempt to make Jesus a "proven divine fact," "a worldly security with which the *homo religiosus* arms himself in his effort to become self-sufficient before God, just as did the Jew in Paul's day by appeal to the law."[6] We now see, Robinson says, that the *kerygma* calls for an existential commitment to the meaning of Jesus, and that this requires risk and is incommensurate with any worldly or historical security. The liberals, in contrast, wanted to avoid this risk of faith and, by applying objectively verified proof, revealed that their enterprise was based on an "unbelieving flight to security, i.e., the reverse of faith."[7]

If the old quest was theologically illegitimate, Robinson goes on, it was also impossible, historiographically speaking, for it presupposed a conception of history which is obsolete. Overly impressed by the success of the natural sciences, the nineteenth-century liberals wrote history with this model in mind. They thought the purpose of history to be the reconstruction of the "past as it really was." This, in turn, dictated a preoccupation with the facts, and these facts were primarily external in nature—names, occurrences, dates, causes, and the like. Consequently, the historical Jesus in this context referred to a chronological and biographical account of his life and ministry. "Jesus" was what emerged after everything supernatural had been carefully expunged by the objective and detached historian.

This old quest can now be seen to be invalid. First of all, it was discovered that the New Testament sources do not lend themselves to this sort of treatment. The Gospels are not objective historical sources but highly interpretative documents which reflect the culture and beliefs of the primitive church. They are, so to speak, the devotional literature of the primitive church. History survived only as *kerygma*. This insight has, in turn, reversed the basic conception of the sources: whereas the nineteenth-century Biblical critics presupposed the accuracy of the Synoptic picture of Jesus except where "doctrinal tampering" was obvious, the twentieth-century critic feels confident in asserting the factuality of details only where their origin cannot be explained in terms of the beliefs of the church.[8] Thus, the burden of proof now rests on one who believes it is possible to write a biographical and chronological account of Jesus' ministry. This burden, Robinson adds, has not successfully been taken up by C. H. Dodd and others who have tried to prove that the *kerygma* does contain chronological elements.[9]

But if it is impossible to paint a chronological picture of Jesus' life, we may ask, does this not make a new quest equally impossible? How can a new quest be successful where the old one failed?

It is at this point that Robinson introduces a new conception of history which he thinks makes a unique contribution to this contemporary theological problem. The possibility of a new quest rests on a "new hermeneutic," a new theory of historical interpretation and of the self, a theory which emerged in the twentieth century as a result of the revolutionary philosophical insights of Wilhelm Dilthey, Martin Heidegger, and R. G. Collingwood. If the nineteenth century conceived of history in terms of an objective, dispassionate reconstruction of external facts, the new view of history, in contrast, is grounded in an awareness that history does not consist in external facts but in the purposes and meanings of selves.

The dimension in which man actually exists, his "world," the stance or outlook from which he acts, his understanding of his existence behind what he does, the way he meets his basic problems and the answer his life implies to the human dilemma, the significance he had as the environment of those who knew him, the continuing history his life produces, the possibility of existence which his life presents to me as an alternative—such matters as these have become central in an attempt to understand history.[10]

In their acts persons reveal who they are, and it is the task of the new historiography not to chronicle actions but to "lay hold of the selfhood which is therein revealed."[11]

It was existentialism, particularly that form of it found in the works of Heidegger, which deepened the concept of selfhood and which revealed the inadequacy of the psychologistic emphasis of the nineteenth-century historians. According to the new view, which Robinson accepts, the self is not to be identified with what we usually call the personality, which is to say, that which is built up of habitual responses to the environment and culture. Rather, the self is that which is "constituted by commitment to a context."[12] The self is not, so to speak, *what* we are but *how* we relate to what we are. The self is always in the process of becoming, and decision is that which determines what form the self will become in any given moment. The self, in this sense, is to be understood in terms of its decisions, decisions that do not simply flow from a given personality but are free and underlie it. Man is a being who can literally lose or win himself. Robinson insists that it would be a basic misunderstanding of selfhood, therefore, "to describe the causal relationships and cultural ingredients composing the personality, and assume one had understood the self."[13] This was, in fact, precisely the mistake of the old historiography with its psychologistic conception of personality.

This view dictates a different method of historical understanding, one which takes account of the radical difference between history and nature. Whereas the old historiography employed the model of the disinterested scientist getting at the facts, the new historiography claims that unless the historian is "open himself to encounter other human beings," that is, unless he permits his own self-understanding to be called into question by the past, he cannot really apprehend or understand that past. The old positivistic historiography absolutized bloodless detachment. The new historiography insists that "one should be *engagé,* with one's whole selfhood at stake, in the 'world' in which one moves."[14] This new attitude does not invalidate painstaking research, to be sure, but it does mean that this research is only a preliminary step in understanding history. The culmination of historical understanding comes when one grasps the possibilities of existence which have come to expression in the past and which are repeatable in the present and the future.

Because this conception of historical method is completely different from the old positivistic one, Robinson argues, it has become "a completely open question" whether one can reconstruct the historical Jesus on this new basis.[15] This is especially true because it is clear that the *kerygma* of the early church has striking affinities with the new history. Just as the historian is confronted with the selfhood of a past agent which challenges the historian in his existence, so, too, the *kerygma* preaches the selfhood of Jesus and calls upon the hearer to make a decision concerning it.[16]

If one asks how it is that the new attempt to ascertain Jesus' existential selfhood is possible, whereas the old attempt to get at his personality and life was not, Robinson's answer is that just because the New Testament preserves history as *kerygma* (i.e., contains the message about Jesus' selfhood), we can expect that

the kind of material which the "kerygmatizing" process would leave *unaltered* is the kind of material which fits best the needs of research based upon the modern view of history and the self. For the kerygmatic interest of the primitive church would leave unaltered precisely those sayings and scenes in which Jesus made his intention and understanding of existence most apparent to them.[17]

The very limitation of the sources which made the old quest impossible, therefore, opens the possibility of a new one. It no longer need be considered disastrous if the chronological elements in Jesus' career are gone. The parables, the authentic sayings, the remembered actions and exorcisms all give "sufficient insight into Jesus' intention to encounter his historical action, and enough insight into the understanding of existence presupposed in his intention to encounter his selfhood."[18] Jesus' history and selfhood, in short, *"are* accessible to modern historiography and biography."[19]

If the new historiography has opened up the possibility of a new quest, this also completely alters the contemporary theological situation, Robinson claims. It not only provides a new way of meeting the challenge of those "left-wing" theologians who would turn the *kerygma* into a symbol of timeless truths, but it also makes it possible for modern man to encounter Jesus independently of the *kerygma* itself. The new historiography has, as it were, opened up a "second avenue of access" to the historical Jesus in addition to that first avenue provided by the *kerygma*. This "second avenue" has not existed since the time of the original disciples "who had both their Easter faith and their factual memory of Jesus."[20] The historian by means of his new method can confront the modern man with the selfhood of Jesus and challenge him to believe. The historian, in short, is in league with the believer.

It is just this new situation which necessitates a new quest, Robinson maintains. For it would be odd indeed if theologians like Tillich and Bultmann, even Barth, were to insist on the indispensable historicity of Jesus while maintaining that it is irrelevant whether one has a historical encounter with him, once this has become a real possibility. "Such a position cannot fail to lead to the conclusion that the Jesus of the *kerygma* could equally well be only a myth, for one has in fact declared the meaning of his historical person irrelevant."[21]

The aim of the new quest, however, is not to prove the *kerygma*, for anyone who understands the nature of the new historiography would see that at most it could establish only that Jesus intended to confront his hearers with a decision, not that he actually revealed God. What the new quest seeks to do, rather, is to compare the self-understanding of Jesus, as it can be seen in the *kerygma*, with the self-understanding of the figure, as recovered by the new historiography. The aim will be to eliminate the *kerygmatic* "coloring of the facts" and to test whether the Jesus of the *kerygma* is the same as the Jesus of the new historian. In this way one could establish the continuity of Jesus with the Christ of faith and so exorcise once and for all the specter of skepticism which haunts dialectical theology.

3 · The Problem of Continuity and the New Quest

Jesus cast his own message in terms of the future coming of the kingdom of God, whereas the proclamation of the church had to do with a past event, the death and resurrection of Christ. Jesus' message was not primarily about himself, whereas the *kerygma* of the church is explicitly christological, that is, the proclamation of a heavenly being who came to earth, was crucified, and taken to heaven as the exalted Lord. This obvious difference, which Biblical criticism had made clear, has always been appealed to by liberal Protestants and others in support of an alleged sharp discontinuity between the so-called religion of Jesus and the religion about Jesus.

Bultmann and the other dialectical theologians tended on the whole to accept the fact of discontinuity, although they interpreted it quite differently, as we have seen, than the liberal theologians did. The dialectical theologians argued that the emphasis of the early church on the death and resurrection of the Christ makes it quite clear that the important thing is not the earthly career of Jesus stripped of all legendary elements but the intervention of God in the history of men. Bultmann and Barth, for example, are quite fond of pointing out that *kerygma* as it is found in Paul and John represents little interest in the objective historicity of Jesus, in the Jesus "after the flesh." So, also, the Synoptic Gospels are post-Easter documents which witness to a supernatural being that corresponds feature by feature to Old Testament prophecy.[22] The Synoptics, it is said, document the fact that the risen Lord was the same Jesus who was crucified; they are not attempts to paint a picture of the Jesus of history.

Although Bultmann does insist on a discontinuity between Jesus and the *kerygma,* his position is actually more complex. And this complexity, as we shall see, is significant enough to mention here. In his polemic against the "German Christians" and the Nazi apologists who, for their own ideological purposes, desired to widen still further the gulf between Jesus and Paul, Bultmann, in 1936, stressed the underlying affinity between them. He pointed out that beneath the quite different forms of expression, there was, nevertheless, a strikingly similar conception of human existence. Furthermore, although it is true that Jesus stressed the future coming of the kingdom and did not make himself the object of his own message, nevertheless he so preached that a decision about his own work constituted a decision about God's reign. Bultmann then drew this remarkable conclusion: "If Paul, like the earliest community, saw in Jesus the Messiah, he did nothing other than affirm Jesus' own claim that man's destiny is decided with reference to his person."[23]

In his later writings, however, Bultmann has not consistently explored this insight; indeed, he sometimes appears to have backtracked from it.[24] Moreover, what continuity he does affirm still seems insufficient to his students, since he does not think that the content of Jesus' life and teaching materially informs faith. Consequently, a number of Bultmann's most influential students—Conzelmann, Bornkamm, Ebeling, Fuchs, Käsemann—have sought to establish this continuity more firmly. They argue that the *kerygma* not only presupposes that there was a man named Jesus but that the what and how of his life are the object of Christian proclamation. The gospel of Jesus Christ as the risen Lord has an essential continuity with Jesus' own life and message.

Although there is formal agreement among the post-Bultmannians on this point, there are, as we shall presently see, interesting differences between them concerning how this continuity should be understood. The questions one should ask in examining these views are: (1) What consensus is represented in these views? (2) What theological inferences can be drawn from this consensus? My argument will be that although the new quest is significant in establishing a kind of continuity, the theological position most consistent with this gives aid and comfort to just that "left-wing" view the "new questers" are concerned to refute. But this is to anticipate; let us turn, then, to some of the arguments characteristically advanced by the post-Bultmannians.

One of the most common arguments concerning the nature of the continuity between Jesus and the proclamation of the church is based upon the phenomenon of Jesus' authority. In one fashion or another, this argument is employed by Bornkamm, Conzelmann, Ebeling, Fuchs, and, to some extent, Käsemann.[25] The view may be roughly characterized as follows: According to the least controvertible view of the New Testament sources, the picture of Jesus which emerges is of a man whose preaching and deeds constitute an extraordinary unity. He proclaims the coming kingdom of God; he teaches with relevance, simplicity, and power concerning the will of God and the forgiveness of sins; and he associates with the outcasts of society, with tax-gatherers and harlots. Infusing all of this is a remarkable directness and authority, an authority which sets him quite apart, Bornkamm believes, from the Jewish environment. All of the scenes in the Gospels, Bornkamm points out, reveal this astounding "sovereignty of Jesus," his capacity to reveal to men what they are and to precipitate a decision concerning his message. This authority has nothing to do with the technical historical question of Jesus' "messianic self-consciousness." It simply points to the fact that he is able to make the reality of God present. "This," writes Bornkamm, "is the essential mystery of Jesus."[26]

If Bornkamm emphasizes the authority of Jesus, this is similar to Conzelmann's argument that Jesus' proclamation of salvation is closely tied up with his own person so that his hearer's decision for or against Jesus is, in effect, a decision for or against the kingdom of God.[27] It is also similar to Ebeling's argument that Jesus' uniqueness consists in the call to faith, which, in turn, is set within the context of Jesus' authority. Since discipleship means sharing in the way of Jesus, Ebeling argues, "understanding his preaching of the will of God means sharing in his freedom, and understanding his message of the rule of God means sharing in his joy, his obedience, and his courage in face of the nearness of God. What Jesus says cannot be separated from his Person, and his Person is one with his way."[28] The same motif is found in the writings of Fuchs. Jesus dares to act in God's stead. His own behavior he regards as God's action. His teachings illumine his conduct rather than his conduct being an illustration of his teaching. The parables, in short, are a witness to himself. Jesus wished to be understood on the basis of his own deeds. Indeed, one may say that the demand of the *kerygma* is "simply the echo of the decision which Jesus himself made."[29]

Now it is this sovereignty and authority of Jesus which the *kerygma* brings to expression and which, therefore, constitutes the continuity between Jesus and the church's proclamation. The Easter faith, it is argued, simply makes explicit what was implicit in Jesus' life and conduct. It proclaims that the earthly Jesus was, in fact, the decisive revealer of God's salvation. According to Bornkamm, the awareness of the sovereignty of the earthly Jesus first awakened the hope that he was the promised one of Israel. But it was only after his death and resurrection—an "event" Bornkamm does not defend, incidentally, as a visible supernatural event—that the mystery of Jesus' person was disclosed.[30] Ebeling has a similar argument. The resurrection, he writes, is not an additional object of belief alongside of faith in Jesus' person. "The faith of the days after Easter knows itself to be nothing else but the right understanding of the Jesus of the days before Easter. For now Jesus appeared as what he really was, as the witness to faith."[31]

In the revised German edition of his book on the new quest,

Robinson reveals himself to be somewhat dissatisfied with this type of argument. Although appreciative of Ebeling's and Fuchs' attempts to ground the claim of the *kerygma* firmly in the person of Jesus, he thinks that their terminology "has at times been too reminiscent of the psychological orientation at the end of the nineteenth century."[32] Robinson is surely correct on this point, for although Fuchs and Ebeling clearly do not intend to lapse into psychologism, their arguments inevitably do. Fuchs is especially vulnerable in this regard. He goes so far as to claim that Jesus' call to decision for faith presupposes that Jesus himself made that decision and, as Bultmann has noted, this "leads to the absurd result that in the parable of the prodigal son (Luke 15:11-32) Jesus did not want to teach the grace of God which is open to the sinner, but rather defends his own attitude."[33] Ebeling, who is more cautious, can also be criticized for this. He speaks rather uncritically about Jesus' "certainty," "surrender," "assurance," "joy," and the like.[34]

Robinson also believes that Ebeling and Fuchs lean too heavily on actual linguistic affinities between Jesus and the early church—for example, the concept of "faith." This, Robinson argues, is too narrow a base. He might have said that it is also a shaky one. Ebeling, for example, argues at some length that Jesus' use of the expression "Amen" brings "out the fact that the truth and reality of his words is the truth and reality of God" and gives expression "to the fact that Jesus identifies himself entirely with his words, that in the identification with these words he surrenders himself to the reality of God, and that he lets his existence be grounded on God's making these words true and real."[35] That represents quite an inference, and it will hardly convince many readers not already convinced.

Robinson rests his own case on establishing a continuity of intention between the teaching of Jesus and the *kerygma,* a continuity between the understanding of human existence embodied in the conduct and message of Jesus and that of the *kerygma.* In this connection, Robinson has been impressed by the work of Herbert Braun.[36] After a very detailed analysis of the christological terminology of Paul, the Synoptics, and the Johannine literature,

Braun concludes that despite the wide discrepancy in the terminology, which is always a function of the cultural environment, there is a fundamental similarity in the basic conception of human existence before God. All three radicalize the human situation by insisting on God's demand. All three conceive of sin as an attempt to avoid that demand by becoming concerned with the world. All three regard salvation as an inner freedom in relation to the world, and all three regard salvation as an event. Finally, all three understand grace to be effective apart from the works of the law and made present in preaching. In short, Braun concludes that it is the anthropology of the New Testament that is the constant factor, when anthropology is broadly conceived as man before God, and it is the christological terminology that is the variable.[37] And although Braun's essay is not primarily concerned with Jesus' teaching, he argues in passing that Jesus' own preaching and conduct express this same *Existenzverständnis* and proclaim his own presence as the event in which grace is given as a possibility to man.

Robinson agrees in many respects with Braun's conclusions but believes that one must go even further. One must say that the *kerygma* actually brings to expression the same understanding of existence Jesus had, that what constituted his person is faithfully proclaimed and believed.[38] If, for example, it could be established that Paul's conception of faith, of being crucified and risen with Christ, represents substantially the same understanding at the heart of Jesus' message and conduct, this would go far toward establishing a material continuity between them.

Robinson attempts to establish this by a very detailed analysis of Jesus' message. His argument is too complex to rehearse here, but roughly it is as follows: If one penetrates beneath the terminological forms in which Jesus' eschatology is expressed, he will discern that the temporal distinction of present-future tends to resolve into a material one in which the intervention of God "is hidden in the midst of the continuing evil aeon," so that life in this kingdom is freedom within lowliness. This, in turn, is so connected with Jesus' own presence that Robinson can claim that "the eschatological coming of God in his action is the act in which his ... [Jesus'] existence consists."[39] Since God does not fail Jesus at his death, the *kerygma* can suppose that union with God's action is one and the same as union with Jesus' existence. So, too, the logia of Jesus reveal an understanding of God in which God forgives sinners and brings to nothing the powerful and prideful. The self-saving life is really lost and those who give themselves find life. This "eschatological occurrence" Jesus also understands to be taking place in his own existence. Now the *kerygma*, which speaks of dying and rising with Christ, has the same essential structure and, by proclaiming Jesus to be Lord (Cosmocrator), demands of the listener that he identify himself with Jesus' understanding of existence. The *kerygma*'s proclamation of Jesus as Cosmocrator brings ontologically to expression what happened ontically in Jesus.[40] Put less abstractly, Robinson claims that faith is the repetition in one's own life of the decision which Jesus himself made. This is what it means, in fact, to be "united with Christ."

4 · The New Quest and the Autonomy and Historicity of the Historian

How adequate is the new quest when it is judged by the criteria derived from the morality of historical knowledge? Does the new interpretation of history underlying it require a thoroughgoing revision of that morality? Or does the morality of knowledge itself rest on a misconception concerning the aims of history? And what about the theology of the matter? Does the new quest really solve the problems left unsolved by the dialectical theology? Does it provide a helpful corrective? What theological significance does the quest have? Is it once more possible to be both a critical historian and a believer?

Now it can scarcely be doubted that the new quest certainly intends to embrace the critical historical method. In fact, Ebeling argues, just as we have done in a previous chapter, that the affirmation of the critical historical method has a deep inner connection with the Reformers' doctrine of justification by faith. "I venture to assert," he writes, "that the Protestantism of the nineteenth century, by deciding in principle for the critical historical method, maintained and confirmed over against Roman Catholicism in a different situation the decision of the Reformers in the sixteenth century."[41] But unlike the dialectical theologians, who also made this point, the post-Bultmannians do not intend to secure the faith against the risk of historicity. The Protestant theologian, Ebeling insists, has no alternative but to expose himself to the insecurity and vulnerability implicit in the work of the historian, "to go ahead with the critical examination of our foundations, to let everything burn that will burn and without reservations await what proves itself unburnable, genuine, true—and to adopt this attitude at the risk that much that seemed established may begin to rock. . . ."[42]

Although the new quest does challenge the aims and assumptions of much nineteenth-century historical research, it would be a mistake, then, to conclude that it rejects the more formal criteria of autonomy and rational assessment and the way in which these two, in turn, are dependent on warrants given in our present, critically interpreted experience. The "new questers" have learned their lesson too well from their former teachers, Bultmann and Gogarten. They know that with the loss of the self-evident character of traditional Western metaphysics, modern man has suddenly become aware of the historic character of his existence. He has discovered the time-conditioned character of every event, and with this discovery there has come the "extraordinary sharpening of the critical eye for the question of dependability and genuineness of sources, for cases of historical dependence, interconnexion and change."[43] One could hardly desire a stronger endorsement of the historian's autonomy and his use of warrants given in present knowledge than this one by Ebeling:

The really decisive and revolutionary thing about the critical historical method came from the fact that the modern historian sees himself compelled to take the sources of the past and set them, too, in the light of the new self-evident assumptions. Not that he foists these new self-evident assumptions on to the witnesses of the past, as if they had been self-evident assumptions also for them, but he does examine the factual content of their testimony on the basis of these self-evident assumptions. Thus he will not accept the truth, e.g. of statements which presuppose the Ptolemaic picture of the world, not even when for the rest the source has a high degree of historical dependability. The modern historian is rightly convinced that he knows certain things better.[44]

Ebeling does argue, to be sure, that the critical method is not a neutral and presuppositionless tool, but he is careful not to appeal to "the eyes of faith" or some other euphemism which conceals special pleading and the avoidance of rational assessment. He does not posit supernatural causes or absolutely unique events but affirms that the historian deals "with all historic and literary phenomena of the past by the same method, *viz.*—the critical historical method, which can certainly undergo infinite modifications according to the nature of the particular historical object, but which cannot be put fundamentally out of currency by any historical object."[45]

This point is worth lingering over, especially because some of the proponents of the new quest, especially those enamored of the "new hermeneutic," are given to a somewhat extravagant series of claims which suggest that the new history "has attained a new methodology."[46] And since a new method seems to imply new canons of assessment, an entirely new process of justifying historical statements, it is important to ascertain whether the new quest does, in fact, require a rejection of the morality of knowledge as I have described it.

Robinson's monograph on the new quest makes two points: (1) The new quest, in contrast to the old, requires the "openness" and engagement of the historian, his willingness not only to question the text but, so to speak, to be questioned by it and to give an answer to it. The historian cannot be detached or disengaged. Understanding, consequently, means to enter into a dialogue with the material issues involved. (2) The subject matter with which the new quest is concerned generally is the understanding of existence which comes to expression in a person or text and, specifically, the existential understanding of Jesus. The old quest, it is claimed, was interested only in external facts or in an objectivizing, rationalistic, psychologistic portrait of Jesus. The new quest goes to the deeper level of his person.

Although it can be questioned whether Robinson's wholesale condemnation of nineteenth-century historiography as "positivistic," "rationalistic," and "bourgeois" is justified,[47] the more important question is whether his emphasis on the "openness" of the historian at all requires a serious modification of my own analysis of the morality of historical knowledge. At first glance, it seems so, since the morality suggests disinterested and rational procedures of assessment which appear to be incompatible with the engagement of the existentialist historian. A closer analysis reveals, however, that the matter is not so simple; first, because what Robinson means by "openness" does not really involve the rejection of historical objectivity, properly understood; and, second, because Robinson's views have primarily to do with the final aim of historical understanding, while my own concern is primarily with the formal criteria by means of which historical claims are justified, whether those claims be about external facts or about the existential understandings of past agents.

The problem of objectivity is a very difficult one, and I shall discuss it at some length in the next chapter. But suffice it to point out here that Robinson so defines "openness" that it does not really involve a rejection of objectivity, if by that one means the rigorous suppression of one's own prejudices, so far as that is possible, and the giving of the best reasons one can for one's claims about the past. All Robinson argues is that the "openness" of the historian is a precondition for understanding some kinds of historical phenomena, i.e., the intentions of a past agent. He does not argue that "openness" guarantees historical understanding or that it functions in such a way as to make possible an appeal to some special data or warrants. Openness, he argues, "involves a willingness to listen for underlying intentions and the understanding of existence they convey, with an ear sharpened by one's own awareness of the problems of human existence, and a willingness to suspend one's own answers and one's own understanding of existence sufficiently to grasp as a real possibility what the other is saying."[48]

It is difficult to quarrel with such a view, but perhaps this is because it is not really so different in principle from the idea of objectivity advocated by many of those nineteenth-century historians on whom Robinson is so hard. When Ranke, for example, called for rigorous objectivity on the part of the historian, he did not mean that the historian should not be interested or open; he meant, rather, that the historian should have a respect for the past as it really was and not as the historian wished it might have been, and that he should refrain from the rhetoric of praise and blame. So, too, the Ritschlians made an analogous distinction between the historian's "office," which was to re-create the past in all of its richness, and his "person," which might have an opinion or value-judgment concerning the meaning of the past for him. However much the nineteenth century tended to conceive of the past in terms of external facts, the formal principle underlying its work is no different from the one Robinson advocates. Presumably, an existentialist historian who wants to understand, say, the selfhood of Caesar also has to make a distinction between how Caesar *really* understood himself (the facts) and what the historian may think about that self-understanding.

There are, of course, two real differences between Robinson's view and that of the Ritschlians. First, Robinson, like Bultmann, believes that the "person" and the "office" of the historian cannot be so sharply distinguished, because the questions which the historian puts to his texts presupposes a certain personal sensitivity and "life relation" to the subject matter. Second, he believes that the historian must make a commitment of some kind about the meaning of the past for him.

The first point may be conceded, but only if the issue is precisely formulated; otherwise, the emphasis on engagement may be erroneously taken to mean that unless the historian has certain specific presuppositions (a certain faith) he cannot understand a given past. But this is not what Bultmann or Robinson really mean. They do not argue, for example, that the Christian historian has a certain set of presuppositions which enable him to understand, say, the intention of Paul, whereas a non-Christian historian cannot. On the contrary, they appear to argue that "openness" is not a special gift of the Christian historian at all but a possibility given, in principle at least, to man as man.

The second point, the insistence that the historian must take a stand on the meaning of the past for him, does tend to violate the nineteenth-century emphasis on detachment, but a closer inspection reveals that the issue here is really irrelevant so far as it bears on the possibility of rational assessment. For even if one accepts the view that the historian should take a stand, surely such a stand is appropriate *only after the determination of the nature of the events in question.* It does not constitute some sort of methodological basis for *making* claims about the past. No statement about the past can be *justified* on the grounds of the historian's stand, because the stand that he takes presupposes some prior determination of *what* it is he takes some stand on. And this prior determination necessarily rests on data and warrants relative to present fields of knowledge.

It could be argued, of course, that this concern for engagement tends to prejudice assessment, and this is precisely what the historians of the nineteenth century argued. In this connection, incidentally, they are supported by at least one of the more capable pilgrims on the new quest, Ernst Käsemann, who is obviously nervous about the language of commitment.

I regard the confusion of understanding and decision as . . . dangerous. . . . The cardinal virtue of the historian and the beginning of all meaningful hermeneutic is for me the practice of hearing, which begins simply by letting what is historically foreign maintain its validity and does not regard rape as the basic form of *engagement.*[49]

The point I am making is that no matter what the personal sensitivity of the historian, his judgments about the past solicit assent, whether they be judgments about external or internal realities. These claims necessarily require appeal to certain data and the assumed validity of certain warrants. The issue here, in short, has to do with the important distinction between getting in the position of understanding (being "open") and justifying the claim to have understood. And nothing advocated by the new quest invalidates that distinction. The appeal to "openness" and engagement, therefore, may illumine the aims of understanding and its preconditions, but it in no way materially alters the criteria implicit in the morality of historical knowledge. In this respect, it does not constitute a new methodology.

This brings us to Robinson's claim concerning the newness of the new quest as compared with the old, namely, that the subject matter of the former is different from that of the latter. Let us concede for the moment that it is, that a description of the self-understanding of a past agent differs materially from a depiction of the external, biographical facts which were so beloved by nineteenth-century historians. Still, as we have seen, this concession in no way alters the logic of rational assessment; indeed, it presupposes it. It presupposes not only the appeal to data but—and this is important to note—it also presupposes the appeal to warrants based on one's present knowledge. The existentialist historian must also make use of the principle of analogy. Insofar as he assumes, for example, that past human beings were moved by the same basic human questions as we are, and that the answers to these questions manifest themselves in speech and deeds, the historian assumes that there is a kind of continuity, an "analogy of human being," that makes historical understanding possible. Indeed, the language of engagement and "openness" requires just this continuity, for how could a historian really believe that the past actualization of a certain self-understanding is relevant for him in the present unless he also assumes that nothing human is alien to any man? In this respect also, then, the new historiography does not really alter the basic logic of rational assessment.

The real newness of the new quest does not consist in its modification of the morality of historical knowledge but in its reconception of the aims of historical understanding, the recovery and encounter with certain possibilities of self-understanding which have been actualized in the past. The true aim of history, it is claimed, is to have one's own understanding of life called into question by the "profound intentions, stances, and concepts of existence held by persons in the past, as the well-springs of their outward actions."[50]

Now it can scarcely be denied that this is a genuine and much needed contribution to the discussion concerning the nature of historical inquiry. It keeps history from being reduced to the dry chronicle of fact, something to be indulged in only by those with antiquarian interests. It reminds us that human action is finally intelligible only as a quest for meaning. In this sense, it may be regarded as the reaffirmation of the humane significance of history. More important, it makes clear that this basic question of meaning comes to expression more vividly in some kinds of texts and events than in others, and that no genuine understanding of these things is possible unless one comes to them with the proper questions. Consequently, this kind of historical inquiry has been extraordinarily useful in the interpretation of religious and philosophical texts, as well as of persons whose lives can best be understood in terms of their conception of the meaning of life. It has, in fact, revolutionized Biblical studies.

But when this conception of historical scholarship is universalized, that is, when it is regarded as the *only* legitimate kind of history, then it can become philosophically mischievous. There are, for example, other kinds of history which have their own integrity and which cannot be very helpfully described in this way. The existentialist model, for example, is not very illuminating with respect to economic, political, military, and cultural histories, to mention a few. Our desire to understand the past takes many forms and springs from many motives. We may want to ask, for example, whether the Settlement of 1815 was a reasonable one, or whether the Negro soldier in the Army of the Republic contributed significantly to a Northern victory, or what the reasons were for the failure of Hitler's invasion of Russia. We may wish to trace the development of Mesopotamian civilization, or the rise and fall of the West. We may want to ascertain whether *The Odyssey* contains fact or fiction. The aims of history are as diverse as the questions men can ask, and it is an unfortunate, and humorless, truncation of the human imagination to argue that only one kind of history is peculiarly entitled to the name.

This criticism would scarcely need noting did it not have a direct bearing on the problem of the justification of historical explanations and assertions. For when one model of history is elevated to the exclusion of others, the tendency has been to isolate one kind of historical explanation as the standard by which all others are to be judged. Instead of examining the diverse kinds of claims and interests of historians and attempting to illuminate them, the philosopher begins to conduct a search for a clear and distinct idea of "historical explanation." This, in turn, obscures the field-encompassing character of history, the diversity of historical judgment, and, consequently, the diversity of the data and warrants to which the historian necessarily appeals. The result is a philosophy of history, a theory of historical explanation, that does not really illumine this diversity, and this, in turn, leads to philosophic reactions which are equally one-sided. Historical judgments are too diverse to lend themselves to any one model.

This criticism brings us near to the Achilles' heel of the new quest. Just because it is so monolithic in its view of the nature of history, just because it tries to make New Testament history conform to this one view of historical understanding, it cannot solve the theological problem of the relationship of faith to history. Indeed, it compounds the problem. By redefining history as it does, it so specifies the object of faith that the burden of faith is made to rest on just the logical type of judgment which can least support that burden.

5 · The New Quest and the Texture of Historical Assent

Although the new quest stands up quite well when measured by the first three elements in what I have called the historian's morality of knowledge, it fails at a fourth point. Although it does justice to the radical autonomy of the critical historian and to his obligation to submit his claims to the rational assessment of his colleagues, an assessment which necessarily presupposes warrants lying in present knowledge, the new quest fails at the crucial point of judgment. It fails to understand the delicate relationship between the *quality,* or texture, of the historian's assent and the type of warrant which justifies that quality of assent. It puts the heaviest weight on just those kinds of historical judgments which, from a logical point of view, are the least capable of bearing it. By regarding historical inquiry as culminating in claims about a person's existential selfhood, it defines historical knowledge in terms of the weakest of its epistemological links. This cannot fail, generally, to lead to cynicism about the possibility of historical knowledge at all, on the one hand, or to highly artificial attempts to justify it as knowledge, on the other. In the case of theology, it leads to an intolerable state of mind in the believer, because the believer's religious certitude must rest on those historical judgments which are least capable of sustaining that certitude.

These criticisms can best be elaborated by pursuing two closely related questions: (1) Can the existential selfhood of any person in the past be grasped except by inferences drawn from so-called external data among which it is important to establish chronological relationships? (2) Are not the warrants which license conclusions about the "deep-lying intentions" of past persons such that, in the nature of the case, these conclusions should be made only with the greatest caution and, in some cases, not at all?

Let us consider the first question. Could a judgment about a past agent's existential selfhood be anything but an inference drawn from certain external data the historian possesses? Lacking any direct memory and not being able to assume that all that is said to be remembered, in fact, happened, the historian has no option but to try to ascertain what events really took place, what words were spoken, to whom, on what occasions, and the like. As Collingwood points out, he must try to reconstruct the thought of the agent.

But thought does not occur in a vacuum. It is itself a highly contextual, conditioned affair. In order to reconstruct it, the historian, unless he has a document in front of him which articulates it step by step, must assume the possible development of the thinker. He cannot assume, for example, that a crucial decision at one stage in a person's life is a typical one unless he has built up an intelligible picture of that person which justifies the adjective "typical." The historian must also reckon with change. He cannot assume that similar actions at separated intervals are rooted in the same reasons; for example, that Lincoln's more mature statements about slavery reflect the same grounds underlying those made when he first stood for elective office. Decisions are historical.

Now "chronology," which the "new questers" so disparage, is simply a roughhewn term for our recognition of development and change, the fact that every decision presupposes antecedent conditions which, in turn, presuppose still prior conditions. To make any heavy claims about these decisions, therefore, one must either have direct evidence of the process of reasoning, like a document in which the reasoning is actually going on, or one must infer what the decision was in the light of other evidence which has enabled the historian to build up a picture of the person deciding. Otherwise there is no basis for the inference.

The force of these observations is to ask whether the new quest requires something like the same sort of data which Robinson claims, against the old quest, it is impossible to have? Consider, for example, whether the type of question preoccupying the "new questers" is really different from that which engaged the old ones: What are the authentic words of Jesus? What is the significance of his use of "Amen"? What was his relationship to John the Baptist? Why and when was he baptized? Did he change his views of the Baptist? What was his attitude towards John's death? Did he regard John the Baptist as the bringer of the "new aeon"? Did Jesus believe himself to be the Messiah or was he looking for another? How did he understand his own relation to the coming of the kingdom? How did he regard the law? Was he, at the outset, in conflict with the Pharisees or did this mount during his ministry? Did that alter his interpretation of his message in any important respect? Did he first intend to take his message to the Gentiles? Why did he set his face toward Jerusalem? Did he anticipate his death? Did he expect the imminent end of the world? How did he interpret his suffering and death? The determination of Jesus' existential selfhood depends on answering all or most of these questions. But can these questions be answered without an extensive consideration of chronology?

Or, more narrowly, consider the crucial question concerning Jesus' relationship to John the Baptist on which Robinson, in particular, stakes a great deal. His argument proceeds roughly as follows: "Since Matthew 11:11-14 has at its root a genuine saying of Jesus, and since the passage is not completely created by the

Church, then Jesus did in fact see in the coming of the Baptist the
shift of the aeons."[51] Since this fact implies that Jesus regarded
himself as standing within the new age, and since he called
upon men to repent because of the reign of God breaking in, and
since he himself "repented of his former selfhood" when he was
baptized, we may conclude, together with Fuchs, that Jesus' call to
repentance is a call to repeat the decision that he himself made.

Apart from the fact that almost every step of that argument can
be, and has been, debated, does it not presuppose just the chronological information Robinson maintains that it is impossible to
have? For surely in order to conclude that Jesus' relationship to
John the Baptist was as it is claimed and led inevitably to his
death, it is necessary to secure one important item of knowledge,
namely, that Jesus never faltered or changed his mind. The "new
questers" must at least eliminate the possibility that between Jesus'
baptism, when we are told that he "repented of his former selfhood," and his crucifixion he may have repented again, or altered
his reasons for dying, or gone to the cross, as Schweitzer suggested, as a despairing man who had thrown himself against the
wheel of history only to be crushed by it. Is not Bultmann correct
when he notes: "The greatest embarrassment to the attempt to
reconstruct a picture of Jesus' character is the fact that we cannot
know how Jesus understood his end, his death"?[52]

These possibilities are not ruled out by common sense (men do
change their attitudes, especially when confronted with the destruction of their missions) nor by existentialist philosophy (the
demand to be "open to transcendence" is posed anew by every
change of circumstance, and no past authentic decision necessarily
guarantees a future one). Do the "new questers" believe that,
lacking all evidence of a chronological nature, a historian should
be able to conclude with a high degree of probability—not to
speak of a certainty—that Jesus did not repent again? However
distasteful such an idea may be to the pious, can the critical historian qua historian rule out this possibility, unless he has just the
kind of evidence Robinson characteristically denies can be had?
Lacking such information, how much weight can the conclusion
bear?

The more fundamental issue here, however, is whether the war-rants which license claims about deep-lying intentions of past per-sons are such that they can solicit heavy assent, that is, whether they can be held with a high degree of certitude. Can one claim to know the real motives of an action? Is the thought behind the action the same thing as the motive? Can one know the thought and not the motive? Must a motive be conscious? Can the historian discern motives which the actor himself was not aware of? These are extraordinarily difficult questions, as the literature on the sub-ject reveals.[53] We know how complex human action and decision are and how difficult it is to infer motives from action and speech.

This problem is the more compounded by Robinson's claim that existentialist historiography is not at all concerned with statements about the "personality" of the agent, and, in that sense, with his psychological motives, but with the self underlying the personality. The personality, he writes, is merely one's "empirical habitus," the "inescapable medium through which the self expresses itself but is not identical with the self. . . ."[54] But how does one get at this self underlying the personality except by some kind of reflection on the conscious beliefs, intentions, and motives of the "personality"? Surely it would be meaningless to talk about a decision in complete abstraction from motives. Would it not, for example, alter our estimate of a decision if we knew it was an especially difficult decision to make, one which went counter to the personality of the actor? If we were to say that a man's action in a given situation was courageous because he had to oppose public opinion, this language is justified only if we knew that he *characteristically* put an inordinate value on public opinion. If he did not—if, say, he was a rebel and had contempt for others' views—we would hardly be justified in calling his action courageous. In short, our estimate of the authenticity of an action is intelligible only against the back-ground of judgments about the personality.

But if judgments about motives are in many cases extremely difficult to make, *how much the more difficult would it be to make claims about the self underlying the motives?* And if, in any particular case, such as that of Jesus, it should be argued that it is impossible to understand his motives, how much the more difficult should it be to recover the existential selfhood behind the motives?

Law courts, psychiatric journals, and the best novelists have always taken into account how difficult it is to infer a man's motives from his actions and speech. If one were to cast this wisdom into the language of logic it would take this form: warrants licensing claims about motives are rarely very tight. But even this generalization is too roughhewn, because we must distinguish levels of motives. It is not difficult, for example, to infer anger from a clenched fist and a punch on the nose. But it is far more difficult to infer loyalty from the words "I love you," and it is more difficult still to infer the quality of religious faith from the act of martyrdom. In the first place, modern psychology has taught something about the complexity of motivation. Put logically, a conclusion about a man's deepest motives is almost always open to qualification, or permits a wide range of possible rebuttals. There is, in certain areas of human experience, no simple line of connection between an authentically appearing deed and an underlying authentic choice. Indeed, the general presumption is that the more a decision touches the deepest springs of motivation and conduct, the more tentative our claims about it ought to be.

There is no necessity here, however, to lean on the authority of psychology, since this might appear to rest on a misunderstanding of what Robinson means by selfhood. But what are we to do with the Protestant conception of man, which is also predicated upon this understanding of the ambiguity of human decision? Luther and Calvin—not to mention Paul, who in I Corinthians 13:3 and elsewhere argues that there is a distinction to be made between the "works of love" and love—were quite clear that one is never justified in inferring faith from a man's speech or deeds. In fact, the purpose of their distinction between faith and works, the "inner" and "outer" man, "person" and "office," was to emphasize the hiddenness of faith and the possible discontinuity between charitable actions—even martyrdom—and the inner man. It is the quite un-Protestant archbishop in T. S. Eliot's *Murder in the Cathedral* who wisely says:

> The last temptation is the greatest treason:
> To do the right deed for the wrong reason.[55]

Now surely this general problem is hopelessly compounded in the case of Jesus because we have such scant historical evidence in his case. If modern historians are unable to decipher the mystery of Abraham Lincoln, even though they possess volumes of authentic sayings, intimate letters, and the accounts of eyewitnesses, are we to believe that we can encounter the real Jesus of Nazareth on the basis of a handful of sayings preserved in no chronological order by a community that was especially anxious to prove that he was the Messiah?[56] Unless we assume in advance that Jesus' selfhood was more consistent with his life and thought than that of other human beings—and as an a priori assumption it can hardly serve the purposes of critical history—surely we must remain silent concerning his own "openness to transcendence."

This is the major reason why the various arguments of the "new questers" are so unconvincing as historical arguments. For however self-evident it may appear to a believer, it does not follow that because Jesus spoke and acted with incomparable authority we can infer that he was himself a man of perfect obedience. There is too much room for a rebuttal or another interpretation of the data. One might point out, for example, that many prophets have spoken with authority and power. Some regarded themselves as saints, while others would have been horrified at the thought that their prophecy justified a conclusion about their own inner lives: "Why do you call me good?" (Mark 10:18). Indeed, it is even possible that a man could regard the rejection of his own message and mission as a rejection of God and still believe himself to be an unfaithful man, or, more probably, a man who lived in "fear and trembling," unsure of his relation to God. By what right does Ebeling infer from Jesus' authority that in his "heart of hearts" he was the embodiment of a complete and selfless sacrifice? There is no right, except an a priori one.

I conclude, then, that the new quest, insofar as it concentrates on Jesus' existential selfhood, tends to corrode the balance of judgment which is the *sine qua non* of critical history. It does not do this, to be sure, in the way that orthodoxy does, by demanding belief in certain supernatural events; rather, it does it by soliciting the heaviest possible assent to a historical judgment which, in this particular case, is most tenuous. It hangs the passion of faith on the slenderest of threads by defining Jesus' own existential self-understanding as the object of faith, as an essential part of the content of the *kerygma*.

6 · The New Quest and the Nature of Faith

But it may now be asked, What does the new quest's understanding of the matter do to the Protestant understanding of faith? Does it not, in the last analysis, equate faith with an assent to a historical judgment that is, in the nature of the case, a dubious one? And does not this equation lay an intolerable psychological burden on the believer, so that the more honest he is as a historian the less possible it is for him to be a Christian, if a necessary though not sufficient condition for being a believer is to assent to the proposition that Jesus was "open to transcendence?" If faith is a liberation of the self, as Herrmann and the dialectical theologians understood it to be, how can a man be inwardly liberated by believing what he knows, on other grounds, to be a highly tenuous historical assertion? Does not such a demand lead either to the inner pathos of Kähler's student or to a desire to prove by historical means that the *kerygma* is not untrue and, thus, to an inauthentic desire for security?

Robinson's attempt to turn aside this criticism is an ingenious one. He argues,

A new quest cannot verify the truth of the *kerygma,* that this person actually lived out of transcendence and actually makes transcendence available to me in my historical existence. But it can test whether this kerygmatic understanding of Jesus' existence corresponds to the understanding of existence implicit in Jesus' history, as encountered through modern historiography.[57]

In short, the historian cannot make the theological judgment that Jesus was the revelation of God, but he can establish what Jesus' selfhood was like, so that one is faced with the question of faith.

Robinson is surely correct in saying that no historian could verify the theological content of the *kerygma*. But does this really speak to the issue? Consider the use of the word "test" in the above statement. What does it mean? It surely means that a historian could establish a lack of correspondence between what the *kerygma* says about Jesus' selfhood and what he can conclude through historical research. Would this not disprove the *kerygma* if a necessary though not sufficient condition for the truth of the *kerygma* is the historical fact that Jesus had such a self-understanding as the *kerygma* says he has and which he then makes available to us? And would faith have no anxiety about such a possible disconfirmation? More important, would not a responsible person be justified in suspending his decision about the *kerygma* until he was satisfied that critical historians could agree on the matter?

Consider this hypothetical case. A Christian historian who has "encountered" Jesus' selfhood in the *kerygma* comes to the conclusion that the available historical evidence indicates a discrepancy between the *kerygma*'s report about Jesus' selfhood and the selfhood that the historian has uncovered by means of critical history. Perhaps he believes that Jesus' denunciation of the Pharisees may reveal an inauthentic hostility or, like Schweitzer, that Jesus went up to Jerusalem in the hope of forcing God to bring in his eschatological reign and died in despair. "My God, my God, why hast Thou forsaken me?" (Mark 15:34).

Does this hypothetical historian doubt the truth of the *kerygma*? It would seem so. Is this doubt capable of being removed, in principle, by historical inquiry? It would also seem so, since it is precisely this kind of issue the new historiography claims to adjudicate. Faith, then, waits on a historical answer, unless, of course, one argues that the historian can believe on other grounds, or that he can resolve the issue by deciding in favor of the "new hermeneutic"—a curious procedure for a critical historian. And what if the historian simply believes that the evidence does not permit a conclusive answer, that is, a firm assent? Shall he believe it anyway?

Meanwhile, what kind of psychological state shall we attribute to this hypothetical historian? Surely he will ask which of the two Jesuses he "encountered" is the real one, which is to say, he will ask whether he ever "encountered" Jesus at all or only thought he had. Furthermore, will he have no desire to resolve the matter? And will his efforts be marked by less anxiety than those of liberal Protestants who also wanted to establish that Jesus lived the exemplary life the Gospels attribute to him?

One might argue that this dilemma is groundless. Just as a man can be confident that a jury will find his friend innocent of a crime—since he "knows" independently that his friend is innocent, although he must wait for the judgment of the jury—so the believer knows that the church's memory about Jesus could never be discredited.[58] But, we could reply, how can faith have such a confidence in advance without restricting historiography to a purely confirmatory role, to be believed when it corresponds with faith and suspected when it does not? Indeed, in what sense can one speak of a quest at all if it is already decided what object is to be found?

The new quest, then, fails not only as historical argument but also as an analysis of the nature of faith. Nor are these failures unrelated, for just because it tends to regard faith as necessarily including assent to a historical proposition about Jesus' selfhood, it stretches the delicate spring of historical judgment beyond its tensile strength. Ironically enough, this was precisely the dilemma of liberal theology, especially the theology of Wilhelm Herrmann, to which dialectical theology hoped to provide a corrective. Now it appears that the new quest's attempt to provide a corrective to the corrective has brought us back again full-circle to our starting point.

7 · The Positive Significance of the New Quest

If the analysis of this chapter be correct, we seem to be faced with an unhappy dilemma. If, on the one hand, we say with the "new questers," as well as with liberal and orthodox theologians, that it is theologically necessary to recover the selfhood of Jesus—whether it be his "openness to transcendence," his "God-consciousness," or his "sinlessness"—then we not only corrode the texture of historical judgment but also sacrifice the meaning of justification by faith which the "new questers" also want to preserve. Instead of providing a corrective to the dialectical theology, the new quest actually involves a retrogression to a view which that theology tried valiantly to overcome. If, on the other hand, we argue that Christian faith does not require any such affirmation, we seem to undercut any view of the uniqueness of Jesus and so regard his life merely as a symbol of some timeless truth. We are faced with the question whether Christian faith is rooted in history in contrast to a myth.

This dilemma, I believe, is a false one, and in the concluding chapter I shall attempt to demonstrate more fully why this is so and to provide the defense of an alternative view. In the concluding paragraphs of this chapter, however, I wish (1) to point out briefly what positive results actually have been achieved by the new quest and (2) to suggest that these results not only do not support the theological position of the new quest but, on the contrary, lend some support to just that "left-wing" view the "new questers" wish to refute, but which they misunderstand.

There is, I think, considerable irony in the program of the new quest. On the one hand, it is an understandable attempt to overcome the formlessness of much of Bultmann's description of faith. Consequently, it aims to go beyond Bultmann and to anchor the *kerygma* firmly in the life of the historical Jesus. On the other hand, it nevertheless credits Bultmann with having provided the classic example of the application of the existentialist historical method to Life-of-Jesus research. But, we may ask, if both Bultmann and the "new questers" are applying the same revolutionary method, how is it that Bultmann is so skeptical about the possibility of recovering Jesus' existential selfhood while the "new questers" are not? Is Bultmann unable to practice properly the very method he so self-consciously introduced into New Testament research?

The answer to this question contains the key to appraising both the significance of the new quest and Bultmann's method. For the truth of the matter is that Bultmann, unlike the "new questers," does not believe that the existentialist method enables one to re-

construct the selfhood of past agents. On the contrary, the viability
of the method, so far as he is concerned, consists in the fact *that it
enables the historian to avoid precisely that question.* For Bultmann, the name "Jesus" actually refers to what he calls the "complex of ideas" lying at the bottom of the layers of New Testament
tradition.[59] By this, he does not mean that Jesus never existed or
was only an idea. He means, rather, that all the existentialist historian can do is reconstruct the picture of a man who subordinated
everything to the proclamation of a certain possibility of existential
self-understanding. This understanding, to be sure, is no system of
timeless truths, if by that we mean something that might enrich our
theoretical understanding. Rather, the possibility is presented as
one that is a concrete matter of choice for whoever takes the figure
of Jesus seriously. At one level, one can speak of Jesus' "intention" to do this. But at another level, no historian can legitimately
say whether he actualized the truth of his own teaching in his
"heart of hearts." All the historian can say is that Jesus was the
"bearer" of this understanding, its proclaimer, and that for the
Christian, at least, the message and "Jesus" are indissolubly
united.

But Robinson and the "new questers" cannot be satisfied with
this. Although they agree with Bultmann that Jesus' proclamation
is the presentation of a possibility of self-understanding, what interests them is whether it was actualized in Jesus' own deepest
(*existentiell*) selfhood. They think that in order to overcome the
formlessness of Bultmann's description of faith they must ground
the *kerygma* in Jesus' own faith. Consequently, Robinson, Fuchs,
and Ebeling speak of Jesus—of his "repentance," "joy," "assurance," and "certitude"—in ways that Bultmann would never do.
They press the existentialist method beyond its legitimate limits in
order to justify this kind of claim, and in doing so destroy the
delicate balance of historical judgment. What they should have
done was to criticize Bultmann for not seeing the way in which the
figure of Jesus, *as Bultmann himself describes it,* does, in fact,
inform faith, the way in which Bultmann's own description of faith
presupposes just the cruciform life that is best exemplified in the
Biblical picture of Jesus. Bultmann's formlessness, in short, is due

not to his historical skepticism but to his refusal to see the inherent possibilities in his own point of view, and this, in turn, can best be accounted for, as I shall suggest in the last chapter, by his uncritical acceptance of the dictum "faith can never be dependent on the results of Biblical criticism." The issue is not whether faith presupposes some historical knowledge but whether that knowledge which it presupposes requires a sacrifice of the intellect.

The significance of the new quest, then, does not lie in the recovery of the existential selfhood or "person" of Jesus, but rather in the application of a method that is extraordinarily fruitful because it enables us to interpret historical events theologically without special pleading or without appealing to some special Christian data and warrants. It permits the theologian to talk about Jesus as the witness to faith without putting an undue strain on the fabric of historical argument. Furthermore, when this method is used to penetrate beneath the various mythological forms of expression, it discloses that there is a remarkable continuity between the understanding of existence which is contained in the message and conduct of Jesus and that contained in the *kerygma* of Paul. This continuity has little to do with the "person" or "selfhood" of Jesus; rather, it has to do with the relationship of man with God. Both Jesus and the *kerygma* proclaim a radical gospel of grace which condemns the boasting of men. And yet both, paradoxically, emphasize the unconditional claim of obedience. Both conceive of sin as a bondage to the world which is passing away and redemption as a freedom from "this world." Both issue a call to responsibility, and both see the precondition of that responsibility to be the acceptance of one's own death. Both understand the true pattern of human life to be "death and resurrection." Both embody the conviction that man is justified by faith.

If this is the case, however, then what is this but to say with the "left-wingers" that Jesus embodies a meaning complex, that his life and death actually serve as a powerful and concrete symbol of a certain possibility of self-understanding, the relevance of which is violated if it is interpreted as having only occurred in Jesus of Nazareth? In short, is it possible that the new quest has provided theologians like Buri and Ogden with the very documentation they needed in order to make their case? Braun, in fact, seems more uncomfortably aware of this than does Robinson, who apparently does not sense the importance of the fundamental distinction between the understanding of existence of which Jesus was the bearer and Jesus' own appropriation of that understanding. Thus, Braun's essay, in which he establishes that the constant element in the New Testament is the anthropology while the variable is the christological form, ends in a tortured attempt to answer the question, "Is then the essential aspect of Christianity, the constant factor, a self-understanding, and therefore, perhaps only an ideal?"[60] In short, is Jesus only the symbol of a timeless truth?

Braun is unable to answer that question satisfactorily because the question is badly posed. It is not possible, as I shall show in the last chapter, to play "idea" and "event," "truth" and "historical occasion" off against one another as he does. But before I can show this, it will be necessary to explore still another attempt to solve the problem of faith and history. Only then will we be able to weave together all the strands into the fabric of an argument.

NOTES TO CHAPTER SIX

1. Rudolf Bultmann in *Kerygma and Myth,* ed. Hans W. Bartsch, trans. Reginald H. Fuller (New York: Harper Torchbooks, 1961), p. 33.
2. Fritz Buri in *Kerygma und Mythos,* ed. Hans W. Bartsch (Hamburg: Herbert Reich Evangelischer Verlag, 1952), II, 85-101; cf. *Kerygma und Mythos,* ed. Hans W. Bartsch (Hamburg: Herbert Reich Evangelischer Verlag, 1954), III, 83-91. See Schubert M. Ogden, *Christ Without Myth* (New York: Harper & Brothers, 1961).
3. Buri in *Kerygma und Mythos,* III, 90.
4. Buri in *Kerygma und Mythos,* II, 94; Ogden, *op. cit.,* pp. 145 ff.
5. See Gunther Bornkamm, *Jesus of Nazareth,* trans. Irene and Fraser McLuskey with James M. Robinson (Harper & Brothers, 1960); Hans Conzelmann, "Jesus Christus" in *Religion in Geschichte und Gegenwart* (3d ed.; Tübingen: J. C. B. Mohr, 1959), III, 619-653; cf. his "The Method of Life-of-Jesus Research" in Carl E. Braaten and Roy Harrisville (eds.), *The Historical Jesus and the Kerygmatic Christ* (New York: Abingdon Press, 1964), pp. 54-68; Gerhard Ebeling, *Word and Faith,* trans. James Leitch (Philadelphia: Fortress Press, 1963), pp. 201-246, 287-304; cf. his *Theologie und Verkundigung* (Tübingen: J. C. B. Mohr, 1962); Ernst Fuchs, *Zur Frage nach dem historischen Jesus* (Tübingen: J. C. B. Mohr, 1960), pp. 100-125, 143-167, 168-218, 238-257, 377-404; Ernst Käsemann, *Exe-*

getische Versuche und Besinnungen (Göttingen: Vandenhoeck & Ruprecht, 1960), I, 187-214.

6. James M. Robinson, *A New Quest of the Historical Jesus* (Naperville, Ill.: Alec R. Allenson, Inc., 1959), p. 44.

7. *Ibid.*
8. *Ibid.*, p. 37.
9. *Ibid.*, pp. 48-66.
10. *Ibid.*, pp. 28 f.
11. *Ibid.*, p. 68.
12. *Ibid.*
13. *Ibid.*
14. *Ibid.*, p. 47.
15. *Ibid.*, p. 67.
16. *Ibid.*, pp. 69, 90 f.
17. *Ibid.*, p. 69.
18. *Ibid.*, p. 70.
19. *Ibid.*
20. *Ibid.*, p. 86.
21. *Ibid.*, p. 88.

22. See Karl Barth, *From Rousseau to Ritschl,* trans. Brian Cozens (London: SCM Press Ltd., 1959), p. 386.

23. Rudolf Bultmann, *Existence and Faith,* ed. Schubert M. Ogden (New York: Meridian Books, Inc., 1960), p. 196.

24. Ogden has pointed this out in "Bultmann and the 'New Quest'," *The Journal of Bible and Religion,* XXX (1962), 209-18.

25. See Bornkamm, *op. cit.,* pp. 56-63, 67, 169, 178; Conzelmann, "Jesus Christ" in *Religion und Geschichte und Gegenwart,* III, 619-652; Conzelmann in Braaten and Harrisville, *op. cit.,* pp. 67 f.; Ebeling, *Word and Faith,* pp. 237, 243 f.; cf. his *The Nature of Faith,* trans. Ronald Gregor Smith (Philadelphia: Muhlenberg Press, 1961), p. 56; Fuchs, *op. cit.,* pp. 143-167; Käsemann, *op. cit.,* p. 206; for a popular treatment of this theme see Heinz Zahrnt, *The Historical Jesus,* trans. J. S. Bowden (New York: Harper & Row, 1963), pp. 109-119.

26. Bornkamm, *op. cit.,* p. 62.

27. See Braaten and Harrisville (eds.), *op. cit.,* pp. 63 ff.

28. Ebeling, *Nature of Faith,* p. 56; cf. *Theologie und Verkundigung,* pp. 124 f.

29. Fuchs, *op. cit.,* p. 157.

30. Bornkamm, *op. cit.,* p. 62.

31. Ebeling, *Word and Faith,* p. 302; cf. *Nature of Faith,* p. 62.

32. James M. Robinson, *Kerygma und historischer Jesus* (Zürich: Zwingli Verlag, 1960), p. 149; cf. Robinson's essay in William Klassen and Graydon F. Snyder (eds.), *Current Issues in New Testament Interpretation* (New York: Harper & Brothers, 1962), p. 91.

33. Bultmann in Braaten and Harrisville (eds), *op. cit.,* pp. 32 f.

34. Ebeling, *Word and Faith,* pp. 237 f; cf. *Nature of Faith,* pp. 54-56.

35. Ebeling, *Word and Faith,* p. 237.

36. See especially Herbert Braun, "Der Sinn der neutestamentlichen

Christologie," *Gesammelte Studien zum Neun Testament und seiner Um-welt* (Tübingen: J. C. B. Mohr, 1962), pp. 243-282.

37. *Ibid.*, p. 272.
38. Robinson in Klassen and Snyder, *op. cit.*, pp. 105 ff.
39. *Ibid.*, p. 99.
40. *Ibid.*, p. 105.
41. Ebeling, *Word and Faith*, p. 55.
42. *Ibid.*, p. 51.
43. *Ibid.*, p. 46.
44. *Ibid.*, p. 47.
45. *Ibid.*
46. See James M. Robinson in *The New Hermeneutic*, eds. John B. Cobb, Jr. and James M. Robinson (New York: Harper & Row, 1964), p. 62.
47. See the criticisms by Van A. Harvey and Schubert M. Ogden in Braaten and Harrisville (eds.), *op. cit.*, pp. 225-228.
48. Robinson, *New Quest*, p. 96, n. 1.
49. Quoted by Robinson in *The New Hermeneutic*, p. 43.
50. Robinson, *New Quest*, p. 39.
51. *Ibid.*, p. 118.
52. Bultmann in Braaten and Harrisville (eds.), *op. cit.*, p. 23. In the German edition of his book on the new quest, Robinson puts less stress on Jesus' decision in the face of his immediate death. "Jesus' surrender to death may not be limited solely to his death in Jerusalem. Rather the existential meaning of his own acceptance of the message of the imminence of the divine reign—and correspondingly his break with the 'present evil aeon'—consists in the fact that he continuously accepted his death. On that account, the historicity of the crucifixion of Christ does not depend on what may have happened on the last day but rather on Jesus' understanding of existence that attests itself in his entire public activity" (*Kerygma und historischer Jesus*, pp. 109 ff.). But surely this raises the question how we can know Jesus persevered in his attitude unless we have chronological information.
53. Robinson's appeal to the hermeneutics of Dilthey and Collingwood in support of his own methodology is unconvincing. Further attention needs to be given to the question whether either of these men can be interpreted in his fashion. Collingwood's view, it could be argued, was not that a man's existential selfhood can be recovered but that a man's ideas or thought qua thought could be rethought in the present. Dilthey's views are, I believe, less clear. Sometimes he argued that one can understand a self in the past by grasping the significance of three kinds of expressions: (1) statements or judgments expressing ideas and concepts; (2) human actions; (3) "vital expressions" (*Erlebnisausdrücke*), such as spontaneous gestures and exclamations, but more importantly, artistic expressions. It is significant that Dilthey had the least confidence in the value of the first two types of expressions, that is, *just those types that are the only ones we possess in the case of Jesus*. Moreover, the third class, Dilthey claimed, give no information about the author at all: ". . . ja es will vom Autor überhaupt nichts sagen" (*Gesammelte Schriften* [Stuttgart & Göttingen: B. C.

Teubner Verlagsgesellschaft and Vandenhoeck & Ruprecht, 1958], VII, 205 ff.). Rickert made some very telling criticisms of Dilthey's theory of expressions and argued that a historian could understand a "meaning complex" but not a "motivation complex." Dilthey, in reply, seems to have withdrawn from his original position when he writes that historical skepticism can only be overcome when "one's method does not need to reckon with the determination of motives" (*Ibid.*, p. 260.). H. A. Hodges interprets this passage in such a way that it does not represent a concession to Rickert, but the reader will have to judge for himself whether Hodges is successful in turning aside Rickert's criticism, which is analogous to my criticism of Robinson's views. See the discussion in H. A. Hodges, *The Philosophy of Wilhelm Dilthey* (London: Routledge & Kegan Paul Ltd., 1952), pp. 154-159, and chap. v.

54. Robinson, *New Quest*, p. 68.

55. T. S. Eliot, *The Complete Poems and Plays, 1909-1950* (New York: Harcourt, Brace & World, Inc., 1952), p. 196.

56. Note the problems historians confront in understanding the character (selfhood?) of Lenin even though he wrote, by conservative estimate, some ten million words and left an indelible imprint on those with whom he was associated. In a book review of three recent lives of Lenin, Henry L. Roberts notes how difficult it is to get back to the man and that "probably the principal difficulty is the personality and mind of the man himself" (*New York Times Book Review*, June 14, 1964, p. 1).

57. Robinson, *New Quest*, p. 94.

58. John Knox argues in this vein in *Criticism and Faith* (New York: Abingdon-Cokesbury Press, 1952), pp. 38 ff.

59. Rudolf Bultmann, *Jesus and the Word*, trans. Louise Pettibone Smith and Erminie Huntress Lantero (New York: Charles Scribner's Sons, 1958), p. 14.

60. Braun, *op. cit.*, p. 276.

VII

The Morality of Historical Knowledge and the Perspective Theory of History

1 · Historical Relativism and Christian Apologetics

THE existentialist philosophy of history that undergirds the new quest was only one of several reactions to the excessive claims made on behalf of a scientific history in the last century. Equally critical of them were the historical relativists, men who, like Carl Becker and Charles A. Beard in America, scoffed at what they regarded as the naive appeal to facts and to the value-free judgments of the historian. History, they said, is a unique discipline, and to conceive of it as a science is to misunderstand both its aims and its methods. Unlike the scientist, the historian has no object upon which he can experiment, no laws that he hopes to discover or on which he can rely, no theory which serves to correlate his data. More important, the historian is not disinterested in the way that the scientist is. What the historian chooses to regard as evidence, what he selects to describe, what interpretation he gives of the facts—all these are intelligible only by reference to the historian's values and assumptions. Indeed, the very idea that the historian's main task is to collect all of the facts and to let them "speak for themselves" is preposterous, wrote Becker, because it is impossible to present all the facts, and even if one could, "the miserable things wouldn't say anything, would say just nothing at all."[1] What historians naively call a fact is in reality a symbol, "a generalization of a thousand and one simpler facts which we do not for the moment care to use. . . ."[2] It represents a selection and this, in turn, is a function of the historian's values and interests. Written history is an "act of faith,"[3] and it tells as much about the historian as about the past he is investigating.

Historical relativism is less a systematic philosophy than a series of loosely knit arguments woven into a somewhat rough but identifiable garment of belief. But it has deeply influenced many Protestant theologians and New Testament scholars. C. H. Dodd, John Knox, H. Richard Niebuhr, Heinrich Ott, Wolfhart Pannenberg, Alan Richardson, to mention a few, have all incorporated the insights of relativism to some extent or other as a means of solving the problem of faith and history. Just because historical relativism is so loosely knit, however, it can be appropriated in significantly different ways. Consequently, any evaluation of its theological uses is somewhat complicated. For that reason, I will distinguish between two basic employments of it. The first I shall call Hard Perspectivism; the second, Soft Perspectivism. Neither type is often found in its pure form in any one author, but this or that author tends to emphasize the characteristic elements of one of them. The differences between them should become apparent from the following discussion.

2 · Hard Perspectivism as a Form of Christian Apologetics

It is not difficult to imagine how historical relativism could be employed by a Christian apologist as a dialectical weapon against the morality of knowledge, and the argument would surely look something like this:[4]

You have, with your so-called morality of knowledge, not only surrendered the Biblical conception of faith but have accepted a naive philosophy of history and then thrown up a moralistic smoke screen around the entire issue by invoking the sanctity of intellectual integrity.

The theological issue at stake is that the central motif of the Christian faith is God's supernatural action in certain historical events which have been interpreted through the faith of the apostles and the prophets. So central are these events that the whole Christian edifice would be found to be built on sand were these events not to have happened in the way they are reported. But if this theological point seems to you to beg the issue, then I can only say that you have accepted a very bad philosophy of history and identified it with intellectual honesty. But the issue is not honesty, autonomy, rational assessment, or any of the other elements you have invoked; the issue is a very sophisticated one concerning the nature of presuppositions. You have assumed that the autonomous reason which rationally assesses claims is a bloodless, disinterested, presuppositionless reason. But that is a fiction. All assessment and judgment take place within a context of interpretation. You might have learned that from F. H. Bradley, to whom you appeal with such approval. Although there is a sense in which there is no substitute for the hard, unexciting collection of facts, the collection of facts is merely a preliminary step preceding the writing of a narrative. But it is erroneous to think that a narrative can be dispassionate and free of value-judgments. A historian, as you also say, must select and interpret his data, and if he does not do this, someone else will, as the "scientific historians" of Germany found out to their dismay. But all interpretation presupposes some criteria, some principles of interpretation, and these, in the last analysis, reflect the faith-perspective of the historian.[5]

Indeed, if the matter were to be rigorously pressed, it is artificial to assume that one can separate one's beliefs and presuppositions from the determination of fact even at the preliminary level of historical investigation, especially when one's deepest convictions are at stake.[6] Consider the various lives of Jesus written since 1834, all of which claimed to be impartial but all of which presented a Jesus curiously representative of the authors' personal faith. The facts themselves cannot be established or clarified apart from value-judgments about them. The assumption that there is a realm of objective fact is not only a bad theory of knowledge, but, if I may invoke Christian categories, sinful, because the pretence to an "undistorted or impersonal vision of the truth of history is but a modern version of the Serpent's lie: 'Ye shall be as God, knowing good and evil.' "[7] What you do not see is that there is no impersonal objective standpoint; that disbelief, with its corresponding doubt about miracles, is not derived from an impartial study of the records but is itself based upon a faith-principle, albeit a positivistic and secular one.

The kernel of your argument is that Christians are incapable of bringing their own truth-claims to the bar of rational judgment and are, therefore, irresponsible fideists. That is false. We are as anxious to demonstrate the truth of our standpoint as you allegedly are. In fact, the entire aim of Christian apologetics is to demonstrate the superiority of the Biblical Christian view of the nature of history and historical investigation over the rival views.[8] But having said this, we acknowledge that we are ultimately dealing with matters of faith and not proof, because it is not communicable to outsiders who operate basically within a different perspective. If you think this is obscurantism, we can only argue that historians do disagree and that their disagreements can be shown to be functions of their metaphysical presuppositions. If you ask how it is possible for a nonbeliever ever to become a Christian, then we must point out that one must choose his perspective, or, if you would permit more religious language, "there must be some prior enlightening of the eyes of the mind before either the facts or their meaning can be seen in their true perspective."[9]

It is for this reason that we resent your moralistic criticism that faith corrupts the texture of judgment. Of course it is necessary to exercise "balanced judgment," to use your vague canon, and to qualify one's assent depending on the force of the warrants. But these are purely formal prescriptions and beg the central issue, namely, the fact that warrants are but functions of one's perspective. Given these warrants it is possible *within* a perspective to exercise different degrees of judgment.[10] We are not committed to all-or-nothing-at-all judgments. The most casual inspection will disclose that there are permissible degrees of opinion among Biblical scholars. They differ, for example, concerning the manner of Jesus' death and resurrection or whether he destroyed a fig tree or a herd of swine. But these are all intramural issues within the perspective which rests on the central conviction that Jesus was raised from the dead and worked the works of the Messiah.[11]

The real issue between us, then, is not whether historians should be autonomous, rational, or of sound judgment, or dependent on present knowledge. The issue is the difference in perspective as to what constitutes present knowledge. You rule out miracles. We say that whether miracles occur or not is not a scientific question, for if they did occur they could not, by definition, be the result of any physical force science could describe.[12] To assert the contrary is to be committed to the view that the only forces in the universe are those science can describe, but that is a metaphysical not a scientific belief. The real issue is the applicability of canons derived from the present, and your appeal to common sense settles nothing, for we are dealing with something quite uncommon in the New Testament. The Christian faith rests on that, and to doubt it is simply to say you do not share the perspective. No one will condemn you for that; only do not equate not sharing it with integrity and sharing it with credulity.

This form of the relativistic view, like so many other ingenious arguments in the history of philosophy, has a puzzling quality about it. It does seem to do justice to certain undeniable—what can one say but—"facts," and yet it fails somehow to satisfy the mind. It does, for example, seem to account for the understandable differences among historians, many of which seem to be reflections of more basic differences of belief. There is no existing realm of fact which the historian bloodlessly describes. The historian does select and interpret. On the other hand, the argument fails to dispel a feeling of dissatisfaction, a feeling that the word "fact" cannot easily be telescoped into the word "interpretation" without a certain loss, a feeling that the word "truth" cannot be defined simply in terms of the coherence of a perspective. We do dispute about facts in law courts, newspapers, and in political debates, and we distinguish quite sharply between these and interpretations. The problem is how to account for the plausibility of the relativistic argument and still not lose contact with our ordinary claims and counterclaims.

3 · *Selectivity and the Standpoint of the Historian*

Consider, first, the claim that since historical narrative is necessarily selective, this selection presupposes the interests, values, and beliefs (the standpoint) of the historian. No one can, of course, deny that it is impossible to describe any event exhaustively or to re-create it in its entirety; what, for example, Lincoln ate on the morning of the Gettysburg Address, what he wore, who he talked with, or how he wrote the Address, the number of drafts he rejected, etc. But what are we to conclude from this truism? That a true re-creation of this or any other event would be a photograph-like picture of it? That an objective account would be a disinterested account? Hard Relativism assumes that selection always involves distortion, that interest and purpose are necessarily antithetical to objectivity. But these assumptions acquire their force only by holding an impossible and irrelevant ideal up before the historian, namely, that he should reproduce the past in the way some divine observer with no interests and purposes would. But this comparison, surely, only breeds confusion. The question whether history can be objective or not is a genuine one only if real alternatives exist.[13] The issue is not whether historians are to be compared with an omniscient divine observer, but whether *within* the limits of human observation, which is necessarily selective, there are some standards for judging the degree of arbitrariness of selection and for adjudicating historical disputes.[14] The question of objectivity is not, "Can a historian see as God sees?" It is, "Are there canons which enable the human historian to judge whether some things are true, even if they run counter to what he devoutly hopes and wishes were not true?"

The irony is that Hard Perspectivism presupposes just the scientific conception of history which it rejects, that is, that the aim of history is to reduplicate the past "as it really was." Then, discovering that this is an impossible absolute ideal, it flees for refuge to the injunction that the historian should select only those things which fit into his perspective. Morton White is correct when he observes:

But this is a non sequitur. Since we cannot present the whole truth we are fallaciously advised to select those truths which interest us. But the net effect of this is not to help the historian approximate his admitted ideal. How can he approximate it if he forswears the task of approximating it and turns to selection guided by his values and prejudices?[15]

This criticism, it should be noted, does not depend on a caricature of the relativist's argument. As T. A. Roberts also points out, Alan Richardson's argument in *Christian Apologetics* is peculiarly vulnerable at just this point.[16] Richardson first identifies objec-

tivity and truth with God's perspective and then concludes that to
desire objectivity and truth is not only impossible but sinful because it is the attempt to see as God sees. Apart from the curious
form of the argument—could it not also be concluded that just as
we are to try to approximate God's love we should seek to emulate
the divine vision?—it is irrelevant because the quest for impartiality and truth is not a quest for divine perfection but for *human*
candor and open-mindedness. It is, in effect, a call for ruthless
honesty and the suppression of all obscurantism, special pleading,
and wishful thinking.

But does selection necessarily involve distortion even within the
limits of human judgment? And does it necessarily preclude the
assessment of assertions which we make within the limits imposed
by our selection? There is a sense, of course, in which selection
means one has not told the "whole truth." And, there is also a
sense in which a selection can be eccentric. But is it true that
selectivity as such involves a distortion of the event, or that an
event is never understood unless all of its relationships can be
exhaustively described? Because every event is related to every
other event, must every termination of description be arbitrary and
false? This would seem unnecessarily restrictive. As Ernest Nagel
has pointed out, B may be no less a cause of A simply because B
has its own causal antecedents.[17] Nor is it difficult to imagine that
certain events have characteristics relevant to different kinds of
inquiries so that one may, for certain purposes, attend to one set
while ignoring, for the moment, the others.[18] Luther's career may
be of interest to psychoanalysts, students of the digestive tract,
political historians, theologians, and students of the history of
Biblical translations. However selective, even narrow, the historian's questions may be, he still should be able to bring forward
justifications for his answers within the limits of this concern. Falsification results only when an exhaustive significance is claimed for a
selective answer, when it is claimed, for example, that Luther's
life can be *fully* explained as a revolt against paternal authority, or
in terms of his constipation, or of his political dependence on the
princes, or of his doctrinal beliefs.

Although selectivity precludes a complete description of any series of events, it is also true, as Collingwood and others have pointed out,[19] that selectivity is the precondition for achieving any knowledge at all, whether it be scientific, historical, or common sense. All determinate knowledge is a justifiable answer to a specific question of some kind. All of our questions are necessarily selective and discrete and involve abstractions. Consider, for example, these questions: What are the indispensable elements of cellular structure? Is the mass of the negative charge of an atom spread throughout its extra-nuclear region or is it concentrated? Why did Hitler on the very brink of defeating England suddenly turn to the East and attack Russia, thereby precipitating the war on two fronts that his entire general staff desperately hoped to avoid? What understanding of life is implied in Socrates' acceptance of the hemlock? Was the assassination of the President of the United States a part of a larger plot or the work of a single deranged mind? Who is responsible for the footprints all over the living room rug? All of these questions are selective ones and may be said, in some loose sense, to involve a host of presuppositions.

The idea of cause itself, for example, is often a highly selective one, as Patrick Gardiner has taken some pains to point out.[20] For common sense, "cause" often functions as a kind of handle, an instrument for achieving some purpose. We use it to select certain factors rather than others as crucial for understanding why something happened in the way that it did. When we say, for instance, that one of the causes of the failure of Pickett's charge at Gettysburg was General Longstreet's delay, we assume that this is not an exhaustive answer. It presupposes many other factors, and it is always possible to ask why Longstreet delayed, which, in turn, could lead us into another direction of inquiry. But, given a certain desire for economy in explanation, the fact that he delayed is a perfectly intelligible reason, although a highly selective one. It does not follow that because it is not exhaustive it is a distortion or an unsatisfactory reason.

The point is this: If selectivity is the precondition for knowing or relating anything at all, how can its existence be used as an argument for the impossibility of any objective historical knowledge? It cannot be, unless, of course, there hovers over the argument some irrelevant standard, like omniscience, against which all human answers are measured and found wanting. But this is just to smuggle into the discussion the idea of a scientific history which the relativist professes to reject.

4 · Objectivity and Involvement

A similar argument may be brought against the claim that the historian's deepest convictions will dictate what and how he will write about the past. Once again this is both true and misleading. It is true in the obvious sense that no scholar is apt to spend much time or labor studying that in which he has no real interest, although some doctoral dissertations seem to be exceptions to this truism. But it is misleading, because, as A. O. Lovejoy points out, the concept of interest is completely general and commits one to nothing until we inquire how it actually affects procedure and selectivity.[21] A historian may be interested simply in understanding, and this may or may not be determined by what John Dewey called the "dominant questions of the cultural period." Indeed, it could be argued that just to the degree a history is written to satisfy the interest of any one "school" or period, it ceases to be of interest to other historians and to succeeding generations. Lovejoy insists this is particularly true of intellectual history. "If any normative criterion for the intellectual historian's selection is to be set up, it is that the selection should be determined, not by what seems important to him, but by what seemed important to other men; for it is precisely this that differentiates historical from any other type of relevance and significance."[22]

It can be questioned, however, whether passion and objectivity are mutually exclusive, if by objectivity one means the capacity to withhold judgment until one has good reasons for making it. Might not a judge who is also the father of a son accused of a crime be even more objective in his search for the truth than one who was less interested? Although many fathers would doubtless be prejudiced in the matter, not all necessarily would, and it is just our use of the adjective "prejudiced" in this case that indicates we recognize this distinction. And although society protects itself against the general proclivity to bias on the part of involved judges by asking them to disqualify themselves when their sons or other acquaintances appear before the bar, it acknowledges exceptions to this loose general rule and thereby admits the possibility of self-transcendence on the part of human beings.

That Richardson, in his defense of Hard Perspectivism, should use the argument that historians cannot be objective in matters where their deepest convictions are at stake has a touch of irony to it. For the conclusion to be drawn from it, as society has done in the case of involved judges, is that we should generally distrust the work of Christian Biblical scholars because *their* deepest convictions are obviously at stake in the inquiry.

As has been frequently pointed out, Hard Perspectivism ignores the distinction between an explanation and the justification of an explanation, between getting in the position to know something and defending what we have come to know, between why we want to know something (psychology) and the grounds (logic) that can be given for saying that we know it.[23] The judge who is also a father may have quite personal and, to that extent, subjective reasons for wanting to find his son innocent, in contrast to his merely being thought to be innocent. But the validity of the reasons he advances for his conclusion, however painful, are logically independent of his desires. Louis Pasteur's imaginative experiments on antitoxins were evidently undergirded by the theological conviction that God, in his infinite goodness, would not permit the existence of any dread disease not having its own cure. But one need not share this basic conviction in order to acknowledge the validity of his particular scientific experiments. In fact, Pasteur's theological conviction was obviously compatible with a number of untrue hypotheses he might have hoped were true but which turned out, in fact, to be false.

The issue, basically, is twofold. In the first place, the question is not whether historians can be objective, but whether some selective judgments about a course of past events are more entitled to credence than others. In the second place, the issue is whether human beings possess sufficient possibilities of self-transcendence to arrive at unpleasant truths, that is, at judgments which run counter to their treasured hopes and desires. Indeed, it is just because we realize that we are not omniscient deities that we impose standards on our judgments.

Hard Perspectivism tends to deny this possibility of self-transcendence and yet, paradoxically, it has to assume it in its own statement of its position. Carl Becker, for example, after informing us that it is useless to talk about past facts because a fact is a present judgment built out of our present needs and purposes, argues that "every man has some knowledge of past events, *more or less accurate. . . .*"[24] Or again, he writes that even people who do not read history have some picture of the past "however little it *corresponds to the real past.*"[25] So, too, Charles A. Beard, who at times embraced a radical relativism, argued paradoxically that he was driven to this conclusion by a study of historiography itself, which, presumably, presupposed his ability to acknowledge the real character of the past in at least one respect, namely, the history of history. And in his *Christian Apologetics,* Richardson, after building his case on relativism, argues that the Christian perspective is the true one because it enables us to see the facts as they really are.[26] But, we are entitled to ask, how can a perspective be rationally evaluated unless the standards in the light of which the evaluation occurs transcend the perspective? This is the crucial question, and one searches the relativistic literature in vain for an adequate answer to it, or for one that does not presuppose what it denies.

5 · *Facts and Interpretations*

The heart of that form of relativism I have called Hard Perspectivism is the claim that it is meaningless to make a distinction between fact and interpretation in history.[27] This claim is put forward in a number of ways, but a characteristic version of it goes something like this:

Before we can speak of history in any significant sense, there must be events which possess an interest and a significance for someone. Historical writing differs from mere chronicle and recorded memory just to the degree it brings out the meaning of events. "We might indeed say that an historical "event" is an occurrence *plus* the interest and meaning which the occurrence possessed for the persons involved in it, and by which the record is determined."[28] But the meaning of events is most truly apprehended by those within the series and not by those related only externally to it. It follows, in conclusion, that the significance of the events of the New Testament can be apprehended only by those who are a part of the community, so that "there can be no true historical understanding of the Bible which is not also devotional, or religious, or theological."[29]

The first thing to observe about this argument is its high level of abstraction. It is so high, in fact, that no distinction is made between "significance," "meaning," "value," "interest," and "interpretation." It is first declared that no fact would be recorded unless it were of interest, interest is then equated with value, and value, in turn, with a specific theological interpretation. Consequently, if one begins by assenting to the truism that no one records events of no interest, he is led up the garden path to the conclusion that the events of the New Testament cannot even be understood unless first interpreted (believed?) in a certain way.

It is important here to keep our minds on concrete cases and not to be seduced by high levels of abstraction. In ordinary experience, for example, events frequently occur that we simply are unable to interpret in any meaningful way. In fact, they constitute a problem just because we do not know how to interpret them. The police files are full of such events, just as are the notebooks of scientists: the unsolved murder, the unexplained reaction of the brain to certain chemical stimulants, the unintelligible cuniform tablet, the discovery of a third-century Roman coin in a first-century ruin, the discovery of a diary that contradicts a widely accepted version of an event. All these require interpretation. They are facts in search of a meaning, so to speak. Now the word "fact' is naturally employed in just such circumstances. It means that there is something that still requires an interpretation or some hard datum that forces us to revise an old one. Although it is true that we are referring in some of these cases to a judgment, this judgment, nevertheless, is of a different sort than other judgments that relate such and such a fact to other facts (an interpretation). We can see this use of the word "fact" in such cases as these: when a political candidate is inclined to argue that a widely publicized case of corruption in his entourage is being used to smear him and we are wont to reply that he cannot deny the *fact* that his associate received the money; or when a writer argues that an accused assassin could not conceivably have fired a certain number of shots from a certain type of rifle in a specified length of time and we argue that a reliable group of experts have shown that it can, as a matter of *fact,* be done. Our everyday arguments are full of such appeals to fact, and these appeals serve an indispensable function in our language.

The use of the word "fact" is especially important in historical inquiry for still another reason. It calls attention to something that this hard form of relativism obscures, the important distinction Marc Bloch noted between intentional and unintentional data.[30] Intentional data are those sources or documents that reflect a conscious intention to inform someone about the nature of an event and the meaning the author attaches to it. Unintentional data, on the other hand, are those types of things that witness to something in spite of themselves, so to speak, and that may be the basis for an interpretation quite foreign to the conscious intention of the author of a document. It is significant that historians rely far more on unintentional than intentional data. Without the former, as Bloch shows, the historian "would become the inevitable prey of the same prejudices . . . and myopias which had plagued the vision of those same generations."[31]

Now the relativistic dictum that the meaning of a series of events is most truly apprehended by those within the series simply does not illumine this practice. Apart from the paradox of the position—it dictates that one cannot call these anomalous facts historical events because a historical event, by definition, is a "fact plus significance"—it contradicts the actual procedure of critical historians.[32] The historian is usually far more attentive to what a document unintentionally reveals than what it intends to communicate. He by no means assumes that those involved in a series of events best apprehend its significance.

There is still another reason, however, for resisting any attempt to collapse the distinction between fact and significance, a reason inherent in the use of the word "significance" itself. The word is obviously a relational term. Something is significant *for* someone. But who is the someone who determines the significance of any given series of events in which more than one person is involved? This is not a trivial question, for it immediately casts into relief a problem historians confront at every turn, namely, the problem of conflicting interpretations of the same event on the part of those involved in it. The relativistic dictum that "history is the event plus the meaning which the occurrence possessed for the persons involved in it, and by which the record is determined" is utterly useless to anyone attempting to reconstruct the course of any given series of events. Who, for example, were the participants that perceived the *true* significance of Hitler's death? Are we to argue that the history of this event is the meaning given to it by those Nazis who were most closely identified with him? Or should we say it is the meaning given to it by those Jews who were persecuted and survived? Or is the true meaning apprehended by the German people?

As soon as we raise these concrete questions, it becomes clear that we are dealing with a muddled idea. We recognize at once that there is no *one* significance to any event. There may be as many meanings attributed to it as there are persons who interpret it. But it is precisely this diversity of interpretation *that forces us to use the rough distinction between fact and interpretation*. By using this distinction, we indicate that although the death of Hitler meant many different things to different people, his death was a fact alike for Nazis, Jews, Germans, Russians, and English historians.

This distinction is admittedly a vague one, but it is difficult for even the relativists to avoid making it. Becker, for example, after telling us that the appeal to fact is naive, insists that the real value of history is that it enables us to correct the "common image of the past by bringing it to the test of reliable information."[33] And Richardson, after arguing that facts vary according to one's perspective, concludes that "Christians believe that the perspective of biblical faith enables us to see very clearly and without distortion the biblical facts as they really are: they see the facts clearly because they see their true meanings."[34] And some practicing historians who reject the fact-meaning distinction in their philosophical introductions, suddenly invoke it, or something like it, as soon as they settle down to the actual business of writing critical history.

This phenomenon can be observed in the writings of certain New Testament historians. Although they are not what I have called Hard Perspectivists, John Knox and C. H. Dodd, for example, obscure this distinction between fact and significance. In one of his early books Knox argues in the familiar vein that there are no such things as bare facts in history and that, therefore, objective historiography is impossible. Consequently, only the church can read the New Testament.[35] But Knox no sooner puts aside these observations than he turns to the concrete question whether the memory of the early church is an *authentic* one. He concludes that although the Gospels rest on "the primitive authentic memory of Jesus, they contain much *which did not belong* to that memory."[36] He tells us that legendary elements have been woven into the *sounder* (factual?) parts of the tradition. He argues that since Matthew and Luke have contradictory birth narratives *both cannot be true,* and that "since no remembered fact threw any light upon why his parents were in Bethlehem . . . imagination was free to explain the circumstance in whatever seemed the most plausible way."[37] So, too, he writes that Jesus' alleged descent from David is probably not true, because the genealogies are contradictory and cannot both be correct.[38] Indeed, the only "facts of which we can be especially sure" are Jesus' origins in Nazareth, his baptism by John, the Galilean locale of his ministry, his execution, and his extraordinarily brief ministry.[39] In all of these arguments, the fact-significance distinction, which the author has rejected in his philosophical introduction, is reintroduced in his actual critical historical work. And not without reason, for it is impossible to write history without having recourse to some word that will denote what any historian would accept as a legitimate claim.

Furthermore, it is noteworthy that just to the extent that Knox believes that the interpretation of the early church did play a significant role in the formulation of the documents, he tends to discount them as factual. For example, just to the extent that he knows that the early church believed Jesus to be the Messiah, Knox distrusts those elements that reflect this belief: Jesus' messianic claims, the genealogies, etc. Dodd, incidentally, argues in a similar way and dismisses the nativity story, the flight into Egypt, and other narratives as legendary because they can be explained as "the imaginative products of the search for fulfilled prophecy."[40]

It is equally noteworthy, however, that when Knox treats of the resurrection, he departs from the use of "fact" and employs his canon that fact and interpretation are indistinguishable. He tells us that the knowledge of the resurrection rests not so much on accounts of the empty tomb and the like as on Jesus' recognized presence within the community. And since we, today, can participate in that community and presence, we, too, can know Jesus as risen. Indeed, it is this present knowledge that forces us as Christians to cease doubting the objective character of the appearances.[41]

And yet, even here Knox cannot completely drop the language of fact, and it is just this that makes his argument so puzzling. For if "fact" is employed in a common-sense fashion when Knox deals with the birth stories, it suddenly is employed in a different way in the treatment of the resurrection. "I have spoken of the resurrection as a fact, not as a belief; and we do not begin to think truly about it until we see it as such,"[42] he writes. Yet this fact, it turns out, is grasped only in faith. But what kind of a historical fact is it that is grasped only in faith? As though sensing that there has been a shift in his usage, Knox falls back on the injunction that we should not be interested in "bare historicity"[43] (bare fact?) but in how Jesus was "remembered," and he was remembered as risen. But, it may be asked of Knox, is not the real question precisely what it means to say "he was remembered"? And if it is possible to separate true from false memories with respect to the birth narratives and Jesus' messianic consciousness, is it not possible to do the same with respect to the resurrection narratives? This is especially important, since he admits that the resurrection narratives are, like the birth stories, hopelessly contradictory and impossible to harmonize. But if the contradictions were grounds enough for rejecting other Gospel stories as fact, why are these irrelevant so far as the resurrection is concerned? But in any case, surely it is inappropriate at this point to invoke the word "fact" at all, since he has previously argued that it is misleading. He does so, I believe, only because the word "fact" serves an indispensable function even for him.

I am not so much interested here in Knox's historical conclusions as in pointing out that (1) as a working historian he is forced to make a distinction between fact and interpretation and employs it regularly until he comes to treat of the resurrection, and (2) he acknowledges that the interpretation frequently given to facts has a falsifying influence. Yet neither Knox nor Dodd seems to see that it is precisely this falsifying influence of the interpretation that raises doubts in the minds of modern readers and forces the language of fact on the New Testament historian and makes entirely unconvincing the dictum that those who are involved in the event most truly apprehend its significance.

The valid point in the relativist's argument, or at least in the form of it advocated by Dodd and Knox, is that the religious significance of the New Testament story will not be perceived by anyone who is *merely* concerned with external fact. They are asking, in effect, for the reader to look with sympathetic imagination at a different dimension of the event; hence their frequent claims that the true understanding of it is a theological one, that the Bible is "from faith for faith." But this insight must be formulated quite carefully. To say this is not to say, as they tend to, that one can only understand what he is already committed to, or that he cannot establish certain facts as facts unless he already shares some specific interpretation of them. To argue in this vein is to argue that it is impossible to understand Nietzsche unless one is first a Nietzschean, or Marx, unless he is a Marxist, or an atheist, unless he is an unbeliever. But this leads to insuperable paradoxes, even for the Christian. For if one can only understand the New Testament when he is already committed to its meaning, then it is also true that the Christian can understand none of the alternatives he has implicitly rejected in the process of becoming a Christian. How can one say he has made a choice between, say, Christianity and Buddhism, unless he has in some sense understood the claims of both and rejected one of them? If he must be a Buddhist to understand Buddhism and an atheist to understand atheism, how, as an atheist, can he ever say he has understood and rejected the claims of Christianity; or how, as a Christian, can he say he has understood and rejected atheism?

As I have suggested, Hard Perspectivism, in the last analysis, is the denial of self-transcendence, the ability of human beings to enter imaginatively into possibilities of understanding and valuation not their own, to appreciate alien claims, to evaluate and assess them, and to commit oneself to them. It is this which the Hard Perspectivist finally denies, and it is this which ultimately strikes the outsider not only as a failure in judgment but as a violation of the morality of knowledge itself, the ethics of belief.

It is for this reason that T. A. Roberts and others suggest that the "fact-significance" terminology be dropped entirely. Roberts argues that it is the function of historical inquiry to establish the true significance of events, and this significance, he implies, should be verifiable.[44] But this criticism suffers from the same disease it seeks to cure. It does not recognize that there are, as we have seen, several levels and types of significance any one event may have. The life and death of Jesus have one sort of importance as events in the history of religions, another from the standpoint of Roman provincial justice, still another as an illustration of man's inhumanity to man, and still another as a disclosure of the meaning of life and death. Some of these interpretations may be judged true or false by the historian; others do not fall within his province. There is no *one true* significance of an event; consequently, to ask what that significance is, is already to deliver the historian into the muddles of this type of relativism.

6 · *Rational Assessment, Degrees of Assent,* *and Hard Perspectivism*

In his book *Christian Apologetics,* Richardson argues as follows: Because our view of the nature and significance of the historical facts varies according to our perspective, it does not follow that all perspectives are equally false. On the contrary, that perspective from which we see most clearly all of the facts, without having to explain any of them away, will be the relatively true perspective. Christians believe that the perspective of Biblical faith enables them to see clearly and without distortion the Biblical facts as they really are; that is, they see the facts because they see their true meaning. Conversely, if the true meaning of the facts as given by the apostolic witness is denied, then the "facts themselves begin to disappear into the mists of doubt," as they actually have in liberal Protestantism and the historical skepticism of Bultmann.[45]

Clearly one of the difficulties with Richardson's argument is its apparent circularity. If someone should argue, for example, that it is his perspective that the President of the United States was assassinated by a group of right-wing extremists in league with the Dallas police, we would argue that this perspective in some way has to be justified; that is, we would ask for an argument that contained certain data and warrants that are commonly acknowledged. If it were then replied that unless we presuppose such a right-wing plot the "facts themselves begin to disappear into the mists of doubt," we would point out that this is precisely what is at issue, namely, what the facts are that justify calling the assassination a plot. A fact is precisely that which we are inclined to accept as indubitable on the basis of certain common data and warrants. So, too, the issue in the case of Christian belief is the degree to which the apostolic witness with respect to the facts is to be trusted. And it will hardly do to argue that unless we assume this apostolic witness we are left with skepticism.

The Christian apologist is, of course, not unaware of this criticism but he seeks to blunt its edge by appeal to the coherence theory of truth.[46] He argues that when we say a proposition is

true, we really mean that it is consistent with all the other statements we are also prepared to accept as true. And what we are
prepared to accept as true itself depends on certain other basic
presuppositions. Truth, in short, is relative to the historian's other
beliefs, to his perspective. This does not mean, however, that one
cannot use his discriminatory judgment within the perspective.
For those who share the same basic presuppositions, it is possible
to assess an argument and to give differing degrees of assent to
various conclusions. It does not follow, Richardson claims, that a
Christian who believes in the resurrection of Christ, for example,
must also believe that Elisha made an axhead float or that Joshua
commanded the sun to stand still. For there is a principle within
the Christian perspective that is the "criterion for determining our
view of the historicity of any particular Gospel or biblical miracle."[47] The resurrection is essential, and the other miracles are
not. The great saying commonly but wrongly attributed to Augustine is applicable here: *In necessariis unitas, in non necessariis
libertas, in utriusque caritas.*

Now this proposed solution to the problem of rational assessment has a certain air of plausibility about it, but we should not
permit it to escape unanalyzed. When we scrutinize it, it becomes
apparent that there are at least two possible uses of relativism; one
is legitimate, the other is not. The difference between them can
best be seen if one asks whether two Christian Biblical scholars
who, by definition, share the same perspective can adjudicate their
own disagreements about facts by appealing to a common but
distinctive set of Christian presuppositions.

When the question is put in this form, it immediately becomes
evident that the appeal to Christian presuppositions is by no means
clear. We might have suspected this on the basis of what was said
in an earlier chapter. There we saw that the term "presupposition"
was itself too inclusive and needed to be "unpacked." History is a
field-encompassing field, and each field of argument has its own
relevant data and warrants. This important feature is obscured by
the umbrella-like term "presupposition." We are not clear whether
the term "presupposition" refers to empirical propositions, assumptions about human nature, rules or criteria, metaphysical

beliefs—all of which may be regarded, in some sense, as presuppositions.[48] To say "every historian has his presuppositions," then, is quite ambiguous until we know what this statement means.

Hard Perspectivism trades on this ambiguity. This is clear when we compare it with another version of relativism put forward by some philosophers. They argue that every historian's judgments reflect certain basic general (metaphysical?) assumptions about reality as a whole or about human nature.[49] Because of the generality of these assumptions, they influence all of the historian's judgments. They apply whether he is investigating the New Deal, the French Revolution, the rise of the Papacy, or the prophetic period of Israel. They apply across the board of history, so to speak. They are a part of the mental furniture of the historian.

But the Christian apologist, who is so eager to defend the uniqueness of the Christian perspective, uses the term "presupposition" in a quite different and more narrow sense. He uses it to refer not to a set of assumptions of wide generality but to very concrete beliefs about a particular set of events reported in the New Testament. Now while it is true that specific beliefs may act in some instances as "presuppositions," the force of the word in this context is opposite to the force of the word as used in this other form of relativism. For the Christian apologist uses the term in such a way as to justify the *suspension* of those normal assumptions we use when interpreting our experience. His point is that the alleged events in the New Testament are so unique *that our normal presuppositions do not apply.* Consequently, whereas the philosophical relativist is calling attention to ingredients implicit in all of our historical judgments, the Christian apologist is asking us to eliminate just those ingredients when investigating New Testament history.

It is important to distinguish between these two meanings of the term "presupposition" because only one of them permits some kind of rational assessment within the limits of the perspective. Two historians, for example, who have the same general presupposition that all human motivation is basically selfish will in any particular case still have to pore laboriously over the evidence in order to decide what particular self-interest seemed served by any given action. The presupposition, in other words, is broad enough that it does not weigh the scales in favor of any particular factual argument. This presupposition does, to be sure, distinguish the standpoint of these historians from those who presuppose, say, that men's actions can be selfless and altruistic. But in both cases it is possible to have differences within the perspective. If, on the other hand, we identify presuppositions with certain specific beliefs about particular events, then there are no more general principles to which one can appeal when differences of opinion arise. In fact, if the beliefs are determinate enough, no difference can arise within the perspective because *the perspective, by definition, has been constituted by a particular belief.*

The Christian apologist is particularly vulnerable at this point because the specific presupposition in question has to do with an event alleged to be absolutely unique, which is to say, an event to which no analogies or warrants grounded in present experience can apply. But if such is the case, it may be asked, how can any meaningful argument concerning that event arise even among those who share the same presupposition or perspective? Indeed, is it not to say that there can be no argument among those who share the same standpoint? Moreover, how can there be discriminating judgments within the perspective? How can there be any degrees of assent to one's claims?

This is the point of our earlier question whether it be possible for two Christian Biblical scholars who, by definition, share the same perspective to adjudicate their own intramural disagreements about facts by appealing to a common but distinctive set of Christian presuppositions. Consider, for example, this very instructive debate between John Knox and Oscar Cullmann as to whether Jesus believed himself to be the Messiah. Cullmann argues that Jesus was constantly tempted to conceive of his messiahship in political terms after the manner of the Zealots. It was, in fact, this temptation which Jesus overcame in Gethsemane. Cullmann writes:

We wish only to indicate the point which is basic to the understanding both of Jesus' attitude and also of his condemnation: namely, that

Jesus regarded himself as the Son of Man who would one day come on
the clouds of heaven. . . . To be sure, the genuine Jewish Messiah is a
victorious national commander-in-chief who conquers all heathen peoples and rules over the world; whereas the Danielic Son of Man comes
from heaven and establishes a kingdom which is not of this world. But
the connections between Messiah and Son of Man are of such a sort
that we can properly speak of Jesus' messianic consciousness. Jesus
was conscious of being the divine emissary, sent to establish the Kingdom of God. Only thus do we understand how Jesus became liable to
the indictment which ended in his condemnation, the grounds for
which were posted publicly on the cross. Jesus' guilt, from the Roman
point of view, consisted in this: that—just like the Zealots—he was
presumed to have aimed at kingly authority in one of the subject
provinces of the Romans. Jesus' condemnation by the Romans . . .
would be incomprehensible if Jesus had not in fact regarded himself as
the Son of Man who came to establish the Kingdom of God in the
world.[50]

John Knox, commenting on this argument, not only notes the *non
sequitur* involved—"are we to have such confidence in juridical
processes in general, and in those of Roman provincial government
in particular, as to assume that Jesus could not have been indicted
and crucified for a 'crime' of which he was entirely innocent?"[51]
—but objects to the idea that

Jesus could have been both aware of himself as "the Son of Man
who would one day come on the clouds of heaven" to establish "a kingdom which is not of this world" and at the same time recurrently or
constantly under temptation to head a Zealot movement to overthrow
the state by force of arms. What kind of mentality are we attributing to
Jesus when we make him subject to this kind of conflict and division?
. . . We repeat our conclusion that a sane man could hardly have
entertained such thoughts about himself.[52]

Now the issue here is not which of the two Biblical scholars is
correct. It is, rather, whether there are any distinctively Christian
warrants to which either does or could appeal to settle their
debate. Clearly there are not, unless one argues that the Christian
presupposition is that Jesus did, in fact, believe he was the Messiah. But this merely begs the issue. Nor does the appeal to

uniqueness help us any. If Jesus was unique, Cullmann would have no right to speak about Jesus' "inner conflict and division," since those terms presuppose certain analogies with our own human experience, and Knox could make no claims about what a sane man could or could not think. Indeed, the most interesting thing about this debate is that the two scholars *actually employ warrants that are not distinctively Christian at all.* And only because they necessarily do employ such warrants is it *possible for them to disagree* within their own Christian perspective.

The logical difficulty with the appeal to the uniqueness of the events in the New Testament is that it undercuts all the formalities of argument. It makes it impossible to isolate data (what kind of evidence testifies to a unique event?), to employ warrants, to offer a rebuttal, or to attach any degree of probability to a claim. The claim that an event is unique, when "unique" is used in more than a trivial sense, is compatible with an infinite range of contradictory assertions. If one historian, for example, argues that certain statements attributed to Jesus reflect a later development in Christian belief and so are not genuine, another can reply that the uniqueness of Jesus was that he could foresee the future. Or if someone objects to the argument that a bodily resurrection of Jesus is compatible with his corpse having remained in the tomb, the answer could be given that we are here dealing with a genuinely unique event. The question that arises in these cases is not, "Which scholar is right?" nor is it, "Did the event happen?" It is, rather, "What are we talking about?" The problem no longer has to do with the truth of the claim but with its meaning. It is not about any particular step in the argument but whether one could identify what a step would be.

Let us dwell briefly on this problem because it is important. Consider the common claim that the resurrection of Jesus is an event unlike any other and so is incapable of being judged by any canons of historical inquiry. When one insists, as Richard R. Niebuhr has, that "the resurrection of Christ does not violate Nature but only death,"[53] the real problem is to determine what we are talking about. Apart from the interesting question whether death is natural or not—and how would one go about deciding that issue?—the fact is that death occurs just often enough to occasion great surprise when we are told that a man suffered it but was resurrected. The surprise is so justifiable, in fact, that the burden of evidence falls on those who make the claim. In such cases, the first question a critical historian will ask is not, "What is the evidence for such an assertion?" but, "What is it that is being asserted?" He will not ask "Did it happen?" but "What does one mean by 'it'?"

Now this question is particularly relevant in the case of the arguments advanced by the author quoted above because, on the basis of historical criteria, he is willing to allow that the empty-grave tradition is a relatively late addition. Yet he insists that the appearance of Jesus involved "identification" and "recognition" and must, therefore, have had some connection with the "flesh insofar as it is the medium of recognition."[54] But the judgment that the empty-grave stories are late legendary additions presupposes just those normal criteria we are asked to suspend when examining the central content of the stories. Terms like "identification" and "recognition" and "flesh" necessarily involve appeal to certain nonunique aspects of human experience. Otherwise, what is the force of the claim that there *must* have been some connection with the flesh since this is the medium of recognition? Yet the qualification "insofar as" suggests a mysterious reservation, an "unfleshly flesh." Our naive minds, therefore, naturally reach out for something concrete, such as an empty tomb or the testimony of two men who talked with Jesus on the way to Emmaus or an appearance in which there was eating and drinking. These stories, it could be argued, express not so much the desire for proof, although that is not as unreasonable as we are commonly told, as the need for some specification of what one is being asked to believe. The critical historian can only turn to a scrutiny of the testimony. But this presupposes criteria of some sort, and this is exactly what the appeal to uniqueness precludes from the outset. There are no criteria for dealing with an event unlike any other.

To say that there is no way of knowing what would constitute a step in the argument is also to say that it is impossible to employ discriminating judgment, for not knowing what would constitute data, warrants, backings for warrants, or rebuttals is to say one does not know what force to give to a conclusion, what weight of assent is being invited from the reader. In fact, it is impossible under these conditions even to achieve the first phase of an argument, the sorting out of the likely candidates for a solution to a question. For our decisions about what may or may not possibly account for a certain testimony or a piece of evidence depend upon reasonings in the light of our normal beliefs about the way in which men and nature behave. Our reasoning is guided by a countless number of notions concerning the relevance of one sort of event to another, of motives to actions, of physical damage to pain, of weight to mass, etc. It is by virtue of these beliefs that we assess newspaper accounts, testimony in courts, the reliability of acquaintances and historians, and that we put question marks after stories of floating axes, suns standing still, asses talking, blood raining from heaven, supernatural births, walkings on water, and resurrections. When we understand this process, we will understand why we should not say that miracles are impossible so much as we should say either (1) that we do not think miracle is a likely candidate for being an explanation for an event, or (2) that we do not know what would constitute data, warrants, or a conceivable rebuttal to the conclusion that one had occurred. Consequently, we do not know how to qualify our conclusions, whether weakly, moderately, or strongly. We simply do not know what would "count for" an absolutely unique event. And when we also realize that miracle stories appear in most religious literature, a quite different explanation assumes the candidacy for a solution. In any event, we can see no reason (warrant) for believing in one set of miracles rather than another. Consequently, it seems to be a case either of accepting the perspective as a whole or of rejecting it, which is to say, of surrendering one's autonomy that is implicit in the critical morality of knowledge. If Christian historians themselves agreed either on their conclusions or their warrants, that might perhaps indicate we have judged too harshly. But it simply is no longer convincing to appeal to the Christian perspective and its presuppositions, especially when one is confronted by such diverse New Testament scholarship as is represented by Markus Barth,

Rudolf Bultmann, Oscar Cullmann, Floyd Filson, Ernst Fuchs, Robert Grant, Ernst Käsemann, C. H. Dodd, John Knox, Otto Piper, James M. Robinson, to mention only a few. We suspect that the differences between them are due not to the possession by some of the "eyes of faith" but must be explained by more mundane and diverse reasons: the uncritical nature of some of their reasoning, the lack of evidence which makes argument possible, the uses of different conceptual schemes to mediate their results, and the like. In any case, we can see no employment of distinctively Christian warrants for the settling of historical disputes.

7 · Soft Perspectivism and "Disclosure Situations"

It is clear that Hard Perspectivism, when used as a model to clarify the problem of faith and history, raises more questions than it answers. Yet, it is difficult to reject relativism outright. There are disagreements among historians and these disagreements do reflect the historians' perspectives. Whether a historian believes as a Marxist that all religious ideas are but epiphenomena of the class struggle, or whether, as a Freudian, he believes that these ideas are but the manifestation of unconscious psychological drives, or whether, as an existentialist, he thinks that they are to be understood as possibilities for existential self-understanding, he will naturally ask different kinds of questions, appeal to various sorts of data, and suggest those types of interpretation that are intelligible only in terms of his own point of view. Every age does rewrite its past, and relativism, it seems, holds this fact before our eyes.

At the beginning of this chapter, I suggested that relativism is not so much a systematic philosophy of history as a series of loosely knit but related arguments. For that reason, these arguments have been used in different ways by theologians. So far, we have analyzed one more or less characteristic form of use, Hard Perspectivism. I have noted, however, that there is another model, Soft Perspectivism, which, although it shares some elements in common with Hard Perspectivism, has distinctive emphases. Soft

Perspectivism employs a more qualified relativism, and, moreover, does so in such a way as not to deny the possibility of rational assessment. Nor does it reject the fact-significance distinction. Indeed, I shall argue that the entire position *rests on this distinction*.

Oddly enough, a good example of Soft Perspectivism is to be found in the most recent work of Richardson,[55] whose earlier work, *Christian Apologetics,* provided a characteristic example of Hard Perspectivism. Elements of his earlier view remain, to be sure, for he criticizes Bultmann and others for their rejection of miracles and the resurrection stories, and he accuses them of having embraced a positivistic history.[56] He also employs the now familiar argument that there are no uninterpreted facts, that what men call objective facts are nothing more than judgments about evidence, and since judgments about evidence reflect the historian's own personal faith, it follows that the Christian historian will accept certain data as evidence where a non-Christian historian will not. "The historian's final judgment of the evidence will, then, in the last resort, and after as rigorous a critical appraisal as he can make, be determined by the kind of man he is."[57]

Despite his frequent reliance on the more untenable sort of relativism, however, Richardson turns at the most crucial points in his argument to a more qualified relativism. The question, he insists, is not whether we are to be relativists but how far we will go in that relativism.[58] Personal viewpoints can be enlarged by discussion and criticism.[59] The "climate of opinion" is a metaphor useful only to a point, "but when it is pressed so far as to suggest that our thinking is totally conditioned . . . leads to absurdity. . . ."[60]

The degree of Richardson's modification of Hard Perspectivism can best be seen when he directs his attention to concrete illustrations of the meeting of faith and historical science. Faith, he argues, can best be understood as a response to a "disclosure situation," which is to say, the commitment to a certain profound meaning perceived in a historic event, the occurrence of which can be known by purely secular historical research. The Old Testament, especially, is concerned with just this kind of event. But the disclosure situations of the Old Testament, Richardson suggests, are not different in kind from those of other histories.

Their distinctive character consists in the depth of their penetration to that ultimate level where the nation, even one's own nation, is stripped of every pretence at self-justification and is brought to the recognition of basic moral issues and of its own costly vocation to serve the righteousness of God in the midst of a concrete historical situation. Though rooted in the particular predicaments of Israel's actual history, these disclosure situations illuminate the truth concerning the predicament of all nations in every age, the real situation of man as man. Israel's history is not unique, except in the sense that every nation's history is unique. . . . What is unique is the faith which arose out of obedience . . . to the moral truth which had been prophetically discerned in Israel's historical experience.[61]

This constitutes a remarkable departure from Richardson's earlier position. It is remarkable, first of all, because, as one reviewer of the later book has pointed out, this idea "is the same one propounded by Bultmann and von Rad," whom Richardson so harshly criticizes.[62] Consequently, Richardson inadvertently testifies to the strength of the very position he despises. But it is also remarkable because, in effect, he abandons any specifically Christian criteria for determining the origins and nature of the events in question, whether they happened at all or in the way they are alleged to have happened. The Christian historian as such has no special canons of evidence. He differs only in his attention to the dimension of depth in the event, to the illumination it casts on the "predicament of all nations in every age." In short, the Christian historian interprets the meaning that a public event has for faith. But this is just to presuppose the fact-significance distinction which Hard Perspectivism claims is untenable.

Insofar as Soft Perspectivism appeals to the meaning of an event, to its illumination of man's situation as man, it is confronted by the same theological problem which, as we saw in the last chapter, haunts the "new questers." If faith is, so to speak, the apprehension of the universal in the singular event, does this not reduce revelatory events to illustrations of timeless truths? If, to put the matter another way, the object of faith is a "complex of meaning," is it not more or less irrelevant whether the Biblical events happened in just the way they are said to have happened?

Richardson himself is obviously haunted by this question, just as the "new questers" were. He accuses von Rad of holding that "what matters is the existential understanding of the individual believer; the relation of such understanding to what actually happened in history is irrelevant."[63] But if this is so, Richardson complains, the existential meaning "becomes what each individual interpreter cares to make it; the one thing which it cannot be is what the Bible itself unanimously declares that it is, namely, the proclamation of God's Sovereignty over history, made manifest through prophetic faith, which discerns his saving acts amidst the crises of Israel's history."[64]

This criticism is scarcely a forceful one. In the first place, Richardson, when referring to the Exodus event as the paradigm of a "disclosure situation," has already conceded that historians are no longer able "to reconstruct in detail the story of 'what happened' at the coming out of Egypt. Perhaps nothing externally happened in Egypt or at the Red Sea or in the Wilderness which we today would not account for by natural means. . . ."[65] But, it may be asked, if no historian can recover what happened, what alternative is left but to say that the important thing was not what happened but the interpretation given to whatever happened by the community? Moreover, insofar as the supernatural elements predominate in the picture of the event preserved by the community, surely these elements must be interpreted as mythological ways of articulating the dimension of depth in the event. What else would it mean to say that the events were not unique in any external sense? Finally, if the significance of the event consists in its disclosure of man's situation as man, is it not probable that the same truth could be disclosed in histories other than that of Israel?[66]

It is clear that the problem, so far as this model is concerned, is the relation between the structure of an event and its meaning and how this can be described so that the morality of historical knowledge is not violated, on the one hand, and the distinctive claims of Christian faith are not sacrificed, on the other. Richardson's model is unable to do this because he clings to the remnants of Hard Perspectivism and because he insists on thinking of faith as belief in the fact that certain supernaturally caused events occurred, such as the resurrection of Christ. Yet, the model of Soft Perspectivism has obvious advantages. It avoids special pleading and permits rational assessment so far as statements about the nature and origins of events are concerned. It simply argues that these same events can have diverse meanings. The question is whether there is some way in which this problem can be resolved and these advantages can be conserved. This brings us to a consideration of the work of still one more theologian who has attempted to provide such a way within the context of relativism, H. Richard Niebuhr.

8 · *Faith and History as Inner and Outer History*

A fully objective history can be reconciled with a valid religious history, argues Niebuhr, only if one accepts the implications of historical relativism, on the one hand, and of radical monotheistic faith, on the other. Historical relativism means that there is no knowledge of things in themselves and that all knowledge is conditioned by the standpoint of the knower.[67] Radical monotheism dictates that God and faith belong together, that there can be no disinterestedness in theology. Consequently, Christian theology must be confessional and begin with revelation as understood from its own historically conditioned standpoint.

The implication of this, Niebuhr believes, is that objective history and religious history are not dealing with two different realities, nature and supernature, existing, as it were, side by side with the beholder's point of view taken as a constant. It was a great mistake, he suggests, when revelation was located in external history, which is to say in miracles and unusual events. The sacred is not to be identified with certain miraculous events not subject to the same type of explanations given for secular happenings; rather, the sacred is a way of talking about the value or significance of the so-called secular realm of events. We are dealing with the same event seen from two different perspectives.

Niebuhr's view is similar in many respects to Richardson's, although the comparison should be reversed, since Niebuhr's is the earlier one by two decades.[68] But Niebuhr's view, unlike Richardson's, is not marred by any attempt to resuscitate miracle or supernaturalism. Furthermore, Niebuhr, more than any other contemporary theologian, has gone on to explore the two major problems this creates for Christian theology: the relationship between the two kinds of history and the relationship between revelation and the wider structures of existence. The first problem will be discussed in this chapter; the second will be reserved for the final one.

Niebuhr explores the relationship between the two perspectives by distinguishing between two kinds of history: an external history, which is written from the standpoint of a disinterested observer, a standpoint that abstracts from the commitments and valuations of persons or selves; and an internal history which is written from the point of view of those whose lives have been decisively qualified by the events in question.[69] Just as there is a marked difference in kind between a doctor's clinical report about an operation in which the sight of a person has been restored and the diary of that blind person who has come to see, so, too, there will be a sharp difference between an objective, dispassionate account of an event and the account given by those for whom the event has a significant value. The data of external history are, Niebuhr argues, ideas, interests, objects, relationships among things. Internal history, on the other hand, is personal and valuational in nature. In external history the historian is concerned with an event's significance in terms of its long-range effects. In internal history, the narrator wishes to communicate the value the event has for selves. In the former, what has no important historic effects is eliminated; in the latter, what cannot be valued is more often dropped from memory. In external history, time is measured chronologically and impersonally. In internal history, what is past is kept alive in memory and continually impinges on the present. In the former, society is a group of atomic individuals, an organization of interests and drives. In the latter, society is a community of persons bound together by a common memory and loyalty.

In the New Testament, concludes Niebuhr, we are dealing with history from an internal point of view. It is a confession of a community that came into being by virtue of a response to a certain event. The community recalls that "critical point in their own life-time when they became aware of themselves in a new way as they came to know the self on whom they were dependent."[70] It is not that an internal history is more true than an external one but that the same reality can be seen in different aspects and in different contexts. Only in some such way as this can we see how "revelation can be in history and yet not be identifiable with miraculous events as visible to an external observer and how events that are revelatory in our history, sources of unconquerable certainty for us, can yet be analyzed in profane fashion by the observer."[71]

What, then, is the relationship between the two kinds of history, between the "I-Thou" character of internal history and the "I-It" nature of external history? Must we live with a "two-aspect theory" of history, a dualism in which one aspect has no intelligible relation to the other? Niebuhr argues that there is no speculative escape from the dilemma, although he thinks there may be a practical solution to it. There is no speculative escape because internal history cannot be absorbed into external history, and one cannot pass continuously from the external, nonparticipant's point of view to the participating history. "Only a decision of the self, a leap of faith . . . can lead from observation to participation and from observed to lived history."[72] So, too, it is impossible to transcend both the internal and external points of view so as to get a synthetic and, thus, superior knowledge of both.[73]

Nevertheless, Niebuhr believes that there is a kind of practical solution to the dualism confronting us. First of all, one can accept external views of oneself and try to make them inwardly significant.[74] To see ourselves as others see us is to have a moral experience and to let it become an event in our internal history. Gibbon's, Feuerbach's, and Kautsky's views of Christianity, for example, can be events in the internal life of Christendom. Actually, the necessity of seeing one's own history from an external point of view is a moral duty, Niebuhr claims. It is the attempt to see oneself as God does, for the deity regards history from both inner and outer points of view. This is a duty also because internal history cannot exist without external embodiment. Although revelation does not refer to historical facts, it occurs in facts. "External history is the medium in which internal history exists and comes to life."[75]

From the standpoint of the morality of historical knowledge and its relationship to faith, this model of Soft Perspectivism is a clear advance over the one offered by Richardson. In the first place, Niebuhr is far less ambiguous than Richardson in rejecting outright any sort of special pleading in the assessment of factual assertions made by Christians. "For sacred events in a secular context," he writes, "must be secularly apprehended and to demand of men that they should exempt certain events in the chain of perceived happenings from the application of the laws or principles with which they apprehend the others is to ask the impossible or to make everything unintelligible."[76] What Niebuhr sees is that the historicity of the historian includes his history as a member of Western culture who thinks with the warrants and criteria of Western man. The inner history of the Christian is not something completely isolated from secular history; rather the rise of secular history is an event within our inner history. The implications of this, as I shall point out below, are very important.

In the second place, Niebuhr's view presupposes a version of the fact-significance distinction which Richardson tends to obscure when he does not reject it. So far as Niebuhr is concerned, affirmations of faith occur on quite another level than do factual judgments. They have a different logic. He sees that it is one kind of problem to ascertain how and why the crucifixion of Jesus occurred; quite another to see in it an event which discloses the love of God or a judgment on one's own way of life. Consequently, there is a leap involved in passing from the external to the internal view, not in the sense of believing something to have happened that violates the morality of historical knowledge, but in the sense of seeing in the event a significance which revolutionizes one's own self-understanding. The discontinuity consists in the difference between believing that such and such occurred and believing that what occurred has such and such a significance for me.

Nevertheless, despite the virtues of this model, there are still certain ambiguities clinging to it. These ambiguities arise from

Niebuhr's too-simple division of history into inner and outer, a division that leads him to a confusing equivocation as to the meaning of external history. On the one hand, external history is analyzed by Niebuhr as disinterested history. On the other hand, external history is a category-bin, so to speak, into which he throws everything that is not the inner history of the Christian community, including all alien *internal* histories that cannot be characterized as either disinterested or objective. As a consequence, many distinctions that are important for the philosophy of history become blurred; for example, the distinction between points of view even within external history taken as a whole. Are economic, political, psychological, existential histories all to be defined as external?

This equivocation on the meaning of external history raises questions about the adequacy of Niebuhr's proposed practical solutions to the problem of the relationship between inner and outer history. He argues that it is necessary for those who stand within the inner history of Christianity to appropriate the external view of their history and to make it a moment of spiritual significance in their own lives. This raises no problems, perhaps, if that external history is merely a disinterested one, concerned, say, with a different set of relationships than concern the participant in an inner history. But if external history is to be defined as including all alien *internal* histories, how is it possible to internalize them, especially since Niebuhr himself seems to argue that we cannot penetrate into the inner histories of communities other than our own without abandoning our own point of view?[77] And yet, when Niebuhr enjoins the Christian to "see ourselves as others see us," he cites Gibbon, Feuerbach, and Kautsky as illustrations of external points of view we should internalize. None of them, however, fits Niebuhr's own criteria of disinterested history.

A related ambiguity arises when Niebuhr argues that an external history of itself is an inescapable duty for Christianity. This duty is laid upon Christians (1) because it is an attempt to see themselves through the eyes of God, who sees simultaneously both from within and without, and (2) because internal history is always embodied in the external.[78] So far as the first is concerned, we must ask whether it is possible to see oneself through the eyes of

God. Niebuhr's entire argument, in fact, rests on the assumption *that it is impossible* for human beings to synthesize inner and outer views or to contain them both in some superior vision. But if this is an impossible ideal, how can Niebuhr appeal to it as a moral duty? In fact, has he not tended to argue that because such an overview is impossible one must accept his conditioned and relative standpoint? Furthermore, in what sense does God see history from both an internal and external view if by external history we mean all internal histories not our own?

As soon as external history is defined as including alien internal histories, one has to reckon with the possibility of mutually self-contradictory internal histories. Does God judge them all to be equally true? If so, then the duty to see as he sees is meaningless. If not, then some internal histories must be judged to be false, and the question returns, how we can judge them to be so without abandoning our own point of view?

So far as the second is concerned, i.e., that internal history is embodied in the external, Niebuhr has introduced still a third meaning of external history, namely, the external facts which internal history interprets.[79] This is especially confusing because up to this point Niebuhr had used external history in a relational sense, that is, history as interpreted from some point of view. One can see the difficulty here if one were to substitute the words "alien internal history" for "external history" in this sentence: "External history is the medium in which internal history exists and comes to life."[80] We would then read it as follows: "Alien internal history is the medium in which internal history comes to life." But this makes no sense.

In the light of these ambiguities, the question arises whether we can preserve Niebuhr's valid insights, and those of Soft Perspectivism generally, while avoiding the ambiguities to which his views lead. We can do this, I believe, if we recognize (1) that his puzzles arise because of the too restrictive division of history into internal and external history, (2) that his own theory presupposes the ability to transcend one's own perspective, and (3) that perspectives are field-encompassing affairs that cannot be abstractly described.

The division of history into internal and external history ob-

scures the fact that there are not just two possible perspectives on
any given event or constellation of events but a plurality of them.
There is a multiplicity of possible inner histories just as there are a
number of possible external histories. From the standpoint of any
given perspective A, all of the others may, of course, be said to be
external to it. But this may be misleading, as we have pointed out.
For not all non-A perspectives are necessarily objective and disinterested in the way Niebuhr has defined them. Many of these non-
A perspectives may also be regarded as internal since they are
value-charged and nonobjective. Consequently, the problem is
really one of ascertaining the kind and level of assertions that
occur in differing perspectives and, in particular cases, discovering
the extent to which they are incompatible and mutually exclusive.

The key to grasping any perspective lies in understanding the
kind of purpose or the basic question that underlies it. In this
sense, Niebuhr is quite right in pointing out the importance of a
fundamental hermeneutical principle, namely, that one cannot
understand what another is trying to communicate unless he attempts to occupy the same standpoint, "to look in the same direction and to use the same instruments of measurement and analysis,
subject to the same conditions, as those which the original observer occupies, regards and uses."[81] For the purposes and questions with which one approaches any event will cause him to attend to some features rather than others and to relate the whole to
other events in quite unique ways.

But, it should be noted, just this principle assumes the ability
to transcend the limits of one's own perspective, an ability most
relativists have been inclined to deny. It assumes that one can
imaginatively enter the standpoint of another, even when that
standpoint is an alien one. Indeed, Niebuhr's own position, although occasionally ambiguous, presupposes this capacity of self-
transcendence by which one can see himself as others see him.

It does not follow, moreover, that once we understand what
another observer was trying to communicate we necessarily have
to agree with him. We may not be able to understand him unless we have put ourselves in his place and asked his questions.

But understanding is not agreement. One may ask the same questions and arrive at a somewhat different answer. We may even understand why the original observer was led to give the answer that he did and still judge that answer to be an inadequate or a wrong one. Indeed, we may even feel that from the standpoint *of his own perspective,* the answer was a poor one. Every historian of ideas sometimes has to make the judgment that he understands his subject better than the subject understood himself.

The difficulty with the overly restrictive division between internal and external history is that it obscures the complexity of standpoints. For any given perspective, as I have suggested many times previously in this book, contains a number of logical types of assertions. Perspectives are field-encompassing. They contain factual judgments, value-judgments, estimates of importance, metaphysical beliefs, assumptions about human nature, as well as procedural rules. This is why it is erroneous to speak as if there were a one-to-one correlation between any given historian's metaphysical beliefs and his concrete historical work.[82] Historians are frequently better, and worse, than their assumptions. One has to know in particular cases how their beliefs actually impinge on any given field and the arguments in that field.

So, too, because perspectives are so inclusive and field-encompassing, they frequently overlap. One might say that internal histories contain many external elements just as external histories are not lacking some of the characteristics of inner history. This is why historical disagreements are rarely, if ever, total in scope. More frequently, historians will agree at one level but disagree at another. It is quite possible, for example, that a Freudian, a Roman Catholic, and a Protestant will agree on a great number of details concerning Luther's career and thought, although they may disagree at other points. But even this example must be put forward with caution, for it is possible to write a Freudian biography of Luther that many Protestants would accept, just as it is true that some Catholic biographers are more in agreement with some Protestant interpreters of Luther than they are with other Catholic ones.

It is misleading, then, to place the Christian perspective over against any given other one as if they were necessarily mutually exclusive. Any modern Christian perspective will contain much that is not specifically Christian. Or, to put the matter abstractly, the historicity of the Christian historian includes the culture of the West (much external history in Niebuhr's sense) as well as that of his own narrower community of belief. The Christian's mind is informed by the physical science, sociology, economics, and psychology of his time, as well as by his own Christian convictions. Otherwise, Christians could not sit on juries with non-Christians or read the same newspapers atheists read. Believers have no distinctively Christian justificatory warrants for ascertaining whether Hitler was mad, Constantine wrote the famous Donation, Luther nailed his theses to the cathedral door, or, for that matter, whether Jesus was raised from the dead. The Christians' insights lie at a different level, at the level of the kinds of significance one attaches to these events which are otherwise known in the way any event can be known.

It is this last point that Niebuhr makes so eloquently and that Richardson sometimes sees when he is not seduced by the apologetic advantages of Hard Perspectivism. But if this model is to be regarded as a valid one, its use does raise a number of theological questions, not the least of which is how revelation can be regarded as a "disclosure situation" and still have the "once-for-all" character most Christians have claimed it has. How can revelation be regarded as the disclosure of a "dimension of depth" and not be viewed merely as an occasion for certain timeless truths? What is the relation between revelation and the wider structures of existence? It is to these questions we must now turn.

NOTES TO CHAPTER SEVEN

1. Carl L. Becker, "What are Historical Facts?" in Hans Meyerhoff (ed.), *The Philosophy of History in Our Time* (Garden City, N.Y.: Doubleday Anchor Books, 1959), p. 130.

2. *Ibid.*, p. 123.

3. The phrase is Charles A. Beard's; see Meyerhoff (ed.), *op. cit.*, pp. 141-151.

4. Although I have created the following argument as representative of a certain point of view, it has clear parallels to Alan Richardson's in *Christian Apologetics* (New York: Harper & Brothers, 1947).

5. *Ibid.*, chap. iv.

6. *Ibid.*, pp. 105 f.

7. *Ibid.*, p. 107.

8. *Ibid.*, p. 108.

9. *Ibid.*, p. 107.

10. See W. H. Walsh, *Philosophy of History* (New York: Harper Torchbooks, 1960), pp. 114 ff.

11. Richardson, *op. cit.*, p. 175.

12. *Ibid.*, p. 174.

13. T. A. Roberts refers to this as the Recording Angel view of history; cf. *History and Christian Apologetics* (London: S.P.C.K., 1960), p. 32.

14. See the discussion in William H. Dray, *Philosophy of History* (Englewood Cliffs, N.J.: Prentice-Hall, Inc., 1964), pp. 30 ff.

15. Morton White, "Can History Be Objective?" in Meyerhoff (ed.), *op. cit.*, p. 195.

16. See Roberts' criticism of Richardson, *op. cit.*, pp. 46 f.

17. Ernest Nagel, "The Logic of Historical Analysis" in Meyerhoff (ed.), *op. cit.*, pp. 209 ff.

18. Arthur O. Lovejoy, "Present Standpoints and Past History" in Meyerhoff (ed.), *op. cit.*, pp. 182 f.

19. See R. G. Collingwood, *An Autobiography* (Oxford: Oxford University Press, 1939), pp. 31 ff.; cf. Rudolf Bultmann, *Essays,* trans. James C. G. Greig (London: SCM Press Ltd., 1955), pp. 252-256.

20. Patrick Gardiner, *The Nature of Historical Explanation* (Oxford: Oxford University Press, 1952), p. 11.

21. Lovejoy in Meyerhoff (ed.), *op. cit.*, pp. 175 ff.

22. *Ibid.*, p. 179.

23. White, in Meyerhoff (ed.), *op. cit.*, p. 199.

24. Becker, in Meyerhoff (ed.), *op. cit.*, p. 135. Italics mine.

25. *Ibid.* Italics mine.

26. Richardson, *op. cit.*, p. 105; cf. p. 147.

27. See C. H. Dodd, *History and the Gospel* (New York: Charles Scribner's Sons, 1938), pp. 25 ff.; John Knox, *Christ the Lord* (Chicago: Willett, Clark & Co., 1945), pp. 1-7; Heinrich Ott, "The Historical Jesus and the Ontology of History" in Carl E. Braaten and Roy A. Harrisville (eds.), *The Historical Jesus and the Kerygmatic Christ* (New York: Abingdon Press, 1964), pp. 142-171; cf. Richardson, *op cit.*, pp. 147 ff.

28. Dodd, *op. cit.*, p. 27.

29. Knox, *op. cit.*, p. 4.

30. Marc Bloch, *The Historian's Craft,* trans. Peter Putnam (Manchester: Manchester University Press, 1954), pp. 60 ff.

31. *Ibid.*, p. 62.

32. Roberts has a devastating analysis of Dodd's formulation of the fact-significance distinction, *op. cit.*, pp. 86-95.

33. Becker in Meyerhoff (ed.), *op. cit.*, p. 136.

34. Richardson, *op. cit.*, p. 105.

35. Knox, *op. cit.*, p. 6.

36. *Ibid.*, p. 12. Italics mine.

37. *Ibid.*, p. 14.

38. *Ibid.*, p. 15.

39. *Ibid.*, pp. 19 ff.

40. C. H. Dodd, *op. cit.*, p. 60.

41. Knox, *op. cit.*, p. 67.

42. *Ibid.*, p. 60.

43. *Ibid.*, p. 61.

44. Roberts, *op. cit.*, p. 113; cf. Christopher Blake in Patrick Gardiner (ed.), *Theories of History* (Glencoe, Ill.: The Free Press, 1959), pp. 341 f.

45. Richardson, *op. cit.*, pp. 105 f.

46. *Ibid.*, p. 147; cf. W. H. Walsh, *op. cit.*, chap. iv.

47. Richardson, *op. cit.*, p. 175.

48. See William E. Kennick, "Metaphysical Presuppositions," *The Journal of Philosophy*, LII (1955), 769-780.

49. See Walsh, *op. cit.*, pp. 103-109.

50. Quoted by Knox in *The Death of Christ* (New York: Abingdon Press, 1958), p. 66.

51. *Ibid.*, pp. 66 f.

52. *Ibid.*, p. 67.

53. Richard R. Niebuhr, *Resurrection and Historical Reason* (New York: Charles Scribner's Sons, 1957), p. 177.

54. *Ibid.*, p. 173.

55. Alan Richardson, *History Sacred and Profane* (Philadelphia: Westminster Press, 1964).

56. *Ibid.*, pp. 139-147.

57. *Ibid.*, p. 203.

58. *Ibid.*, p. 250.

59. *Ibid.*, p. 251.

60. *Ibid.*, p. 254.

61. *Ibid.*, p. 226.

62. See the review by Norman Perrin in *The Christian Advocate*, VIII (Oct. 22, 1964), 19.

63. Richardson, *History Sacred and Profane*, p. 233.

64. *Ibid.*

65. *Ibid.*, p. 224.

66. Richardson appeals to I. T. Ramsey's "most valuable clarification of terminology." But Ramsey's use of the term "disclosure situation" refers to certain common features (covering law) any historian would have to acknowledge and which are clues to understanding *other historical situations in the present.* See, *ibid.*, p. 224, n. 1.

67. H. Richard Niebuhr, *The Meaning of Revelation* (New York: The Macmillan Co., 1946), p. 7.

68. Oddly enough, Richardson makes no mention of H. R. Niebuhr.

69. H. R. Niebuhr, *op. cit.*, pp. 59-90.

70. *Ibid.*, p. 72.

71. *Ibid.*, p. 82.

72. *Ibid.*, p. 83.
73. *Ibid.*, p. 83 f.
74. *Ibid.*, p. 84 f.
75. *Ibid.*, p. 90.
76. *Ibid.*, p. 76.
77. *Ibid.*, p. 82.
78. *Ibid.*, p. 88 f.
79. *Ibid.*, p. 89.
80. *Ibid.*, p. 90.
81. *Ibid.*, p. 13.
82. I have tried to show this in the case of Strauss; see "D. F. Strauss' *Life of Jesus* Revisited," *Church History*, XXX (1961), 191-211.

VIII

Faith, Images, and the Christian Perspective

1 · In Retrospect

IN the preceding chapters, I have attempted to show that there was much truth in Ernst Troeltsch's prophetic claim that the emergence of the historical-critical method presupposes a revolution in the consciousness of Western man so profound that it necessarily requires a reappraisal of many of the basic assumptions of Christian belief. By exploring the morality of historical knowledge I have tried to indicate how and why this morality seems to conflict with the implicit ethic of belief that has been normative for most of Christendom. I have suggested that this conflict is so profound that much of recent Protestant theology may be regarded as a series of salvage operations, that is, attempts to reconcile the ethic of critical historical inquiry with the apparent demands of Christian faith. They are efforts to turn aside the criticism that one can be a believer only at the price of sacrificing the standards of truth and honesty which have dominated the scholarly community since the Enlightenment. We have noted that there is considerable pathos in these apologetic efforts. It was, after all, Christianity itself which tutored the Western mind to believe that it should know the truth and the truth would make it free. But now that the student has learned to prize the truth, he has discovered, with pain both to himself and his teacher, that it can only be gained at the cost of rejecting the one who first instilled in him the love of it.

To some readers, the foregoing analysis must appear to be largely negative in its import, wholly determined by a systematic criticism of the alternatives proffered by others. He might ask, then, whether the author has nothing positive and constructive of his own to propose. Has he no castle that he is willing to defend after he has finished his sallies against the fortresses of others?

This is a fair question, although the warlike metaphor too easily reinforces the tendency to think that my analysis has been wholly destructive in kind. For if modern analytic philosophy has taught us anything, surely it is that a systematic "unpacking" of the issues can itself have a therapeutic function, that criticism can itself prove illuminating if it reveals in any given case why an alternative is deficient. For only when we know what went wrong and why, will it be possible to construct a more enduring castle. Furthermore, it is not true that the criticisms were totally annihilating. Although each of the proffered solutions did prove to err in some important respect, they did not all err in the same respect. This also is instructive. It suggests that each alternative has something positive to contribute to, as well as something negative to be avoided in, a new solution.

Consider, first, one of the positive things achieved by a systematic "unpacking" of the issues. It has delivered us from the deceptive lure of such abstractions as "the historical method" or "historical reason" or "the presuppositions of history." By blurring fine but important distinctions, these abstractions tempt us to look for wholesale answers to what are, in fact, retail questions. Although these omnibus terms are, like a terminological shorthand, sometimes useful, they too easily become substitutes for patient and careful thought. I have tried to show, for example, that the morality of historical knowledge is not one thing but many related things. It refers to the autonomy of the historian, but this autonomy, in turn, is meaningless unless it is seen as a part of the process of rationally assessing justificatory arguments. Justificatory arguments, however, have a complex structure. This structure may be viewed as a skeletal framework of data, warrants and their backings, rebuttals, and conclusions. This structure casts considerable light on the quality of the historian's assent and why this quality plays such an important role in the evaluations historians make of one another.

When we inspected the role of warrants in historical arguments, we noticed another interesting feature, namely, that there are no warrants peculiar to history as such. History is a field-encompassing field. Since this is so, we immediately suspected those revolutionary programs in which one model of history is declared to be the only valid one. We rejected the idea that there is one clear and distinct conception of true historical understanding, whether it be rethinking past thought, or the deductive use of laws, or "the grasp of existential selfhood," or a dispassionate description of the facts. We saw that these programmatic models create needless puzzles and paradoxes: Is an irrational action historical? What laws did the biographer of Hitler use? Is the history of a plague to be counted as history? Must a historian tell all the facts? Analysis, happily, delivers us from the need to wrestle with these puzzles, because it has already delivered us from the assumption that there must be one paradigm for understanding the work of the historian. Is this to be dismissed as a negative result?

Or consider how the "unpacking" of the issues has been therapeutic in still another way. It put us on guard against a well-known but deceptive phenomenon: a badly formulated thesis not only creates needless puzzles and paradoxes but often generates an equally unclear antithesis. The history of philosophy is replete with examples of this, and so is the debate over the problem of faith and history. Consider, for example, the sweeping assertion that "all good historical inquiry is without presuppositions." This claim has generated an equally sweeping counterclaim: "Every historian has his presuppositions." Both claims are not so much false as crude, and lead, therefore, to confusion. It is false to argue that the historian is without presuppositions, as if his task were merely to discover the facts and let them speak for themselves. But it does not follow from this concession that "every man is his own historian." Historians have presuppositions but these are of different sorts. They vary in tightness from field to field. Some may be indubitable, some more or less well-founded, others arbitrary and false. One must always look at the individual case and the respective field. This illumines, as we have seen, why it is so misleading when a Christian apologist argues from the premise that every historian has his presuppositions to the conclusion that the Christian historian has his own faithlike presupposition. The field-encompassing nature of history immunizes us against such arguments. We see that historians do not carry around monolithic sets of warrants that apply in the same way in every field.

Consider still another example of the way in which a rough assertion may dominate a discussion just to the degree it has been permitted to go unanalyzed. Take the familiar dictum "Christian faith cannot be dependent on the probabilities of historical research," a dictum that was accepted in essence if not in wording by Lessing, Kierkegaard, Herrmann, Kähler, and the dialectical theologians. This dictum is immediately countered by another one: "The Christian faith must take the full risk of the ambiguity of the historical." If our analysis is correct, both of these assertions are muddled. The thesis is confused because, as we have seen, all of our beliefs presuppose a knowledge of the past and are, in that sense, dependent on historical inquiry. As Collingwood pointed out, there are historical components in all of our knowing. This is as true of the white-coated scientist and of the mathematician as it is of the professional historian. The scientist and the mathematician have to read the texts and the scribblings of their colleagues, that is, they have to reconstruct past thought and thus, in their own way, are historians. Since this is so, it would seem odd, indeed, if Christian belief did not depend on some historical knowledge. And if historical criticism is but a more exacting and formalized procedure for sorting out the true and the false, how can faith be independent of all historical criticism? Even the "picture of Christ" in the New Testament, of which Kähler and Tillich speak as though it were independent of criticism, can be abstracted only by an act of the historical imagination. And Bultmann's *kerygma* can be reconstructed only by a highly sophisticated process of historical reasoning.

The real issue, then, is not whether faith is independent of all historical criticism but whether Christian faith requires certain specific historical assertions that, in the nature of the case, are dubious or not fully justified. But if this is the issue, one must examine such assertions piecemeal. One must ask in each particular case what degree of certitude is warranted. Once we engage in such a procedure, we will immediately see why the counterassertion "faith must take the full risk of the ambiguity of the historical" is also undiscriminating. The point is that some historical judgments require more of a risk than others. It is one thing to stake one's faith on the veracity of the story of the three wise men, another on the messianic consciousness of Jesus, still another on his crucifixion. The first two beliefs require risks that are not entailed by the last. The dramatic call to take upon ourselves the full ambiguity of the historical conceals this important fact.

There is a second point at which the "unpacking" of the issues has had a positive function. Although all of the various theological salvage operations seem inadequate, they are inadequate in quite different respects. The new quest, for example, is inadequate for quite different reasons than Hard Perspectivism is. Correspondingly, none of the various solutions is wholly wrong. Each has certain strengths. Dialectical theology is important because it makes clear that the so-called secular morality of knowledge cannot be dismissed merely because it is a child of rationalism. It has important affinities with the Protestant conception of justification by faith, with what H. Richard Niebuhr has called "radical monotheism." All of the dialectical theologians, including Karl Barth in his early period, argue that the conflict with historical inquiry arises only if faith is regarded as assent to certain historical propositions. The problem with dialectical theology, however, is that it did not know what to do with this insight. This, in turn, is not unrelated to (1) its uncritical acceptance of the dictum "faith cannot be dependent on the probabilities of historical research," and (2) its attempt to conserve the once-for-all saving act of God in Jesus of Nazareth. The radical idea of faith coupled with an avoidance of all historical assertions leads, on the one hand, to a certain formlessness. The attempt to conserve the language about a decisive saving act of God in Christ, on the other hand, contradicts the radical idea of faith and precipitates a conflict with historical criticism, which is just what the dialectical theologians hoped to avoid.

The theologians of the new quest quite properly react against the formless description of faith. They sense that the Christian consciousness is unintelligible without reference to the concrete image of Jesus, that it is precisely the content (*das Was*) of this image, in contrast to the mere fact that something happened, that constitutes its power. The new quest, however, makes the fundamental error of identifying the content of the image with a dubious historical judgment about Jesus' existential selfhood. By tying the content of faith to the faith of Jesus, they link the certitude of the believer to a historical judgment that is least able to support it. This is not only intolerable from the standpoint of the ethic of historical judgment but it inevitably undermines faith itself.

The failure of the new quest also illustrates our earlier point, that a too quick reaction to a false thesis often leads one to embrace an equally false antithesis. By overreacting to the positivistic claim that history is concerned only with the facts, the "new questers" make the fatal error of trying to justify an opposite but equally monolithic program for historical understanding. Instead of patiently showing how positivism contains some truth but obscures the varieties of historical judgment—its field-encompassing nature—the new quest goes to the opposite extreme and absolutizes one model of historical understanding.

The new quest is not without its positive aspects, however. Insofar as it properly employs the existentialist model of history, it makes clear that there is a way of interpreting historical events and texts that has its own integrity and that does not require a sacrifice of the intellect. There is a way of asking questions that does not so much involve a rejection of other kinds of understanding as it simply reflects another perspective, another angle of vision, so to speak. Unlike the traditional Christian historian or the Hard Perspectivist, the theologian of the new quest does not argue that the Christian historian has a different standard for the determination of fact. He insists only that a fact may mean different things to different standpoints and that there is one standpoint at least from which one may pose certain basic and fundamental human questions.

By practicing this kind of interpretation, by asking what possibilities for self-understanding may be seen beneath the various and conflicting first-century modes of thought, the "new questers" discover that there is a profound continuity between the teaching of Jesus and the *kerygma*. This is an important point. In the first place, it blunts the edge of the sharp distinction between the Jesus of history and the Christ of faith. In the second place, it suggests a new theological possibility, namely, that the heart of both the *kerygma* and the proclamation of Jesus is a certain understanding of man before God, that it is the anthropology which is the constant and the christology that is the variable.[1]

The proponents of the "new quest" are unable to explore this insight freely because they are afraid of giving aid and comfort to the "left-wing Bultmannians," like Fritz Buri and Schubert Ogden, who, it is alleged, want to reduce the *kerygma* to the symbol of a timeless truth. But, it may be asked, is this another of those false and artificial distinctions? What if symbol and event, timeless truth and history, are not strict alternatives?

The conclusion which we reached at the end of the chapter dealing with the new quest was buttressed by our analysis of Soft Perspectivism. For Soft Perspectivism also makes use of the idea of a perspective, a "disclosure situation." The difference between the believer and the unbeliever is not whether a given event occurred; rather, the difference lies in the way the event is interpreted, the significance attributed to the event. This difference in perspective may be such that the two descriptions of the same event also differ, but the two descriptions are not logically incompatible in the way that two differing claims over whether it happened or not are incompatible. It is one kind of debate, for example, whether or not Luther ever did revolt against the church; it is quite another whether or not that revolt can best be interpreted in psychoanalytic terms or in religious terms. Any given historical event, so to speak, makes claims in several different directions, and not all of them are mutually incompatible. Moreover, these interpretations presuppose that there is some "given" to be interpreted and, as we have seen, it is just this insight we presuppose in the rough distinction between fact and interpretation.

The cumulative effect of our analysis of dialectical theology, the new quest, and Soft Perspectivism, therefore, is to suggest that this perspective model is the one least open to objection from the standpoint of the morality of knowledge. The task, then, is to explore its theological possibilities. I am aware that this task can scarcely be accomplished with any degree of rigor in the final chapter of a book; indeed, nothing less is required than a systematic reappraisal of Christian theology in the light of the historicity of the theologian. Nevertheless, it might prove fruitful to sketch the outlines of a model and to suggest at important points how one might deal with the obvious objections that will arise in the reader's mind when he considers it. It is to this task that I now turn.

2 · Paradigmatic Events

In his book *The Meaning of Revelation,* H. Richard Niebuhr suggests that revelation might best be understood as an event that so captures the imagination of a community that it alters that community's way of looking at the totality of its experience. It is an event that strikes the community as illuminatory for understanding all other events. Just as we are sometimes perplexed by a complicated argument in a difficult book and suddenly come across a luminous sentence from which we can go forward and backward and so attain a comprehension of the whole, so revelation may be understood as an event that makes other events meaningful.[2] Niebuhr had been struck by a similiar insight that occurs in Alfred North Whitehead's *Religion in the Making.* "Rational religion," Whitehead wrote, "appeals to the direct intuition of special occasions, and to the elucidatory power of its concepts for all occasions. It arises from that which is special, but it extends to what is general."[3]

There are many suggestive aspects of this model. First of all, there is the idea that certain concrete events or experiences have the capacity to bring about a new orientation. in thought. They impose, so to speak, a certain perspective on us. When viewed in the light of a certain question, they call forth a new understanding or resolve. Second, there is the suggestion that such events or experiences capture the imagination because they seem to be bearers of a wider meaning or significance. They have a paradigmatic or iconic character. The event fuses, so to speak, singularity and universality. Third, Whitehead, especially, makes a distinction between the concrete image cast up by the event and the concepts that are abstracted by the reason. The imagination is dominated by the image, but the image may be rationalized because it contains the universal in the particular.

The notion that there are events that *impose* a perspective upon us may be misleading because it does not take sufficient account of the creativity and spontaneity of the knower, that there are any number of possible contexts in which an event can be interpreted. On the other hand, there is a sense in which certain events more than others thrust certain questions upon us and lend themselves more naturally, therefore, to certain kinds of interpretations. This is especially clear with respect to a person like, say, the Buddha. His life was apparently so focused, his action and conduct so intentional, that certain kinds of questions and interests come effortlessly to the mind which confronts him. Consequently, we call him a religious figure, although his life might be interpreted from a number of other points of view, all undergirded by different interests. Or, appealing to less obvious examples, we might note that although the figure of Socrates can be variously interpreted, philosophical and ethical categories are more germane to understanding it than those, say, of sexuality or mathematics. To say that certain events impose their own categories is to say that these events have the power to demand a consideration on their own terms, so to speak, that there are some ways of interpreting them less eccentric than others. They intrude certain questions and images upon us because they seem to touch human experience and feeling at some primordial level. They speak to our hopes and fears. Consequently, they provide us with the symbols and parables for the interpretation of our existence.

An event may be significant in different ways, and some events have the capacity to intrude not one but several important questions. There will be others whose range of meanings is more circumscribed, whose force, so to speak, is concentrated at one point.

So, too, there are various levels of meanings any event may have and, depending on the level and kind of meaning, it will tend to evoke certain qualitative responses, such as fear, admiration, disgust, horror, pity, awe, ethical resolution. Consequently, certain events lend themselves to immortalization. A community preserves the event in legend or song and uses it as a vehicle for expressing its own self-understanding and for inculcating the young in the values and ethos of that community. History casts up archetypes, and in relating oneself to these archetypes one can relate himself to an entire constellation of beliefs that are implicit in them.

There is nothing esoteric about this phenomenon. Consider, for example, the assassination of President Kennedy. This event was significant in many different directions, which is to say, it was a historic event. The chief of state of perhaps the most powerful nation in the world was murdered by a neurotic and hate-filled youth. That fact alone causes to arise certain basic historical questions: What was the effect of the President's murder on the struggle between the East and the West? What alterations of power did it occasion within the Democratic and Republican parties here in America? What did it reveal about the stability of presidential succession in this democracy?

But there was another dimension of meaning to the Kennedy murder, a dimension that, in the nature of the case, intrudes other kinds of questions. He was obviously more than a chief executive. To countless numbers of people, he was also the symbol of a new style of patriotism and leadership. To an age that had known two world wars and was disillusioned by their aftermaths, the President represented a new possibility for understanding political involvement. A hero in war, a man of reason, wit, self-confidence, tolerance, urbanity, and realism, he seemed to many to epitomize the ideal of the twentieth-century man.

Given this basic image, it is intelligible why the murder of Kennedy touched deep human feelings, why it awakened more powerful questions than those historical ones above. There were, in fact, thousands of people thrown into silent despair by this event, a despair that may be explained in terms of personal loss, though not wholly so. The event seemed also to symbolize the senselessness of existence itself, the murder of a man of style and reason by a Dostoevskian underground man who had no sense of either.

There were those living in Dallas who felt something like this even more acutely because what they respected in Kennedy seemed mocked by the violent and fantastic deeds that both preceded and followed his murder: the smoldering political hysteria in the city that erupted in a physical attack on the ambassador to the United Nations only a month before, the abuse of the civil rights of the President's assassin, his own murder in the jailhouse, the cheering in the streets about this news by women who themselves were presumably grieving for the man of reason, the self-righteous attempts of the civic leaders to assure the nation that Dallas was a "friendly city," the economic reprisals taken against those who dared to suggest that all of these things revealed how sick the city was. Amidst this nightmarish series of events, there appeared on television an interview with Governor John B. Connally, Jr., who was himself recovering from a near-fatal wound inflicted by the same weapon that killed the President. Asked by the reporter what his reflections were, he remarked that he had been haunted by the question why the President had been killed and he, the Governor, remained alive. Had he any kind of answer to such a question? Only this, he replied,

that the President of the United States, as a result of this great tragedy, has been asked to do something in death that he couldn't do in life—and that is to so shock and so stun the nation, the people and the world of what's happening to us—of the cancerous growth that's been permitted to expand and enlarge itself upon the community and the society in which we live that breeds the hatred, the bigotry, the intolerance and indifference, the lawlessness that is, I think, an outward manifestation of what occurred here in Dallas. . . . I'm not the least fearful of any foreign enemy so long as we have within ourselves not hate but human understanding, not passion and prejudice but reason and tolerance and not ignorance but knowledge and the willingness to use that knowledge. This is the only answer I can give . . . why he's gone and I'm not.[4]

For some, Connally's witness formulated the meaning the entire series of events must have for them, not in the sense of providing a providential explanation for why one man was alive and another dead, but in the sense of providing an occasion for resolving once again to embody and foster the self-understanding that was epitomized in the Kennedy image and that Connally represented in his word about the martyred president. And there were those who, then and there, covenanted with themselves and others to preserve just this significance and never again to let political slander or bigotry in their city go unchallenged.[5]

Abstractly expressed, every event has a number of potential meanings. Furthermore, the kind of meaning one sees in it will dictate appropriate postures and attitudes. It would, for example, seem strange indeed for a future historian to commit himself irrevocably to the thesis that Kennedy's death altered the relationship between Russia and the West, or to the proposition that it disclosed the stability of the processes by which presidential power was transferred. But it would not seem odd if this historian were to be strangely moved by this event to raise the question about the meaninglessness of existence itself and should resolve to embody certain ideals of reason and charity henceforth in his own historical work.

A paradigmatic event is one that fuses concreteness and a wider meaning. The more fundamental the meaning, the more the event becomes capable of being transformed into myth, where "myth" does not mean a false story but a highly selective story that is used to structure and convey the basic self-understanding of a person or a community. A pattern is abstracted from the event and becomes the formalized parable that is used to interpret larger tracts of history and experience. This parable is preserved and retold in order to reaffirm the faith and values of the community and to communicate them to its young. The images derived from it constitute the key to that community's elemental confidences.

Martin Buber uses the term *"Sage"* to illustrate this mythologization of history in the Old Testament.[6] By *"Sage"* he means the preservation, often in poetic and rhythmical form, of the immediate response of the community to an event it regards as decisive for its life. It is not scientific history in the sense of an exact reconstruction of what really happened; on the other hand, it is not fantasy. It is the expression of a profound wonder and enthusiasm that has gripped a people. Buber even goes so far as to argue that the poetic form of *Sage* attests its authenticity; because if it did not attain strict form at the time of the event, it would lend itself to the elaboration of later narrators. One need not agree with this conclusion to argue that there is a sense in which *Sage* represents something more like a bas-relief, or what Peter Munz has called "telescoped history."[7] A significant pattern has been worked loose from the event, a pattern that reflects, of course, the specific interest and perspective of the community. But the pattern is not an arbitrary one. *Sage* is not a myth which is then projected into history; it is a creative and interpretative response to a historical event.

The distinctive characteristic of religious paradigmatic events, in contrast to those of political or national groups, is that these events are believed to focus some insight into the nature of reality itself, or more precisely into the nature of reality so far as it bears on the human quest for liberation and fulfilment. To be sure, every political or national paradigmatic event may have some implicit or indirect bearing on the religious quest and, therefore, the lines between political and religious events are frequently hazy. Nevertheless, a religious paradigmatic event is one that intrudes the most fundamental questions concerning the character and trustworthiness of being itself. It constitutes what William A. Christian has called a "suggestion," a central focus of illumination that provides the basis for interpreting life as a whole.[8] This is the reason why these images can be rationalized into theologies and metaphysics. They contain concepts that provide an orientation for thinking about existence itself. Religions arise from the special but they extend to what is general.

3 · *Religions as Symbolic Perspectives*

A religion, abstractly speaking, may be regarded as a perspective, a standpoint, in which certain dominant images are used by its adherents to orient themselves to the present and the future.[9] It may be understood as a way of looking at experience as a whole, or better, as a way of interpreting certain elemental features of human existence. This model, I believe, is a very useful one for helping us deal with the problem of faith and history. It sheds much light on the relationships between events and symbols and the kinds of certitude one has. Since this model has also been used by those philosophers who have argued that religious perspectives are noncognitive ones, I believe myself obligated to clarify the model at points that might not otherwise seem directly relevant to the discussion in the preceding chapters.

The very use of the term "perspective" suggests a visual and, correspondingly, a spatial analogy. It calls to mind a situation in which some given object, like a coin, is seen differently depending on the location of the observer. Thus the coin will appear as a vertical line to one, an ellipse to another, and a circle to still another. This visual analogy is not the most helpful one, however, because it relies too heavily on our perceptual, in contrast to our conceptual, experience. It does not, therefore, sufficiently illumine the distinctive aspects of theoretical or interpretive perspectives. For when we speak of an interpretive standpoint, we are not so much calling attention to the inherent limitations on perception as we are to the various possible ways one can organize any given experience. We are pointing out the ways in which the aims, purposes, and questions of an observer influence the way he describes an object and relates it, in turn, to other objects of his experience. We are noting the way a model can enable us to see a pattern in things we otherwise would have regarded differently, or how a suggestion can change our perspective on other facts. If an artist and a scientist, for example, talk differently about the redness of a sunset, it is not because they have a different visual standpoint but because their interests dictate different kinds of descriptions, explanations, and language.[10]

Underlying the model of an interpretive perspective is the insight that the mind is not a mere receiver of sensations, a blank slate on which experience writes. The mind, rather, is active and selective in its thinking and experiencing. It comes to reality with determinate questions that presuppose certain purposes, and these, in turn, incline it to attend to these rather than those features and to make these rather than those possible distinctions. Reality does not dictate its own categories; rather, the mind organizes and conceptualizes its experience under the dominance of certain interests. Nor can any one concept exhaustively describe an object, for our concepts reflect our apprehension of certain relationships and these, in turn, are relative to some concern. Our concepts are always selections and abstractions in the light of some subjective aim. They always contain an interpretive element.

Some students of language have been so impressed by the way in which even our ordinary language, not to speak of our technical vocabularies, presupposes interests and aims that they have argued, as Ernst Cassirer has, that language itself makes perceptual distinctions possible. They insist that the distinctions do not lie in reality itself but are created by language. It follows, so it is alleged, that it is meaningless to talk about the inherent structure of things, because the only structures humans can apprehend are those already constituted by language. The structures of existence come into existence through the process of naming them.[11]

It is not possible or necessary here to debate this question. One may say that Cassirer's basic intention was a valid one. He wished to call attention to the various possible and autonomous ways of organizing experience in contrast to those philosophers who have insisted that there is only one legitimate mode of cognition, namely, science. But it is confusing, I think, to argue that the structures of existence come into existence by naming them, if by that we mean that the mind is, so to speak, a prisoner of its language and can perceive nothing but what its tyrannical jailor permits. It would be more accurate to say that language itself arises out of certain needs to discriminate among given structures and relationships. Although language imposes restrictions, it also is an extraordinarily adaptable instrument. We are constantly experimenting with and altering our categories so that we can deal more adequately with our environment. Our basic categorical schemes may in some sense be arbitrary, but they are not completely arbitrary. Given certain purposes, some are more adequate than others, and this is impossible to explain unless we presuppose some objective and given structures. If, for example, we are told that the Haida language classifies all objects according to their shape (long, slender, round, flat, angular, etc.) to the disregard of all other possible relationships and structures, this does not mean that the classification is completely subjective and has no relationship to the external world. The shapes are there and presumably could be recognized even by a person who did not know that language or who possessed one based on a different classification scheme. Language does not create the structures; rather, the knower discriminates among objects and relationships by means of language.

The concepts and symbols we use, the means by which we isolate and attend to some pattern of things rather than others, arise out of lived experience and may be understood as presupposing an objective order and an interpretive response to that order in the light of some predominant concern. Now there are, of course, any number of possible concerns, but any observer of human culture cannot help but notice three or four predominant types: the scientific, the aesthetic, the moral, the religious. Within these overall types of basic human activities there is an extraordinary wealth of diversity. But given a dominating interest, certain features of experience will tend to require explanation and symbolization in contrast to others.

Actually, the single term "religious" is somewhat misleading. There is no religious perspective as such any more than there is a scientific or an artistic perspective. There are only religions, scientific theories, and artistic forms of expression of various types. Nevertheless, there are family resemblances among these forms of human activity that justify classifying them as one or the other. And of those family resemblances that characterize religions, the chief one is the preoccupation with certain universal and elemental features of human existence as they bear on the human desire for liberation and authentic existence. The most obvious of these elemental features are finitude and contingency, the perpetual perishing of everything that is, the fact of order, and the fittingness of certain kinds of being for other beings (value).[12] In one way or another, these basic elements appear in different guises in all of the great world religions, the differences being a function of the priorities assigned to this or that feature, the qualitative characteristics associated with them, and the dominating conception of how human life can best be fulfilled in relation to all of them.

The great religions are total in scope. They are ways of relating the subject to the whole of life; their objects of devotion and basic symbols are, therefore, always cosmological and metaphysical. On the other hand, these metaphysical beliefs are always viewed in their relationship to the human quest for liberation and fulfilment. Consequently, religious language and symbolism are rarely abstract and theoretical in character but are expressive and prescriptive. Religions dictate "right knowledge" and "right conduct." The truths to which they point are always seen as constituting "the way." Nevertheless, within and underlying these prescriptive utterances is an implicit ontology, a descriptive element. It is just this feature that accounts for the believer's conviction that his religion is true, for there is enough correlation between symbol and reality to seem to justify his confidence in his beliefs. It also accounts for the fact that observers may extract theoretical elements and offer philosophical translations of religious symbols. Religions are interpretive perspectives, albeit of a unique logical type.

Many contemporary philosophers of religion, as well as some theologians, resist the idea that religions are interpretive of anything, which is to say, they argue that they are noncognitive.[13] These philosophers point out that statements about the whole of reality are not falsifiable in the way that scientific judgments are. Consequently, they conclude, religious assertions are not about anything. They are really statements about certain human attitudes and commitments. They are the expressions of one's intentions and values.

This analysis, I believe, is too crude. First of all, it fails to illumine the complexity of religious perspectives, the fact that they contain many logically diverse kinds of assertions: metaphysical, historical, anthropological, valuational, aesthetic, moral, etc. There is no one thing that qualifies as a religious judgment any more than there is one genre of language called religious language. Secondly, it is one thing to say that the metaphysical beliefs implicit in religions are noncognitive in the sense of not being falsifiable in some precise way; it is quite another thing to say that they are not *about* anything, that they refer to nothing. In one sense, of course, they do not refer to any particular thing. In another sense, however, they are referential because they are attempts to symbolize certain basic elements that characterize all things: contingency, change, order, value. These beliefs are, to be sure, "logically odd," but to say they are odd is only to say that they are odd, not that they are nonreferential.

It is R. M. Hare who, perhaps, first uses the word *blik* to point out that there are ways of looking at experience that rest on deeper assumptions which the linguistic philosopher must of necessity consider to be logically peculiar because these assumptions cannot be empirically proved to be true or false.[14] Yet these assumptions are so important that were they to be denied, these ways of looking and interpreting would have to be radically changed. Hare attributes this insight to David Hume who, he says, taught us that our entire commerce with the world rests on such logically odd beliefs. As an example, Hare asks us to consider the belief that everything happens by chance. In one sense, this statement does not assert anything that could be proved to be true or false, since this belief, as well as its contradictory, is compatible with anything happening or not happening. On the other hand, if we believed this, we could not plan or explain anything, since planning and explanation presuppose that everything does not happen by chance. So it makes a great practical difference whether we do or do not have this particular *blik,* or perspective.

Hare's suggestion is a fruitful one insofar as it calls attention to the way in which certain beliefs may be said to be referential without being cognitive in the narrower sense of that term. We may, for the time being, say that these basic affirmations do not constitute knowledge, but they do constitute beliefs and beliefs of a quite distinctive order.[15]

Now many of the basic images of religion are attempts to symbolically express these beliefs which refer to certain fundamental features of existence. But just as it is possible for any given event to be interpreted and categorized in a number of ways, so, also, is it possible to interpret any basic element of reality in various fashions. The perpetual perishing of all things, for example, may be interpreted as a blind, meandering flux indifferent to any realization of significance or value. On the other hand, it might be regarded as a boundless creativity in which each entity is seen as contributing briefly to the richness of the whole. If the process is regarded as fatelike and indifferent, certain attitudes will necessarily follow, and certain actions and conduct will seem appropriate to inculcate and foster. If the process is regarded as creative and benign, still another set of prescriptions will naturally arise. So, too, the sense of absolute dependence may awaken horror and a contempt for finite existence or, on the other hand, when interpreted from a certain perspective, it may awaken a sense of gratitude and awe.

It could be, and has been, reasonably argued that classical philosophy is a series of reflections on these primal features of being as we apprehend them and that religions are symbolic forms of interpretation of these same features in the light of a certain basic concern for beatitude and fulfilment. But this is simply another way of saying that the way in which one relates to these elemental features is influenced by certain assumptions about human nature. But human nature is also subject to various possible interpretations and symbolizations. Are men basically dependent or independent? Are they separate individuals or so bound together that individuality is an abstraction? Is man's glory and crown his reason, his passion, or his will? Does his sense of identity testify to a perduring ego or is his individuality merely a characteristic pattern of traits that create the illusion of selfhood?[16]

These basic anthropological judgments influence the interpretation of the metaphysical beliefs just as the metaphysical beliefs influence the basic affirmations about human nature. If the Therevada Buddhist considers man basically to be an individual whose beatitude is not dependent on the salvation of others, the Mahayana Buddhist argues that liberation is dependent on seeing that the ego is an illusion and the source of pain. This, in turn, is closely related to their respective views concerning the experience of absolute dependence and the kind of order that is regarded as fundamental. Is man absolutely alone or is there a grace that sustains all? Is life to be found in solitude and escape from the wheel of existence or is it to be found in compassion and the promotion of the harmony of life with life? Each interpretation finds expression in certain powerful symbols and images. Each interpretation calls for an appropriate style of life.

If one asks why religions differ, the only answer that can be given is the same that must be given to the question why metaphysicians and philosophers, even linguistic philosophers, differ. Each one is struck by the importance of a given model.[17] Sometimes these models arise out of some special occurrence. Some event or experience strikes the person or community as especially relevant. They are "suggestions," to use Christian's term. They provide an illumination for the whole. Consequently, they are immortalized in legend, song, and myth. And the images that arise from these experiences acquire a special sanctity because they are emblematic of a particular self-understanding.

4 · The Meanings of "Jesus of Nazareth"

It should not be said, as it often is said, that Judaism and Christianity are the only religions rooted in paradigmatic events. Nevertheless, there is a sense in which these religions are preoccupied with history in a way that most other religions are not. The events which Judaism and Christianity celebrate are so interpreted as to direct attention to history. They guide these communities in their responses to other concrete historical events. The paradigmatic events, in other words, do not direct the community away from history but have as their focus the life of responsibility in history.

The basic occasion that constitutes the originating and formative event for the consciousness of the Christian is, of course, Jesus of Nazareth. Like all events, this one is amenable to the inquiries of historians, and, like all events, it can be interpreted in different ways and in different contexts. One can say, then, that there are different possible meanings for the proper name "Jesus of Nazareth." The problem is how we might understand the significance of this event for the Christian community without so stating it that one necessarily collides with the morality of historical knowledge. The solution to this problem will take the form, then, of sorting out the various possible levels of meaning of "Jesus of Nazareth" and the relationships among them.

Now when we use a proper name in historical inquiry, we normally refer to an actual and past person in the concreteness of his lived relationships. The name "Jesus," then, refers to a man who lived two thousand years ago and had a quite determinate pattern of relationships with his family, friends, disciples, and enemies. We mean, to use language we can scarcely do without, Jesus as he really was. At the same time, we are also aware that this actual Jesus really points to a limit of thought. No actual figure in the past can be fully recovered or described, and this is especially true in the case of Jesus, since we possess only a very few stories and sayings from the last months of his relatively brief life.

We can also mean by Jesus of Nazareth what is commonly called "the historical Jesus." As has been often pointed out, "the historical Jesus" is actually an ambiguous term because it may refer both to the actual Jesus and to the Jesus that is now recoverable by historical means. For clarity's sake I shall use "the historical Jesus" in the latter sense; that is, what can be fairly said about the actual Jesus on the basis of inferences from our present sources. It might be argued that the phrase "what can be fairly said" is itself question-begging because historians differ as to what can be fairly said about the actual Jesus. This is true, but it is also the case that there is some consensus among historians who otherwise disagree, and it is important to distinguish this level of consensus from those assertions that are most debated. And this consensus must, in principle at least, be distinguished from the actual Jesus.

The historical Jesus can only be recovered from documents that were preserved by those who had some contact with the actual Jesus. This is not to say that all of the New Testament materials were written by eyewitnesses; it is only to say that some of the materials do reflect a memory-impression of Jesus. We have, for example, certain sayings, parables, teachings, and some remembered deeds and actions. Now this memory-impression was obviously a highly selective or perspectival one. Its basic features were obviously abstracted in the light of some interest. In this sense, this image is not unlike a bas-relief in which everything irrelevant from the standpoint of those who preserved it was carefully chiseled away. There may, to be sure, have been other perspectival images —for example, the one in the minds of the Pharisees, or in the minds of the followers of John the Baptist, or of the Roman soldiers—but we no longer have access to them. The only memory-impression we have is that of the earliest Christian community.

If we judge this memory-impression to be an authentic one, we might say that this perspectival image is, in some sense, the historical Jesus. I say "in some sense," because some might object to this equation of the perspectival image with the historical Jesus. They would complain that we have already defined the historical Jesus as that which can be reconstructed by the best scientific means. There is some merit in this objection, provided that we realize that a perspectival image is not necessarily less true because it was not arrived at by modern historical research; otherwise, we would have to discard most of the memory-impressions of our families and friends. But if modern historical research discovers that this image does, in fact, represent a memory-impression, then, in an important sense, the historian has judged that the memory-impression does have some real correlation with the historical Jesus and the actual Jesus.

The fourth possible meaning of Jesus of Nazareth is what I shall call "the Biblical Christ." By this I mean to designate the transformation and alteration of the memory-impression (or perspectival image) under the influence of the theological interpretation of the actual Jesus by the Christian community. In this sense, the Biblical Christ includes the idea of pre-existence, the birth and temptation narratives, many of the miracles, those stories which clearly reflect Old Testament prophecies, the resurrection and forty-day traditions, and the ascension. The Johannine Christ is a good illustration of what I mean by "the Biblical Christ." Now as we shall see, the Biblical Christ, just because it is a transformation of the memory-image, is not a complete distortion of it. It also contains some elements of the memory-impression and, therefore, some elements historians can use for the reconstruction of the historical Jesus. The point, however, is that the Biblical Christ is an alteration and transformation—as can be seen most clearly in the Fourth Gospel. Consequently, we can identify the memory-image and the Biblical Christ only at the price of a profound confusion, as we shall see below.

To sum up, then, we have these various components to relate to one another: (1) the actual Jesus, (2) the historical Jesus, (3) the perspectival image or memory-impression of Jesus, and (4) the Biblical Christ. I want to turn now to the third of these elements because it is crucial for the solution to our problem.

5 · The Perspectival Image of Jesus

Although New Testament scholars differ among themselves about many aspects of the historical Jesus—the extent to which his message was determined by a belief in the immediate coming of the Kingdom of God, whether he believed himself to be the Messiah, how he interpreted his death—they nevertheless agree that the basic outlines of a memory-impression exercised some restraining influence over the obvious tendency to remold and recast the central tradition in the light of Old Testament prophecy and Hellenistic religious motifs. Although it is difficult in many cases to know exactly where the imagination of the Biblical author begins and authentic tradition ends—did Jesus, for example, really heal the sick, or is this a messianic tradition put in historical form?—there are many elements that are unintelligible unless we assume that they represent an authentic tradition: Jesus' ministry in Galilee, the baptism by John the Baptist, his consorting with the flotsam of his society, his crucifixion, and, above all, the basic outlines and form of his teaching.

The image of Jesus that exercises this control is, of course, a highly selective one. First of all, it is confined to the last few months of a life that spanned some thirty years. Secondly, it represents an abstracted pattern that is intelligible only in terms of the basic religious interest of the community that preserved it. To use the analogy I have employed before, we are presented with something like a bas-relief in which everything unessential from the standpoint of the sculptor has been chiseled away until nothing remains but its basic pattern, or *Gestalt*. Everything that might have cast some biographical or psychological light upon Jesus has been eliminated. His boyhood, his psychological relationships with his family and friends, his personal dreams and wishes, his character traits, his physical appearance, his private opinions and beliefs have all been removed in favor of a picture of his teachings and deeds. Yet we have every reason to believe that the image of his teaching and deeds is a trustworthy one, despite the additions and interpolations and the lack of chronology and significant detail.

Two possible objections at this point are worth considering. The first has been advanced by Paul Tillich. He argues that the accuracy of any picture is dependent on its details, and that it is useless, therefore, to talk about a *Gestalt* limited to the essentials while leaving the particulars open to doubt.[18] The second objection is that the memory-image cannot be trusted just because it is so highly selective.

It is true, of course, that a total picture is derived from, and therefore dependent upon, particulars. But it does not follow from this that when one wants to convey an impression of one person to another he must re-create those particulars in literal detail. One may, in fact, alter or telescope this or that fact in order to bring the essential image into clear focus, as when we tell a characteristic story about an acquaintance or a friend. As John Knox has pointed out, it is possible to have a vivid and true picture of some intimate, such as one's father—his typical way of speaking, behaving, or of responding to crisis situations—without being able to recall the accurate details of any single past situation or to remember a precise sentence he has uttered.[19] Indeed, if we confined ourselves to what we literally remembered of our friends, we might not be able to communicate our overall impressions at all.

All of our ordinary imaginal abstractions are highly selective. This selection is a function of many things: the basic interest we have in our minds, the role of the person, the relationship he bears to us. All images represent the impression upon us of some subject in some definite context. If we say, for example, that some teacher has left an enduring impression on our minds as to what it really means to be a teacher, this image necessarily presupposes a fairly delimited relationship. And when we try to communicate this impression to someone else, we assume that this image has no necessary reference to the teacher as lover, husband, father, or any number of other roles he might have performed. The images are partial and perspectival, but they are not necessarily untrue or unrepresentative of what was grasped in the concrete relationship.

Now there is every reason to believe that the actual Jesus had a powerful and profound impact upon a little group of people called his disciples and that the impression he left upon them was a function (1) of the basic concern he awakened in them and in the light of which they eliminated everything irrelevant to that concern, and (2) of his own role in relation to them, the role of one who had given them a picture of a new possibility of self-understanding and who had the power of awakening their faith. The basic concern was a religious one. Whether we may presuppose that the disciples came to this event with a religious question or whether the event itself raised the question for them, we need not decide. At any rate, this figure thrust upon them a decision, and they judged that the most important thing about him was his ability to bring this decision into clear and powerful focus. This was what they judged to be typical, and this is what they preserved. His role was that of having raised and answered the basic human question of faith. It was this role which made him the paradigm of God's action, for he had taught them to think of God as the one whose distinctive action it is to awaken faith.

There are three interrelated elements in the perspectival image of Jesus: the content and pattern of his teaching and preaching, the form of his actions, and his crucifixion. These three motifs reinforce and condition one another. The teaching provides the context for interpreting his actions, and his actions are symbolic exemplifications of the teachings. Both of them acquire a peculiar power by virtue of the crucifixion. So much is this the case that the crucifixion can itself become a selective emblem representing the entire ministry.

There is no need here to rehearse in any detail the basic structure and impression left by Jesus' teaching.[20] We know that it was dominated by the theme of the sovereignty or reign (kingdom) of God, although this formal designation of it scarcely does justice to its richness or to the unique way in which he envisaged that sovereignty to be exercised. It is exemplified, yet hidden, in the growing of lilies, in the fall of the sparrows, in the raining on the just and the unjust, and, especially, in the call to faith that comes to expression in Jesus' own witness. This theme, in turn, is the basis for the subordinate themes concerning the law and the new righteousness. This new righteousness, paradoxically, is said to manifest itself in the acknowledgment of one's lack of righteousness and in concern for the neighbor. The call to faith is the call to confidence and trust in that last power that is said to hold and sustain and limit men in their being and powers.

The witness is characterized by an uncompromising sense of urgency. "The hour is at hand" and men are not permitted to be indifferent to it. This sense of urgency doubtless found expression in some form of apocalyptic imagery, although it is difficult to know how central this was, partly because, as I have suggested above, there is a profound naturalism in many of the most trustworthy sayings attributed to Jesus. But it is hard to conceive of this urgency in terms of the apocalyptic imagery alone, for it appears to have been a manifestation of Jesus' peculiar ability to precipitate a crisis in the lives of those with whom he came in contact. Men could not remain indifferent to him or his message. This, in fact, constitutes Jesus' "authority," for he did not teach as the scribes taught. He so posed the demand and the possibility of faith that it came to men as their last chance, a decision that could not be put off as other decisions could. Indeed, whoever rejected Jesus' witness is said to reject God, not because Jesus himself claimed to be God but because the content of his teaching was that God's call to faith is directed to men in their present existence; hence to postpone the decision or to reject the witness is to turn away from the reality to which the witness points.

Jesus' actions seem calculated to the same end. Like many of the prophets in the Old Testament, he apparently regarded his actions as symbolic, as re-presentations of the content of his teach-

ing. Thus, if his preaching could be regarded as the verbal manifestation of God's claim, so, too, his deeds could be interpreted as a
sign, as an embodiment that gave concrete content to the form of
God's sovereignty. But just as the sovereignty of God as it is
depicted in his teachings is a sovereignty that seems paradoxical,
so, too, that reign expressed in his action is equally surprising. For
the reign of God is not naked power but the sovereignty of *agapē*.
Consequently, it represents a radical reinterpretation of the concept of righteousness and of the ideas of God's power held by
those who hoped to be justified by the law. Jesus consorts with
the outcasts and the sick and the weak, those the "righteous" call
unrighteous. His concern is for those who are aware that they are
in need of a physician. Thus, his behavior gives force to the
parable of the great supper (Luke 14: 16-24) in which the host,
having had his invitations to the banquet refused by intended
guests, instructs his servants to extend invitations to the poor and
the blind and the lame. Jesus' conduct illustrates the parable of
God's sovereignty, and by it, too, men are asked to make a decision concerning its meaning for them.

It is quite important to note how the perspectival image preserves and interprets the relationship between Jesus' teaching and
his conduct. For it is precisely the relationship that defines it as
revelation so far as the texts are concerned. His preaching and
teaching specify how his actions are to be understood, and his
actions, in turn, give concreteness and embodiment to the content
of his teaching. Otherwise, the facts of his life, his behavior, could
be, and have been, interpreted differently. They were, for example, undoubtedly interpreted by some as the deplorable predilections of a rebel who enjoyed the company of the outcasts of
society more than that of the powerful and self-righteous. They
have been interpreted by others as the actions of a sinless human
being who displayed an incomparable human love. The teaching,
however, makes it quite clear that the psychological question is an
irrelevant one, just as is the predication of sinlessness. For whatever his personal predilections—"Why do you call me good?"
—the only real decision the observer has to make is whether the
witness is a true one, that is, whether the last power with which

men have to do can be trusted. The aim both of the action and of the preaching is to force that decision, and the admiration or the denigration of Jesus' character, personality, or motives only clouds the essential question: Is this man the disclosure of God's intention for human life?

The last and decisive element in the memory-impression is the crucifixion. If Jesus' teaching and action may be said to be mutually dependent, the cross focuses the meaning of the entire story. For the cross raises in the most powerful form the basic question of the truth of Jesus' witness. For what kind of righteous power is it that permits this witness to be reviled and rejected by men?

Unfortunately, the history of Christian reflection on the death of Jesus has obscured the way in which the crucifixion actually functions in relation to the teaching and deeds. By interpreting his death as a foreordained event or as a necessary and vicarious sacrifice for sin, Christendom has tended to isolate the cross from the content of Jesus' message and deeds. Happily, this has made no actual theological difference, because so long as it is believed that this death was the vicarious sacrifice of the Son of God, the same question—Is God gracious?—has been raised and answered. But for those to whom vicarious sacrifice and atonement are unintelligible, it must be pointed out that the crucifixion of Jesus, when viewed in the context of his teaching and deeds, simply represents the question whether both of these are in any sense true, whether, in fact, they constitute a revelation of anything at all except the meaninglessness of existence. Is this the way the world ends? Are the Christs crucified while the Pilates die in their beds? What kind of a world is it where this parable of a hanged man is thought to be the crucial one? Can the inscrutable last power who permits this to pass be called righteous? The cross does nothing more or less than recapitulate the whole content of Jesus' message and deeds.

Because the cross does recapitulate the content of Jesus' message and deeds, it can become the image or symbol that is emblematic of the entire story and its meaning. It at once symbolizes God's sovereignty, which appears as weakness in the eyes of men, as well as the cruciform character of Jesus' ministry. But the cross touches more primordial elements of human experience, as the history of religion makes clear. It can symbolize the death of the self which is the path to new life, the stupidity of men when confronted with goodness, personal courage, the suffering of God, and the intersection of the divine and human. This iconic significance in part accounts for the persistence and power of this image, but for the Christian all this is subordinate to the question the cross raises for faith.

The Christian church emerged with the confession that Jesus was the Christ, which is to say that he was in fact the revealer. And because his life was a revelation, the proclamation necessarily took the form of representing the pattern of his life as the disclosure of the divine righteousness. I agree with Ebeling that it is in this context that the resurrection-ascension belief must be interpreted. This belief, Ebeling argues, is not an additional *credendum* to the conviction that Jesus was the revelation; it is nothing else but the expression of "the right understanding of the Jesus of the days before Easter."[21] In the resurrection belief—Jesus is "raised to the right hand of God"—Jesus is confessed to be what he really was, the decisive witness to and awakener of faith. Whatever we believe to be the historical occasion for this resurrection belief—a resurrected body or a visionary appearance of some sort—the point is, as Ebeling indicates, these appearances are not regarded as making faith any easier, and those who do not experience them are put at no disadvantage. It follows that all men are "without excuse." Christian faith is not belief in a miracle; it is the confidence that Jesus' witness is a true one. This faith is not made easier or more difficult by the occurrence of a miracle. Here, too, Ebeling is correct: the so-called appearances can be interpreted only as the "concomitant phenomena of the faith-awakening encounter with Jesus."[22] The resurrection-faith is that Jesus is, in fact, the Word, that this image does, in fact, provide the clue to the understanding of human life.

Now all of this can be said, as I have suggested from time to time, without any implicit or explicit reference to Jesus' person, sinlessness, or existential selfhood. All of these are understandable but unnecessary ways of protecting the truths that it was in and through Jesus' witness that Christians grasp the content of faith and that they find the proclamation of this event to be efficacious still in awakening faith. To say more adds nothing to faith, and it precipitates, as we have seen, the collision with the morality of historical knowledge.

6 · The Memory-Image of Jesus, the Biblical Christ and the Truth of Faith

Once we have sorted out the various possible meanings of "Jesus of Nazareth," it is possible to deal more discriminatingly with some of the problems that have bedeviled contemporary theology. Consider, for example, the oft-repeated claim that it is impossible to get behind the Biblical picture of Christ and to reconstruct the historical Jesus. The force of this claim is to set certain methodological limits upon historical inquiry, and once these limits have been set, faith feels itself liberated from any anxiety concerning the results of that inquiry, because faith is said to have as its object the Christ of faith and not the Jesus of history. I will argue that this claim is erroneous, that the theological argument coupled with it has a valid element but is misleading, and that another theological possibility must also be considered.

When it does not rest on dogmatic assumptions (that Jesus by definition is unique and thereby defies all historical reconstruction), the claim that one cannot get behind the Biblical picture of Christ is based on the partially justifiable assumption that the New Testament sources already depict an interpreted Christ. It is true that the image of Jesus in the New Testament is a highly selective one and, therefore, that many of the questions a historian might legitimately ask cannot, in the nature of the case, yield any productive answer. Nevertheless, the assumption is only partially justifiable, which is to say that it is misleading, because it obscures the important fact that there are not one but two possible meanings of the term "the interpreted Christ." The so-called Biblical picture of Christ may refer either to what I have called the memory-impression or it may refer to the Biblical Christ. But, as I have suggested, these are by no means the same. Although the former may be said to reflect an interpretation, it is an interpretation that stays in close relationship to an authentic historical tradition. The latter, by contrast, alters and transforms that tradition. The former, to be sure, represents a selection; but the latter imaginatively transforms even that selection under the influence of christological dogma.

This distinction is no mere piece of logic-chopping because it has both methodological and theological ramifications. The first is this: If one makes the distinction, as I have done, between the memory-impression and the Biblical Christ, this suggests that the historian *can compare the perspectival image with the Biblical Christ,* whereas the reference to a single Biblical picture of Christ obscures this possibility. Such a comparison is not unimportant; in fact, just such a comparison has actually made it possible to establish the important differences between the Synoptic Gospels and the Fourth Gospel, to note the crucial differences between the parables and deeds of Jesus in the former and the christological utterances and symbolic actions attributed to him in the latter. Although it is true that the Gospel of Mark also represents an interpreted Christ, the point is that the interpretation stays in closer relationship at crucial points to what the historian calls "fact" than does the Fourth Gospel. This distinction between levels of interpretation is not at all illumined by the sweeping statement that one cannot go behind the Biblical picture of Christ.

The second methodological consequence of this distinction between two levels of interpretation is that it enables us to attack the arbitrary restriction placed upon the Biblical critic by virtue of the assumption that one cannot get behind an interpreted picture. We must say that everything depends on the kind of interpretation. If an interpretation is more like a selection than a transformation and, consequently, preserves some historical tradition, then the historian is not prevented, in principle, from testing the general reliability of the selection. And insofar as the selection has some presumed relation to fact, it may *inadvertently provide the basis for a criticism both of the selective image itself and of the Biblical Christ.* To understand this point, one must keep in mind the distinction that was made in an earlier chapter between intentional and unintentional data, between what a witness intends to tell us and what he unintentionally reveals in the process of telling us. Frequently, the latter is far more interesting and important to the historian than the former. Sometimes, a witness unintentionally forces the historian to raise certain questions about the truth of a selective portrait or causes him to see it in a different light or even to reject it as unreliable. Just as a psychiatrist who is "listening with the third ear" to a woman client describe her late departed and beloved husband may find unintentional data in that description (interpretation) that suggest a somewhat different picture of the loved one (or require, at least, that the doctor interpret differently the things the client says), so, also, a historian may find elements unintentionally preserved in the perspectival image that require him to criticize that image itself in certain respects or to take account of some systematic bias that permeates it. The historian may now be required to suspend judgment about some things, to give a different weight to others, to maximize what might have been minimized, and to alter the whole in various important ways. No critical historian simply takes his sources at face value or throws up his hands in skepticism when he is presented with an interpreted figure. If he were to do so, he would cease to be a critical historian, because all of his witnesses will present him with interpretations of some sort. There are no uninterpreted pictures. The historian's task is to interpret the interpretations. Otherwise, his job would be merely that of transmitting received traditions and trying to harmonize them.

If this is the case, however, then we can take one further step in our argument. Not only can the New Testament historian compare the memory-impression with the Biblical Christ, but he can, in principle at least, test the former to see the extent to which it can be trusted. But this is just another way of saying that he *can test the perspectival image to see to what degree it says something which the historian can accept as true,* i.e., as the historical Jesus. It could be replied, of course, that although this test is possible in principle, it is not possible in the case of Jesus. But this rejoinder, it should be noted, already involves a significant retreat from the grounds for the initial and sweeping claim that it is impossible to get behind the picture of the Biblical Christ. More than that, the rejoinder is actually false. New Testament historians have in fact worked over the perspectival image and have concluded that it does contain enough intentional and unintentional data to warrant a number of significant conclusions.

Consider the processes of historical judgment that are at work in the following examples: (1) The historian notes that the New Testament sources preserve the story of the baptism of Jesus by John the Baptist, yet that this baptism is obviously a source of embarrassment to those same sources. Could Jesus have willingly undertaken a baptism of *repentance?* Does this baptism not constitute the basis for the claim of the disciples of the Baptist that he was superior to Jesus? From this the historian infers that there must have been a natural tendency to suppress this story or to alter it in such a fashion that it could not be used by the followers of the Baptist in defense of their claim. If this is a reasonable conclusion, then it suggests that the actual fact of Jesus' baptism by John was so widely known that it could not have been eliminated from the sources and that the story had to be told in such a fashion as to prevent what the Christian community regarded as a misinterpretation: hence, the confession of unworthiness put in the mouth of the Baptist, the sign from heaven in the form of a dove, etc. (2) The historian observes that the sources preserve certain sayings in which Jesus refuses to traffic in miracles and signs. On the other hand, many signs and miracles are attributed to him. The historian believes that this apparent contradiction is sufficiently important to reflect about the matter. He concludes that the apologetic situation of the primitive church continually tempted them to try to prove the divine significance of Jesus in terms of signs and miracles. This conclusion is borne out by the elaborate miracle stories in the apocryphal literature also used by early Christians. Yet the tradition remains that Jesus refused to work miracles. Moreover, this tradition seems to reflect a certain theological understanding of the nature of faith that can also be detected in many of Jesus' teachings: It is a "sinful generation that seeks a sign" (Matt. 12:39, 16:14; Mark 8:12; Luke 11:24). The possibility arises, therefore, that, like the earlier example of Jesus' baptism, we are dealing with a memory-impression that could not be erased. This possibility suggests to the historian that he should re-examine the whole tradition in which Jesus claims to be the Messiah, such claims naturally being bound up with miracles and signs. He notes the odd and, when it was first noticed, startling fact that the early church preserves no unequivocal claim by the historical Jesus to be the Messiah. What, then, are we to make out of the messianic titles "Son of Man" and "Son of God"? The historian notes, in the light of all of the rest of his reasoning, that this is a very complex matter, that the Aramaic equivalent of the former title may simply have been in some cases "a man" and that in other cases Jesus seems to have used the phrase to refer not to himself but to another. So, too, what is one to make out of the so-called messianic secret? Was this a convenient way of interpreting to the Gentiles the remembered fact that Jesus did not actually claim to be the Messiah, or is it a far less self-conscious use of a current Gnostic myth of the hidden savior-god who came to earth incognito? But these two possibilities may not have been incompatible. Perhaps the myth was used just because it fits the memory-impression in which Jesus claimed no messianic role or function. This, in turn, causes the historian to look at that otherwise unintelligible retort Jesus is said to have given to the rich young man, "Why do you call me good? No one is good but God alone" (Mark 10:18). So, also, what is one to make of the consistently enigmatic replies Jesus makes to John the Baptist's entreaties to say whether he is the Messiah or not? How could the church have passed up such an obvious apologetic opportunity to cinch its case against John's disciples? All of these things seem intelligible only if we assume that the memory-impression reflected in the preserved sayings is authentic.

The point of these examples is not to attempt to prove that the memory-image is authentic, but to illustrate the complexity of historical reasoning involved, a complexity so great that it cannot be described abstractly. It is also intended to show that it is an untenable restriction upon historical inquiry to argue that because we have an interpreted image we cannot ever presume to go behind it. Indeed, it is just because the New Testament historians have presumed to go behind it that we have been able to make such progress as has been made in the interpretation of the Synoptic materials.

I suggested at the beginning of this section that even though the methodological restriction is an untenable one, the theological claim accompanying it has a certain validity. That claim, it will be remembered, is that faith does not depend on getting behind the Biblical picture of Christ. The validity of this claim is that the degree of Christian faith is not proportionate to one's factual knowledge about the historical Jesus. Indeed, if we understand properly what is meant by faith, then this faith has no clear relation to any particular set of historical beliefs at all. Faith has to do with one's confidence in God, which is to say, with one's surrender of his attempts to establish his own righteousness and his acceptance of his life and creation as a gift and a responsibility. It is trust and commitment. This awareness, to be sure, may be linked in the minds of some people with certain historical beliefs, but it is by no means clear that it must necessarily be so linked. Indeed, it could be argued that the history of the Christian church—not to mention the histories of those outside of the church—indicates that countless members of that body of belief have perceived this truth in and through stories that are, judged by modern criteria, mythological, which is to say, factually untrue. Can one seriously question, for example, that the Johannine Christ has provided a powerful medium for communicating the meaning of grace and, therefore, constitutes a call to faith even though we now know that this Christ bears only a slight likeness to the actual Jesus? Or can one doubt that the mythological doctrines of the sending of the only-begotten Son and of the vicarious atonement have been, for some persons, extraordinarily forceful vehicles for apprehending the suffering nature of the divine *agapē* and, therefore, a new understanding of human existence? And is it not, therefore, a peculiar lack of insight into the nature of faith when D. M. Baillie argues that the faith of Christians who lived in the age of authority and before the recovery of the historical Jesus was an "impoverished one"?[23] The faith of Augustine, Clement, Bernard, Francis of Assisi, Thomas Aquinas impoverished?

The conclusion one is driven to is that the content of faith can as well be mediated through a historically false story *of a certain kind* as through a true one, through a myth as well as through history. Everything depends on the form and structure of the symbolism and the myth. But having said this, one must also say that the conditions of belief change from age to age. What may have been intelligible to and valid for Augustine and Francis may not be so for those of us who live after the advent of Biblical criticism. And it is just this fact that enables us to consider another option, namely, that the call to faith may be made far more powerful for modern men if interpreted in terms of the memory-image of Jesus, who proclaimed the righteousness of God, associated with tax-collector and harlots, and was crucified, than in terms of the only-begotten Son who existed before all worlds, came to earth, was crucified as an atonement for sin, was raised from the dead, and exalted to heaven. We may understand now why that symbolism and mythology took the form it did, and we can, therefore, seek to interpret it, which is to say, to demythologize it. But for many of us, this same truth can best be mediated through the story of the despised man Jesus. Put rather starkly, is it not as possible to hear the call to faith through the image of Jesus as through the Biblical Christ? Are there not at least two avenues, so to speak, to the truth of faith?

It is precisely this possibility, as we have seen, that has been discovered by the new quest, although, paradoxically, the pilgrims on that quest do not seem to see the significance of their own work. If the understanding of man before God implicit in the perspectival image of Jesus, and implicit also, then, in the historical Jesus (when that refers to a certain kind of historical reconstruction) is the same understanding that is given through the *kerygma* of a dying and rising savior-god, then the decision of faith in both cases is the same: Can the last power be trusted? Is God gracious? Is my life significant in some sense that transcends the world?

7 · *Symbol, Event, and Once-for-Allness*

If one thinks of revelation as a paradigmatic event that casts up images that alter our interpretation of all events, this requires that we distinguish between two kinds of belief, and, accordingly, between two kinds of certitude: the belief that the actual Jesus was as the perspectival image pictures him, and the belief that the perspectival image does illumine our experience and our relationship to that upon which we are absolutely dependent. The former is a belief about a contingent fact remote from my own experience. Consequently, it can never have the immediacy of an event that impinges on my own life, although I may, of course, have a high level of certitude about it, depending on the data and warrants. The latter is also a belief, to be sure, but of a different order. In the first place, it is not a belief about a past event but a belief that an image cast up by a past event illumines some present experience. Consequently, this belief has to do with the present and can have an immediacy no remote event can acquire. In the second place, it is not a belief about one unique contingent event but has to do with the adequacy of an image for interpreting the structure and character of reality itself.

No remote historical event—especially if assertions about it can solicit only a tentative assent—can, as such, be the basis for a religious confidence about the present. Even if it were historically probable, say, that Jesus was a man who was completely open to transcendence, this belief in no way makes it any easier for someone two thousand years later to be so open—unless, of course, the silent presupposition is present that the object of faith is the same and can be trusted. But this silent presupposition is precisely what is at issue in the decision of faith, and no reference to a past event can establish that. Or even if we were to believe that the corpse of Jesus was resuscitated, this fact could be the basis for a religious confidence only if that event were already interpreted as revelatory of the being with which one has to do in the present. But this, again, is precisely the affirmation of faith.

The difficulty with all the traditional orthodox attempts to ground the credibility of revelation in something objective like miracles or the fulfilment of prophecy is that they fail to see that there is no intrinsic connection between such external events and faith, *unless faith is already presupposed.* This, in turn, tells us something about the nature of faith. As Luther so clearly saw, history says nothing unless a "why" is discerned in it, unless it is "for us." This is why Luther's interpretation of miracles tends to relativize their importance. So, too, Herrmann and the dialectical theologians never wearied of repeating that faith is not believing things but the fundamental attitude one has toward the whole of existence. It is basically confidence in the nature of being itself.

This confidence must have some basis in one's present experience. No event or miracle that others tell us about can acquire the force of something we know for ourselves, and if one has the experience for himself, the appeal to a past fact is important largely because it provides us with an image to which we can return again and again and use in our present relationships with others. A fact cannot provide the ground or the object of faith when faith is properly understood, although it can awaken faith and provide the symbols that faith uses.

Actually, Christendom has always preserved some such insight as this, by distinguishing between the Christ after the flesh and the living Christ, or between Jesus Christ and the Holy Spirit. The doctrine of the Trinity, it could be argued, is a way of preserving the formative significance of a past event for interpreting a present and living reality. The Holy Spirit is the power that opens one's eyes to the Logos of all reality that was embodied in the man Jesus.

This argument should not be taken to mean that the image of Jesus has no correlation with the actual Jesus, since we have historical reasons for believing that it does. It means, rather, that this correlation is not itself an object of faith, that the truth of faith is not dependent upon such a correlation. Faith finds its certitude, its confirmation, in the viability of the image for relating one to present reality. In this sense, we could agree with Kähler and Tillich that it is the picture of Christ that has created and preserved the community of faith, were it not, as we have seen, that this terminology is systematically ambiguous. The power of the Christian message is mediated through the image of Jesus. It is this image which the Christian finds to be a reliable one for relating himself to the beings around him and to the power acting in and through all beings. Jesus Christ is the key image in a parable which the Christian uses to interpret the more inclusive reality with which all men are confronted and of which they try to make some sense.

The situation is not so much that the Christian has access to realities to which the non-Christian does not, or that the Christian believes that certain entities exist which the non-Christian finds doubtful. The situation is, rather, that both Christian and non-Christian are confronted with the same realities but interpret them differently. They regard them from different perspectives. If, for example, other men who do not call themselves Christian are struck, as we are told Ludwig Wittgenstein was often struck, by the feeling "How extraordinary that anything should exist?" and should testify it was always accompanied by the "experience of feeling absolutely safe,"[24] the Christian need not argue that this is an illusion or deprecate it because Wittgenstein did not believe in Jesus Christ. Rather, with the aid of the image of Jesus, the Christian will attempt to understand both his and Wittgenstein's common experience. Or, to use a slightly different example, if all men note that the rain falls equally on the lazy and diligent alike, and some men interpret this as a sign of cosmic indifference, there are others who may realize that they also are tempted so to interpret it but, with the aid of a suggestion out of their past, may see the same phenomenon in a different light, as the sign of a cosmic generosity. Or, if all men have been terrified at times by the awesome creativity of being, some have, with the aid of an image, been able to see this as the manifestation of an infinitely creative and boundless power that delights in the sheer multiplicity and richness of life.

A perspective is a function of the weight and valence attached to this or that experience and the way in which these, in turn, influence the symbols and categories men use to relate themselves to other experiences in the light of certain interests. There is clearly some such logic as this illustrated in William James' reflections on the difference between the inner life of the Greeks and Romans and ourselves. The Greeks and Romans celebrated rectitude, virtue, character, and self-sufficiency. Although they knew these were not easily achieved, they nevertheless were not overly troubled by the experience of hypocrisy and the corruption of virtue itself by self-righteousness. It was Luther, James suggests, who broke through this crust of naturalistic self-sufficiency, who saw that from one standpoint, at least, all humanly accepted excellences and safeguards of character are childishness. And what was determinative of this new self-understanding was another experience, an experience "of an unexpected life succeeding upon death. By this I don't mean immortality, or the death of the body. I mean the deathlike termination of certain mental processes within the individual's experience, processes that run to failure, and in some individuals, at least, eventuate in despair."[25] This experience of a new range of life succeeding on our most despairing moments engenders (suggests) a still wider belief, of "a world in which all is well, in *spite* of certain forms of death, indeed *because* of certain forms of death—death of hope, death of strength . . . death of everything that paganism, naturalism, and legalism pin their faith on and tie their trust to."[26] And this belief James goes on, leads to another: the "tenderer parts" of our personal lives are continuous "with a wider self from which saving experiences flow in."[27]

Now these reflections of James hardly constitute an argument in any strong sense of the word, but they do aid us in understanding something of the structure of a perspective; and it is with structure that I am primarily concerned here. An argument would necessarily take a quite different form. It would take the form of attempting to demonstrate that a given perspective has a viability, intelligibility, and comprehensiveness that the alternative perspectives do not, that it is less eccentric, better able to account for those experiences and structures to which the alternatives attach special weight, as well as for those elements the alternatives seem to ignore or take no notice of. Yet having said this, it is important to stress that the existential certitude of the believer lies in the brute givenness of these experiences, although, if he is not a "blind believer," he will seek to compare these experiences with those of other men and to test his interpretations in all of the ways that seem possible.

The basic objection to some such model as this, I am aware, is that it reduces Jesus to a symbol of some timeless truth. By resting all the weight on the illuminatory power of the event, on its content, I have interpreted Jesus, it may be alleged, as an occasion for faith in contrast to the object of faith. Or, as Kierkegaard put this objection approximately a century ago, I have treated Jesus like a Socratic teacher who, having once put the learner in mind of the truth, is no longer needed.[28]

This criticism itself, however, rests on certain questionable assumptions. In the first place, despite Kierkegaard's insistence on faith as a passion and his polemic against objectification and belief, his own view basically hangs on the identification of faith with propositional belief, although in this case the proposition is claimed to be an absurd one. But, it may be asked, what is saving about believing an absurdity? And if one tries, as Kierkegaard did, to argue that some absurdities are more relevant than others, does this not once more require him to make some appeal to our present and general experience? In the second place, this view, unless one is willing to take it to the lengths Kierkegaard did—he argued that it was sufficient for faith to believe only that God assumed human form and nothing more in the way of knowledge was required[29]—merely raises all the problems that are endemic to any position which insists that Christian faith is independent of all historical knowledge.

A third and more important difficulty with this kind of objection, however, is that it rests on the crude juxtaposition of symbol and event that, in turn, rests on a quite unhistorical view of human nature. The distinction between timeless truths and events is simply too crude for theological or philosophical purposes. As our discussion of perspectives has attempted to show, the power of a paradigmatic event is precisely the fusion of universality and particularity. And once this principle is grasped, then symbol and history, as H. Richard Niebuhr has argued, are not opposites.

For history may function as myth or as symbol when men use it (or are forced by processes in their history itself to employ it) for understanding their present and their future. When we grasp our present, not so much as a product of our past, but more as essentially revealed in that past, then the historical account is necessarily symbolic; it is not merely descriptive of what was once the case.[30]

The greatest difficulty with Kierkegaard's objection, however, is that it fails to appreciate the implications of the historicity of human existence for theology itself. Consequently, it prejudices the radicality and universality of God's grace. Kierkegaard's argument depends on the misleading analogy of religious truth with mathematical truth, an ironic error in one whom many regard as the first existentialist. The truth which Socrates taught to the slave boy had to do with geometry. There is a sense in which those truths could have been taught as well by another teacher, because the content of the knowledge is quite unrelated to the way it was mediated. But this analogy is singularly inappropriate with respect to self-knowledge. When it comes to this kind of knowledge, to the question of who I am, what I have learned is indissolubly connected with my teachers.[31] I am this person with these images just because I have this historical past. In the realm of existential knowledge, teachers are not mere occasions. Their images stamp and condition the consciousness of those whom they have taught. The slave boy of the *Meno* could have been taught as well about the angles of a triangle by Alcibiades as by Socrates, but so far as the image of what it means to be a teacher who loves the truth and sacrifices everything to teach it, the content of that idea, as the history of the Western world indicates, cannot be abstracted from the picture of Socrates. Abraham Lincoln's conception of federal union might have been just as valid had it been held by Stanton, but this idea is indissoluble for most Americans from its embodiment in Lincoln. Human existence is historical existence. We are what we are, and our interpretations are what they are, because certain truths are indissolubly and powerfully wedded to certain persons in our historical past.

Having said this, however, it is important to realize that the confession that we have achieved such and such an understanding by means of this past is not to say that these realities can only be so apprehended. When we speak of revelation, we cannot mean that only in and through these particular events the divine has been disclosed. When we speak of revelation we cannot mean that God is making up for some previous lack of action or disclosure. Revelation, as John Oman once expressed it, can be better understood if it is regarded as God's way of dealing with the alienation which can see no gracious relation of God to us in any manifestation. In strict accuracy, we should speak of a historical reconciliation, rather than of a historical revelation, yet, seeing how God's manifestation is non-existent for us, or is even turned into sheer conflict and cause of distrust, till we are put into a position to interpret it aright, it is in effect a historical revelation. . . . Yet we should remember that it is revelation only as climbing an eminence affords us a prospect because the landscape is there already.[32]

We call Jesus the Christ because he discloses that reality encompassing every man but that not all acknowledge and interpret aright.

It is wrong to argue that this position is a new Gnosticism. It is but a modern restatement of an ancient theological alternative that goes back to the Logos theologians, that has emerged again and again in Christian history, and that has been reformulated more recently by such men as F. D. Maurice, H. Richard Niebuhr, and Karl Rahner. If one is searching for labels, then let it be called a radical historical confessionalism, for it is a position that tries to take with utmost seriousness both the Protestant principle of justification by faith and the historical character of human existence, of which the morality of historical knowledge is but a formalized constitutive part. The Christian community cannot disavow its own historical past, a past that constitutes the Christ event as the decisive one for its self-understanding. Consequently, it has no other vocation than to represent the proclamation about Jesus again and again. On the other hand, the significance of Jesus lies precisely in the relevance of his image for understanding that final reality which confronts men in all events. Christians turn to Jesus not in order to rehabilitate any exclusive claim that a defensive Christianity wishes to make but because it understands that human beings only seem to decide concerning the truth about life in general when they are confronted by a life in particular. The Christian community confesses that this has happened to it and that this can happen again to those who would attend to this image. This is its historical destiny. It is most faithful to that destiny and the image of him who initiated it when it simply accepts and rejoices in that destiny and ceases to claim for this historical reality an exclusiveness that, when claimed, surrenders the very truth to which it witnesses.

NOTES TO CHAPTER EIGHT

1. When I speak of the New Testament anthropology, I mean the understanding of man before God. I do not mean that theology can be reduced simply to statements about man.

2. H. Richard Niebuhr, *The Meaning of Revelation* (New York: The Macmillan Co., 1946), p. 93.

3. Alfred North Whitehead, *Religion in the Making* (New York: The Macmillan Co., 1926), p. 32.

4. From an interview with Martin Agronsky as recorded by *The New York Times*, November 28, 1963, p. 23.

5. In the presidential election of 1964, a personal friend of the author who was a volunteer helping transport Negro voters to the polls reported the following incident: "In one case, I was asked simply to take a lady home who had already voted and had been promised a ride back. When she got in the car and I asked where I could take her, I was surprised to learn that she no longer lived in the immediate vicinity, but had recently moved to Oak Cliff. Having failed to record her change of address, she had been able to vote only by coming all the way back across the city to her former precinct. Obviously, I thought, here's a person for whom the right to vote means a good deal. To have come all that way by bus and in a drenching rain could only mean that she was far more serious than many of the rest of us. And as we talked, it became clear that this was in fact the case . . . . But the thing that sticks in my mind is her simple, matter-of-fact testimony to how all this had come about. Like most other Negroes in the South, she said, she had at first had little interest in politics or even in voting. This, like everything else, was a white man's affair, and her voice wouldn't be heard anyway. But then had come the event of November 22, 1963. All at once, she confessed, she knew that this attitude was wrong. 'If he could give his life for our country, then I knew the least I could do was vote!' And so, on a rainy afternoon almost a year later, this woman had kept covenant with herself and with that event and had voted."

6. See Martin Buber, *Moses* (Oxford: East and West Library, 1946), pp. 1-19.

7. See Peter Munz, "History and Myth," *The Philosophical Quarterly,* VI (1956), 1-16.

8. See William A. Christian, *Meaning and Truth in Religion* (Princeton: Princeton University Press, 1964).

9. I am happy to acknowledge my general indebtedness to the following: Ernst Cassirer, *The Philosophy of Symbolic Forms,* trans. Ralph Manheim (3 vols.; New Haven: Yale University Press, 1953, 1955, 1957); Dorothy Emmet, *The Nature of Metaphysical Thinking* (London: Macmillan & Co.

Ltd., 1945); H. A. Hodges, *Languages Standpoints and Attitudes* (London: Oxford University Press, 1953); Immanuel Kant, "What Is Orientation in Thinking?" in *Critique of Practical Reason and Other Writings in Moral Philosophy,* ed. Lewis White Beck (Chicago: University of Chicago Press, 1949), pp. 293-305; Susanne K. Langer, *Philosophy in a New Key* (New York: Penguin Books, Inc., 1948).

10. See Stephen Toulmin's discussion of the bearing on reality of various possible contexts of discourse in *An Examination of the Place of Reason in Ethics* (Cambridge: Cambridge University Press, 1961), chap. viii.

11. Ernst Cassirer, *Language and Myth,* trans. Susanne K. Langer (New York: Dover Publications, Inc., 1946), p. 24.

12. For a very suggestive interpretation of the way in which religions may be viewed as responses to certain elemental features of human experience, see Philip H. Phenix, *Intelligible Religion* (New York: Harper & Brothers, n.d.).

13. See R. B. Braithwaite, *An Empiricist's View of the Nature of Religious Belief* (Cambridge: Cambridge University Press, 1955); cf. Paul M. van Buren, *The Secular Meaning of the Gospel* (New York: The Macmillan Co., 1963).

14. R. M. Hare, "Theology and Falsification," *New Essays in Philosophical Theology,* eds. Antony Flew and Alasdair MacIntyre (London: SCM Press Ltd., 1955), pp. 99-103.

15. Immanuel Kant, of course, explored this insight with extraordinary subtlety. See "What Is Orientation in Thinking?" in Beck, *op. cit.,* pp. 293-305.

16. For a way in which these differences have influenced the development of Buddhism, see Huston Smith, *The Religions of Man* (New York: Mentor Books, 1959), pp. 128 ff.

17. Emmet, *op. cit.,* pp. 197 ff.

18. Paul Tillich, *Systematic Theology* (Chicago: University of Chicago Press, 1957), II, 103.

19. John Knox, *Christ the Lord* (Chicago: Willett, Clark & Co., 1945), pp. 55 f.

20. For a good summary of what represents a wide consensus concerning the structure and form of Jesus' ministry, see Gunther Bornkamm, *Jesus of Nazareth,* trans. Irene and Fraser McLuskey with James M. Robinson (New York: Harper & Brothers, 1960).

21. Gerhard Ebeling, *Word and Faith,* trans. James W. Leitch (Philadelphia: Fortress Press, 1963), p. 302.

22. *Ibid.,* p. 301.

23. D. M. Baillie, *God Was in Christ* (New York: Charles Scribner's Sons, 1948), p. 52.

24. Norman Malcolm, *Ludwig Wittgenstein, A Memoir* (London: Oxford University Press, 1958), p. 70 n. 1.

25. William James, *Radical Empiricism and A Pluralistic Universe* (London: Longmans, Green & Co., 1943), p. 303.

26. *Ibid.,* pp. 305 f.

27. *Ibid.,* p. 307.

28. Sören Kierkegaard, *Philosophical Fragments* (Princeton: Princeton University Press, 1936).

29. *Ibid.*, p. 87.

30. H. Richard Niebuhr, *The Responsible Self* (New York: Harper & Row, 1963), p. 156.

31. Schleiermacher was keenly aware of this and it forms the basis of his theology. See *The Christian Faith*, eds. H. R. Mackintosh and R. S. Stewart (Edinburgh: T. & T. Clark, 1948), p. 13.

32. John Oman, *Grace and Personality* (2d ed. rev.; Cambridge: Cambridge University Press, 1919), pp. 156 f.

Index